THE
TESTOSTERONE
FILES

My Hormonal and Social Transformation from
FEMALE to MALE

MAX WOLF VALERIO

The Testosterone Files
My Hormonal and Social Transformation from Female to Male
Copyright © 2006 Max Wolf Valerio

 Published by
Seal Press
An Imprint of Avalon Publishing Group, Incorporated
1400 65th Street, Suite 250
Emeryville, CA 94608

ISBN-10 1-58005- 173-1
ISBN-13 978-1-58005- 173-6
9 8 7 6 5 4 3 2 1

Library of Congress Cataloging-in-Publication Data

Valerio, Max W. (Max Wolf)
  The testosterone files : my hormonal and social transformation from female to male / Max Wolf Valerio.
    p. cm.
  ISBN-13: 978-1-58005-173-6
  ISBN-10: 1-58005-173-1
  1. Valerio, Max W. (Max Wolf) 2. Transsexuals--United States--Biography. 3. Sex change--United States--Biography. I. Title.

V35A3 2006
306.76'8092--dc22

2005037674

Cover design by Gia Giasullo
Interior design by Amber Pirker
Cover photo by Kyle Zimmerman
Printed in Canada by Transcontinental
Distributed by Publishers Group West

In order to respect the privacy of individuals mentioned in the book, the author has changed their names.

For all transsexual men—manly, real, and impossibly brave each day—joyous

This one's for you guys

CONTENTS

PART THREE AFTER TESTOSTERONE

PROLOGUE:
THE JOKER'S WILD

In millennial culture, the joker's wild.
—Mark Dery, "Joker's Wild: Mark Dery Deconstructs
the Psycho-Killer Clowns," *World Art,* 1995

I watch myself in the mirror, shirt off, pants slung down past my hip bones. The scars are fading and the contour of my chest looks tight. My pecs have definition; the nipples and areolas are well placed, not too high and not too low.

My areolas are small, the size of nickels. When I turn to the side, there's a slight indentation between my pecs, muscles defined, a symmetry. If I work out I'll get more cut. When I do, the results show right away. That's different from before, when I was a woman.

An old girlfriend once remarked that most men tell war stories—
"Back when I was in the war . . ." Now I would say, "Back when I was
a woman . . ."

For thirty-two years I lived inside a woman's body. Although I resisted
femaleness on and off throughout my life, I learned to speak the language
of women, to pass unseen among them. I was both part of their world
and apart from it, peer and alien, feeling male inside yet living the life of
a woman. I learned a lot. What I learned is still with me, even as I transform, even as my emotional moorings shift and my body re-creates itself
from female to male. *I'm an agent provocateur, behind the lines, a translator.*

This is the unthinkable thing, a *sex change*. The clinics and doctors
don't try and persuade you to have one; they'll do anything to *dissuade* you.

People like me have always existed, in every era, on every continent.
In some cultures, we were allowed to assume the roles and lifestyles of
our preferred gender, but now we can go further than we ever could
before. Because of the discovery and synthesis of the sex hormones estrogen and testosterone, which induce the development of primary and
secondary male and female sexual characteristics, I'm able to do more
than live in the world in the male role. I can actually become chemically,
hormonally male and transform physically into a man.

My life is one of the extravagant experiments of the twentieth century.

You never know whom you are talking to. You never know what you
will do someday, what you are capable of.

Changing sex is an act of subverting nature's implacable authority. Of
uncovering and displaying nature's hidden cacophony, its subtext of sabo-
tage and dissolution. Transsexual men are *real*. Nature is an evolving para-
digm of conflicting tendencies and escalating discoveries; transsexuals hold
a fun house mirror up to nature. We reimagine identity, sexuality, biological sex, and gender. We get to live out our childhood fantasies.

I bathe in the delightful and sensuous machinery of sexual differ-
entiation.

I look good in the rude perfume of decaying boundaries.

I've gone through a number of rites of passage, and some have taken me by surprise. Although no longer subject to sexual harassment on the street, I've been threatened with explosive physical violence more times as a guy than as a woman.

I live my life inside an ongoing paradox.

Ambiguity and peril.

Postmodernism suits me. And sorcery . . . A shaman has three marks to indicate that he or she has completed initiation: scars, a new name, a secret.

In many cultures, transsexual, transgendered, and intersexed people were shamans and tricksters—jokers.

I have donated my body to science.

The joker is wild!

Transsexuality is a phenomenon. Awesome with cloaked paradoxes, unknowable, ranging far from accepted cultural beliefs and practices. Instigating reexaminations of identity as well as the methods and practices that enable us to know or perceive identity.

Identity as will, as having the agency to restructure the very body it inhabits.

Transsexuality is a crime of passion. A nearly savage act of body modification occupying a charged realm far beyond our culture's current obsession with "safety."

Transsexuals are agents provocateurs on the edges of a culture hurtling headlong into a century where technology will interface on an escalating basis with our bodies and consciousnesses. We are the furthest, most extreme expression of manipulation of the body, almost as though that body, that human stretch of flesh, were a piece of plastic, a synthetic, malleable substance. We restructure our glands, our body fluids, our skin, nerves, and genitals. Our lives are recovered by science, the oblique point of reference for an expanding arc of transformation.

We are thieves of technology for the will of an inscrutable and delicious fate. Some call it choice, others—destiny.

How many people have had the experience of living both as a man and as a woman? Of experiencing the hormonal surges, of wearing the skin and muscles, the shifting moods, the social, spiritual, and historical onus of both sexes?

Because we have lived the impossible, what was previously only dreamed of, we must demand to be known and understood. We are prophets of a richly complex net of perceptions and dialogues. We are radically violent instrumentalities of transformation concerning sex, gender, body modification, and identity. Ancient archetypes whisper to us that we are connected to archaic, abiding images of man and woman in our essence, even from within our seeming contradictions. We intensify the archetypes of maleness and femaleness in order to see through them, to live past them, to fully and completely reconfigure their meaning.

By becoming a man, I became all men and developed a new compassion for maleness and femaleness as it is lived in this culture. What previously appeared to be sexist posturing or empty role-playing took on the texture and vulnerable complexities of a passionate panoply, richly lived, *real*. Real, as in abiding, reasonable, rooted in experience that is lived. Not conspired, contrived, or counterfeit. A reality with contradictions, genuine feeling, and insoluble—although tangible—meaning.

I've come to a more complete understanding of why people act in the ways they do. I'm not as quick to judge men or, for that matter, women. I no longer have subtle feelings of superiority from being on the "politically correct" side (in my case, the feminist side). I'm not as dogmatic or defensive. I feel more human, although I'm actually more spectacular and strange than ever before. I feel freedom now that I've served my deepest will and shattered my old life in the course of it.

Because of my transformation, I've had to reexamine my assumptions concerning sexuality, the differences between men and women, the social and biological constructions and foundations of gender identity, the motivating impulses constructing culture.

This transition brings great opportunities to transsexual people if we are willing to take them on. These include freedom, knowledge, and the ability to participate in mystery. The mystery that our lives become once we have changed our sex and eluded all expectations of how and who we are, and the mystery we find the world to be as we take part in it from the vantage point of complete strangers, alien to and yet intimately familiar with each sex. Unlocking the mystery of knowing that just as we are not simple, nothing and no one else is either. The world is a stretching, shaking net, wild with biologically rooted instinct, flashes of intuitive, abstract thought forms encoding and creating culture, inchoate dream sequences, yearnings that search and destroy all assumptions and all dogmatic wishful thinking. It's a jungle, and we're in it.

I have changed my sex. Future generations of transsexuals will only do it more thoroughly as biotechnology becomes more refined. The previously unthinkable range of that transformation actually weds us more deeply to the rest of humanity. From the margins, the periphery, the middle expanses are most easily viewed.

Changing sex is radical because it is extreme, far-fetched, and magical, not because of any imagined alliance to any particular political ideology.

Being transsexual has nothing to do with being part of a unilateral political movement, a religion, or a cult. It is not my particular job to reeducate society and change it to some utopian, or possibly dystopian, multigendered glob. I believe that transsexuals must fight for our civil rights, for affordable, competent healthcare, for the right to live as ourselves with respect and dignity. But I am not interested in a sanctimonious "movement," where being "transgendered" becomes a self-referential lifestyle or is tethered to an ideologically arch set of political values.

Transsexuality is not, as some would now contend, a natural extension of lesbian feminism or of any other type of feminism. While not necessarily in opposition to feminism in its many permutations, it is distinct. Transsexual identities must be defined and expressed on our own terms. Our voices are unique and, until recently, unheard and incompletely imagined.

There are infinite permutations of identity, now identified as "transgender," currently in vogue in queer communities: "FTM dyke butch," "dyke boichix who cross-dress," "genderqueer tranny fag boi," and "biofemme transgender lesbian." Let there be no mistake: Everyone has a right to be who they are or think they are at any moment, to shock, to piss off, to repossess, to realign their scrotum, tits, attitude, skin color, hair color, outfit, and cheekbones! Everyone has a right to be admitted to that exclusive, sexy party. And it's beginning to look as though everyone wants to be. That said, I am skeptical and ultimately wary of enthusiasm for these new "queer" self-congratulatory and self-conscious "transgressive transgendered identities." After all, the desire to have all your options open and never close a door behind you is very American. The belief that you should be able to make *any choice at any time.* We consume commodities, lifestyles, and now identities with the avidity of jackals with one finger on the remote control and another on the index to our crotch. Each lifestyle or "identity" choice is a sweating, heated mélange of images, a loopy potpourri, a postmodern snuff film. We leer at our former identities as they wither and die. We feel triumphant in the voyeurism, the distance our most recent self-invention has opened. Finally, all our various and assorted lifestyles, conflated sexual orientations, and gender identities become just another tidy item for consumption, reproduction, and mass-marketed self-congratulation. We aren't beings with identities, we are consumers in search of a euphoric identity. A slight and whimsical euphoria that can be measured, quantified, and processed into a "safe" space. An identity that is simultaneously final and open, that cancels out the fatality, the palpable limits of choice, chance, or destiny. A contrived identity hyphenated and situated beyond certainty or doubt.

I prefer simplicity—the awkward, close edges of a naive yet emphatic truth-telling, the discerning yet ecstatic voice of authenticity.

I'm interested in inquiry, imagination, the transmutation of elemental psychic energies. I don't have an ax to grind in terms of making everyone give up the "bipolar" gender system. Hey, I like being a guy and I like it when women enjoy being women. The man/woman dynamic turns me on big-time. Boy/girl like animals rutting. Basic. Old-fashioned. Bipolarized.

Politics of the Left and Right bore me. They strike me as short-sighted. Too much bad art, too many dead bodies. Chairman Mao, Stalin, and Hitler had a lot in common. Fidel Castro jails queers and writers. These people thought (or, in the case of Castro, still think) that the control of thought, bodies, and destinies is for the greater good. They believed in a totalization of identity, a "movement," a structured utopia.

I'm in league with nature's lucidity and hunger. With Blake's devil whose "energy is eternal delight," as well as the primeval, mischievous id that drives Pan to manhandle and seduce any sex goddess you can think of with his big hairy hands and his pipes. I'm in league with technology and big dreams that ignite people with hope and pleasure—the future, an escalation of biological invention we can't yet imagine.

Freedom, brisk and invigorating. Not a Hallmark experience, not a therapy. Nothing trite or sentimental, nothing preachy or unctuous—nothing so easy, *safe,* or formulaic. No comfort zones masquerading as truth.

I'm searching for an unpredictable, body-wrenching experience.

INTRODUCTION

The *Testosterone Files* is about transformation in the arena of sexual politics, theory alchemically translated from the flesh. It careens through my first five years of transition from female to male, detailing the physiological, psychological, and social transformations of that dramatic phase in my sex change. My focus in this book is on hormones, not surgery—unlike many transsexual memoirs—as I believe that taking testosterone was actually the most definitive and crucial aspect of my transformation. I recount how testosterone shaped and revolutionized my perspective on life and my take on sexual politics from an explosive vantage point, the perspective of an offbeat punk rock bohemian lesbian feminist in the process of becoming a heterosexual man.

By injecting testosterone, I began to experience the entire world from a perspective I could not have anticipated. Testosterone, the "male hormone," is actually a sex hormone that everyone has, but men possess this virilizing chemical in astronomical amounts compared to women. When I changed my sex, I altered my ratio of testosterone to a male range. The result was not only an amazing physical transformation evident to anyone who meets me, but also an even more amazing and unexpected change in my perceptions, sex drive, and emotions. Mesmerized as my internal landscape and body morphed, I was able, through astute observation, investigation, and constant questioning, to better comprehend the ways in which men and women are actually very different. I also came to a deeper understanding of the male role, and of the role of socialization in constructing the realms of behavior, feeling, and expectation peculiar to each sex. Many beliefs that I had previous to transition were shaken and had to be reevaluated. Although I don't pretend to have the definitive answer to every question about gender and sexual politics, nonetheless, I come to you as a kind of oracle who has been through a unique, intensive fire.

This book is divided into three parts: Beginning, which introduces the reader to me as I begin my transition; Before Testosterone, which narrates the events and internal discoveries that led to my decision to change sex; and After Testosterone, in which the reader is invited to witness my perceptual, emotional, and social transformation from female to male. The book is a mixture of narrative and in-depth treatment of particular phases or subjects relating to my life and transition. Each chapter, particularly in the After Testosterone section, is therefore a kind of "file." I focus in these files/chapters on various aspects of the transition: emotions, sex drive, male violence. So, some of the chapters will follow a narrative thread and others will appear to go back in time and trace my development forward in these specific areas. Also, the After Testosterone section discusses various social aspects of my emerging life as a man, including my relationships with women and experiences at work. Social construction and biology intersect and mesh; maleness is constructed even as it is biologically informed and created.

Throughout this work I use the word "nontranssexual," or sometimes "genetic," to refer to people who are *not* transsexuals. I first heard the term "nontranssexual" used by my friend Anne Ogborne, a transwoman activist and strong advocate of transsexuals being able to construct the world from our perspective. Also, the term "biomale," now in vogue, is problematic as transmen become a form of "biomale" when we inject testosterone on a regular basis. "Genetic" has fewer problems as to its accuracy, although it may be true that some transsexual people have genetic anomalies. Furthermore, it's safe to say that transsexual men are generally XX.

Although I do talk about the personal motivations for my change and capture a portion of my life up to when I made the decision to become a man in the Before Testosterone section, I tend to agree with the Gryphon in *Alice's Adventures in Wonderland* who impatiently told Alice, "The adventures first, explanations take such a dreadful time." It is my intention to foreground changing sex as an adventure, an investigation, and an opportunity to live beyond the given and the commonplace. My rite of passage to manhood was not the common one, but I did endure and enjoy many initiations. Although driven by a deep and unyielding personal necessity to become a man, my transition felt like more than simply a medical solution to a personal problem; it soon expanded into an exploration, an erotically charged boundary-crossing, and a risk-filled journey. I am imparting some of the knowledge gleaned from that necessary adventure to you, the reader, now. I hope that you will find something of value here—an anecdote, a perception, a sexual fantasy, some wild and irreverent humor—that you can use to understand the enigmatic and volatile binary of male and female.

PART ONE
BEGINNING

Am I willing to give up everything I have,
in order to have everything I ever wanted?

—Max Wolf Valerio, from the film "Max"

CHAPTER 1:
RAW POWER

Unscrew the locks from the doors!
Unscrew the doors themselves from their jambs!
—Walt Whitman

Every week there's some small transformation. My voice cracks, my shoulders broaden. There's new, coarse, dark hair on my legs and feet. Today, I see a new pattern in the skin on the back of my hands. As I'm crossing the street it becomes apparent to me slowly, an awakening recognition. I stare at my hands, straining, trying to determine what is different. My pores have become larger, opened up; the crisscross pattern of skin is wider. My skin must be getting rougher. . . . The tiny creases on my knuckles are deepening. In the middle of the day, in the middle of the street, nearly by accident, I notice these subtle changes. And I feel different, more energetic somehow. Objects appear more three-dimensional, the line separating one surface from another is more defined. Although I've always felt more male than female, until I began taking testosterone to alter my body biologically, I never knew what biological masculinity felt like. It's another world, a shift of consciousness.

I take testosterone by intramuscular injection once every two weeks. I've learned to give myself my shot, but it's hard. I prefer to have someone with me. My heart races, my palms perspire. It's a long, thick needle that I push deep into the muscle of the buttock or my front thigh. Slowly, I push through the skin. That's the toughest part, the initial piercing, the puncture of flesh, sliding the length of the long needle down. Register; pull back the plunger. Check for blood; if any shoots up that means I've hit a vein or artery and the thick liquid could create an embolism. If no blood shoots into the transparent barrel of the syringe, I push the oily liquid inside. A twinge of nerves . . . It gets easier each time.

I got my first shot of testosterone on March 20, 1989. The first day of spring, as the sun crept into Aries, sign of the ram. Ruled by Mars: planet of war, lust, and intrepid, flamboyant masculinity. That afternoon at four o'clock I went to the office of Dr. Argopolis—a tiny, balding man with finely tuned, alert features.

Black horn-rimmed glasses weigh down his small face, accenting the looming alacrity of his dark eyes. Dr. Argopolis peers at me without restraint across the metal expanse of his desk. "Which direction are you going?"

My friend Gene tells me I'm going through some profound, mysterious process. My gestures have "become more male." Although I'm contemplating the nuances and subtle cues of maleness and femaleness as never before, I'm surprised by this assessment. I'm not deliberately trying to alter my gestures. That would be cheating. I wasn't aware that the way I was moving seemed different. Apparently, even before I sat in this chair, steeled with anticipation, a process of letting go of any effort to conceal my sense of male identity was well under way.

I have also felt an overall sense of relief. "I'm going from female to male," I declare to a bewildered Dr. Argopolis. Peering at the wispy dark hairs stranded atop his shiny balding head, I worry about whether this doctor has much experience with female to male transsexuals (FTMs).

"Are you sure you want to do this?" Dr. Argopolis asks.

In my hand I clutch a letter from my counselor, Joanne. The necessary "hormone letter." My passport to this office, to a physical examination, an initial shot, and a prescription for testosterone. I'd gotten that letter, earned it in a way, after seeing Joanne for three months. That was the minimum requirement. She determined that I wasn't psychotic, that I understood the process of "sex reassignment," that I was aware of the risks and understood what I could and could not realistically expect from testosterone treatment and, eventually, surgery.

Dr. Argopolis asks to see my California driver's license. I hand him my California state ID card, which I've already changed to my new name, Maximilian Wolf Valerio. He eyes the picture and name for a long time before glancing up over the top of his glasses to announce, "Maximilian. That is a very masculine name."

"Uh, yeah . . ." I notice how much I'm smiling and nodding. Walking the line. I don't want to say anything that'll make him decide not to treat me. The fact that I changed my name on my ID should be proof of my commitment to a male life, a certificate of sincerity.

"You will grow hair," he points out, gesturing toward his chin.

"Yes, I know—just as long as I don't lose it," I quip.

I knew what I was getting into.

I check Dr. Argopolis out with a dubious eye. *Is this guy a quack?* I glance around the room. *There* is *a certificate.* . . . He isn't an endocrinologist, but I can see he is at least a doctor. I'd heard that genuine endocrinologists charged three times as much. These specialists ran test after test, and sometimes put you through a six-week waiting period just to test your nerve. All that felt like a game. I know what I want and I'm anxious to get on with it. Through reading and talking with transsexual men who are further along, I understand the parameters of hormone treatment. I'm aware of the risks.

From the beginning, I had strategized to accomplish my transition as expediently and as cheaply as possible. Initially, I had gone to a therapist at a gender center who had peered at me skeptically and asked why I couldn't just remain a lesbian. The prospect of having to explain this tired fact to him for six months to a year was simply too expensive and time-consuming. I opted for Joanne, a transwoman counselor, who was supportive and discerning and didn't pretend to be skeptical simply to give me a hard time. Otherwise, I felt as though I would be trying to game the therapist to get what I wanted. With Joanne, I could be honest and expect her to follow through appropriately and not waste my time or money. I could also get supportive feedback that I could trust from someone who had been through transition.

Dr. Argopolis feels my liver to see if it's swollen, placing a hand just below my rib cage and squeezing. He weighs me, asks a few questions relating to my general health. My blood pressure, low as usual. "Do you feel faint if you get up suddenly?"

I laugh and say, "No, not usually. . . ."

"Well, it's okay, but it is very low." Resting heart rate also low, everything's fine. Next is a liver panel to check my enzymes, a test that will become routine—every six months to a year—to make sure that my health isn't adversely affected by the testosterone.

"Goodbye." I gaze into my face in the mirror above the sink in his small bathroom. My female self is receding as I watch my eyes. I memorize the moment. Stretch the crossroads out. This first shot is what I've waited and plotted for, my walk off the precipice.

Dr. Argopolis draws up the shot from the small bottle. "Here, get ready . . . here is the medicine." The doctor squints into the barrel of the syringe as it fills up with the virilizing potion.

From that first shot, I've lived each day as though I were already physically the man I decided to become. I've injected a powerful elixir, the workings of which hurtle me into a web of energies and impulses I couldn't have anticipated. The doors are blasted open. I begin to enter the realm of male life.

There's a lemon tree outside. I can see it through the glass door of my basement studio apartment. The lemons are fresh, clean, bright. Their yellow color itself looks edible. I sit and watch them suspended above the yard with a fragile agility. I have time now to contemplate their shapes, just as I contemplate the changes I'm going through.

The atmosphere is textured with life. Colors squeeze into my eyes from every direction as I walk on the street. It's the summer of 1989. I'm thirty-two years old. I've taken time off from working to wait out the first round of physical, perceptual, and emotional changes from testosterone.

Previously, my skin was smooth, the pores finely drawn, almost hidden. I study men walking by, scrutinize their faces and hands. Skin like a lemon or orange peel, thicker, their bodies armored. I hadn't noticed this distinction between the sexes so clearly before. Hadn't contemplated it with any resonance of thought; it slipped past me. I'm starting to become aware of the minute, nearly atomic differences between the sexes—skin, brow, hips, jaw, hairline. As I watch my body and see, hear, and feel it transform into a man's body, I learn about these contrasts. All those characteristics we clock unconsciously in a flash when we meet someone in order to decide: Is this a man or a woman?

My thighs have become compact, harder. I look at them in amazement. The fat where my legs join my hips is gone. And my hips are disappearing fast. I've never actually realized how much straighter and narrower men's hips are than women's until now. Mine are beginning to conform to that shape with biological precision.

I've never noticed my body as much as I'm noticing it now.

I worry about my hands. Most transsexuals do. Hands don't change a great deal in size and shape because of hormones. My hands are smoothly textured, with long fingers. They aren't dainty or tiny, but they aren't masculine, either. I'm acutely aware of this. *How can I live as a man with these hands?* I observe their delicate fingers and feel disconnected—*these hands are not mine.*

When I was twenty-three, I'd gone to see *Raging Bull* with a friend. We'd sat there and watched Jake LaMotta trash his house, beat his wife in jealous rages. In one scene, he raised his hands up, looked at them with hard eyes, and complained that they were too small, "like girls' hands."

I thought, *Yes, like mine. I know how he feels. My hands are small, like girls' hands. . . .* Like girls' hands. I couldn't understand what this feeling meant. I breathed, unconscious, in the dark theater. I told my friend afterward that I understood how he felt. "I have girls' hands, too." Without being completely aware of it, I was saying, *I am a man with girls' hands.*

My friend listened, tossed her head back, and laughed. I was, in fact, a young woman. Lithe, with long auburn hair past my shoulders, slender arms, and smooth hands. Fine skin that shone tight across high, rounded cheekbones. It was unsettling, this thing in me, dark and urgent. It summoned recognition.

Understanding this disparity, between my secret, half-conscious conception of myself as male and my physical female form, was to involve a long unraveling. I had to be overwhelmed by the pain of that contradiction, understand the ramifications of what I took for granted—a persistent, ongoing identification with maleness, with men, with their bodies and experiences.

Now, I hold my hands up and look, and although they are still smaller than average, they have acquired a rougher appearance. With a persistent certainty, my hands become somewhat broader, stronger. My skin gets thicker, and I even see the beginnings of hair on my fingers, but no veins yet. My friend Will's hands are really rugged, with veins popping out, straining. He says he had veins sticking out even before hormones, but not like now. And the veins are beginning to extend up his arms, riding on top of hard ridges of muscle.

Will is ahead of me in this change by a year. Already he looks completely masculine. Five feet four inches tall, Will is half Irish American and half Jewish with the shadow of a gymnast's build beneath a thickening waistline, strong forearms and shoulders, black hair, and the beginnings of a dark, thick beard. He's shaving regularly, and his hairline's beginning to recede. It's already hard to believe that Will was ever a woman, and he's only been on testosterone for one year.

Even though I've just begun, he's optimistic about my potential. "In five years," he claims, "no one, not even another transsexual man, will be able to tell that you were ever female."

My body unfolds its masculinity in increments. I'm not sure how I'm going to turn out. It's a risk. Every day my body discloses another small change; it abandons another facet of its female character. Walking past the mirror, I stop and look with a new intensity. My face is nearly another face. There's a muted sensuality, a thickness to my features. I look a long time, in wonder, trying to gauge what has altered. Is it my nose? My lips? My jaw seems wider, stronger. And I know that this is only my first male face, the face of my second adolescence. In a few months, it will be different.

I bind my breasts in order to flatten and conceal them. I use a posture belt, a device that's usually worn around the lower back. Hike this elastic band up and wear it around your chest and it becomes a breast binder, constricting but effective. Before I get my top surgery, a specialized operation that will give my chest a male appearance, I have to live in this binding. There's no other way to present myself as male and not invite odd stares or ridicule.

And my voice is beginning to change. There's a tightness in my throat. Hoarseness, real hoarseness, making it difficult to speak. And small shifts from low tones to my former, higher voice, then back down into a deeper register.

The energy continues. I find myself grinding my teeth, setting my jaw tight with the sheer tension of this new, cranked-up energy. I take long walks every day; I can't stay inside. Not wanting to spend as much time lying down in bed, I'm restless.

Will tells me, "You can hardly sit still." My energy is like a teenage boy's—moving, pacing, shifting in my seat, speaking in wild bursts. I'm interrupting people in conversation, suddenly overcome with bolts of enthusiasm—I can't hold back!

I feel more confident, expansive, cocky. It's a pounding-on-the-chest kind of feeling, a swagger, a strut. Testosterone is an androgen, an up, pure raucous power. "Raw power!" as Iggy Pop sings. I'm beginning to understand certain things in waves of sharp relief. The adolescent boys who whip past me on skateboards—shouting, grinning, turning wild tricks, jumping curbs, weaving in and out of traffic oblivious to skinned knees or passing cars. Men in groups—loud, boisterous, joking with maniacal enthusiasm. Gay men in Castro bars—sweating, stripped to the waist, dancing to throbbing, relentless music. It's *that* energy—sizzling, pounding, surging, thrusting, a little loud or tight-eyed, paranoid around the edges, territorial, tense, on guard, expansive, cranked up. Testosterone is *party* energy. I'm finding it hard to contain. If I lie down, I beat off. If I get up, I feel like walking, walking, and walking. I wake up with a start in the mornings, charged. I wish I could channel it.

I talk to nontranssexual men about my experiences. "Gee, I wish I felt like that," they tell me. I imagine they did when they were teenagers. But nontranssexual men are used to a different energy level. Because they never experienced estrogen at the levels I did when I was female, they don't have anything to compare their energy level to.

On estrogen, I was more relaxed. I couldn't have known it; I had no means of comparison. I felt submerged in a sweet, dense fog, like walking through liquid—slow, languid.

Friends begin to comment that my energy seems more focused with the testosterone. I give an impression of being more compact. Am I becoming more aggressive? It's hard to gauge what the intentions of my energy look like from outside myself. Aggression appears to be an intention, an outer manifestation of an inner configuration of force. The intensity of it. I catch myself feeling more impatient. Standing in line to get a BART ticket, it's easier to feel frustration. The frustration feels red. It shoots up through my body hot, a whisk of flame.

Although both of us considered ourselves very sexual before, Will and I talk about sex like it is some new discovery. It's an unrelenting obsession; I see sex everywhere. At some point, I realize that I'm beating off three, four, five times a day. It dawns on me, *You are doing this many times, every single day, every single day.*

Initially, there is a tingling in my clitoris. It starts about a week or so after I take my first shot of testosterone. My clitoris is starting to grow. Tingling. I feel aroused by things that don't normally arouse me—soap operas, television game shows, beauty pageants.

I'm seeing something previously hidden from me; another dimension is slowly being revealed. I can't believe all the sexual imagery and innuendo on television: women's asses, ripe breasts nearly spilling out of dresses, the angled arch of a woman's foot as she slips on a shoe, a man stripped to the waist holding a woman close, the way men and women look at each other. *How come I never noticed all this sex before?*

I find myself paying more attention to women on the street, their breasts and asses in tight clothes. I'm hypnotized by their body parts.

This starts out subtly; then I notice myself staring, taking long, lingering looks. It's nearly comical in its intensity—a caricature of sexual feeling, the Tex Avery cartoon wolf with the popping eyes and dripping, salacious tongue. I'm awakening to a drive that is a relentless hunger.

It must be serious. The other night I watched *Wheel of Fortune* and Vanna started to look extremely sexy. I leaned closer to the television, squinting in concentration. I had never really noticed her form before. She was wearing a shining red dress that hugged her ass and hips. Her proportions seemed to take on a glow, a seductive meaning I hadn't intuited previously. *That dress, that body!* I thought. Then I realized, *This is Vanna White! I mean Vanna!* She was smiling with an aching vacancy. But god, she had a body!

Will tells me that what I'm experiencing is the sexual surge of male adolescence. This dramatic elevation in sexual drive evens out a bit after a while, or maybe you just get used to it. Maybe over time it just feels more familiar; you adjust. But the initial surge of fantasy and desire can be overwhelming. In the beginning, Will also felt that everything on television seemed to have a sexual subtext. He'd watch the eleven o'clock news and imagine that, be nearly convinced that, all the news announcers were naked from the waist down, that each newsman had an enormous hard-on, and that the women, too, were ready and anxious, lusting with glee behind their wedgelike smiles, their tight cheeriness. After the broadcast, *he knew,* they would all fuck each other with abandon, in every possible position, legs splayed, knobby knees on the cold floor of the newsroom.

I've gone to porn stores and sat in the video booths and beaten off, surfing through the channels. Flipping the dial feverishly, looking for the "good" stuff—fucking, fucking, and more fucking! Men ramming their hard cocks into women from behind and on top; young women sitting on dicks, moving their hips back and forth, moaning.

This elevation in sexual fantasy and interest feels primal. An outburst of instinct. Before taking testosterone, I could never have imagined this intensity of sexual drive. Will and I laugh about it. "It's madness!" But I am consumed, and still a little in shock.

How to explain this to women? There is this thing about men that they cannot completely know. Few people I know want to believe that there could be a real chasm, a chemically induced difference of sexual drive between the sexes. Few want to believe there might be any difference at all that is not socially constructed. The possibility that men and women are biologically on opposite sides of a steep divide driven by hormonal differences sounds too primitive, too out of our control.

The women who come closest to understanding are the prostitutes, strippers, phone sex operators. It's something they've suspected. This is why these guys are so eager to part with their hard-earned cash for a peek, a fondle, a tease, a quick lay.

When I was female, I wondered why men seemed so preoccupied with sexuality. Walking down Mission Street at age twenty—braless, in tattered jeans and a T-shirt, my long brown hair hanging loosely down my back—men would stare and hiss snake sounds, calling out "Hey, baby!" At twenty-six, I overheard a group of businessmen talking about a young woman walking down the street within view of their office window. "Look at that. She's something, man. Watch those tits jiggle, bouncy, bouncy, bouncy!" I eavesdropped and was astonished. Surely, I thought, this crude appraisal of this anonymous woman's body parts was motivated by some kind of hatred of women, some free-floating hostility. It was actually, I understand now, just pure lust. Lust is not hostility.

I'm beginning to understand many aspects of sexuality from the gut, from both sides. I observe these feelings in myself now, as a man, and remember what it was like on the other side, as a woman perceiving that a man had these feelings.

I remember how it feels to be watched, leered at. It is wrong to make women feel that way, appraised, objectified. Quite simply, it's rude to stare at anyone on the street. So I curb my desire to stare, to watch. I'm beginning to understand that maturity as a male, becoming a man instead of an adolescent boy, means learning to control or sublimate these impulses. Some guys never make it.

Even so, this impulse to watch women's bodies and not notice or care about the rest of them overwhelms me. There's a natural propensity of the male sex drive to objectify. A biological component that is compelling. If one becomes aware that this "urge to ogle" is a fiction of the body, chemically driven, one can cultivate a distance from its influence.

As my sexuality changes, I grow increasingly cynical, tricksterlike, a roguish troublemaker. Sex fires through me, a transgressive impulse. My sexuality doesn't feel as dependent on emotional associations. There's a cold clarity to this drive that hardens my imagination, stripping sentimentality from my humor just as it's stripped from my perceptions.

Will tells me that I say over and over again, "If you'd told me five years ago that I'd be just another dude standing at Frenchy's gawking at girlie magazines or beating off in video booths, I would've said you were crazy."

Before I began hormones, I told my lesbian friend Kate not to worry, I wasn't going to become "the kind of straight guy who puts pinups of nude busty women on his bedroom walls and lifts weights."

My values and beliefs undergo a cataclysmic reevaluation as I transform. I can't be sure where I'll end up. What will I be like in five years, in ten? Will I still be a feminist? Will I become a Republican, an insurance adjuster, an evangelical Christian? Will I become a misty-eyed liberal in the suburbs in a suit and tie with a briefcase and a diversified investment portfolio? Will I start collecting copies of *Soldier of Fortune* magazine? Kate jokes with a swig of sarcasm in her voice that I'm going to be a "nice, sensitive, caring man, like Phil Donahue or Alan Alda." Will I finally become the attorney my mother always wanted me to be? Will I go into corporate middle management and beat drums in the woods on the weekends to get in touch with my "wild man within"? Will I grow my hair to my ass and join a rock band? Go to the game on the weekends? Take ballet lessons? Will I get into punching bags and boxing techniques? Hang out in strip joints obsessed with high heels and bustiers? Try hard to "get in touch with my feelings"? Will I be able to do more handyman things around the house than just screwing in a lightbulb?

I wonder whether or not I'll have the same sense of humor. Will I suddenly go gay or bisexual? It happens.

Perhaps my tastes in sexual partners, food, music, politics, and art won't change. After all, this isn't a brain transplant. Yet all sorts of unforeseen things happen to people when they change their sex. A person can develop in any number of unanticipated directions once they are freed from the pretense of a body that feels unnatural.

And how will other people perceive me? Will women find me attractive? Will I be able to get a girlfriend?

My friend Gene quips I'm going to become a "weird guy." I'm not even sure I understand what he means. I worry and wonder . . . a guy with a wacky laugh who writes strange, infernal poetry? A dreamer, the man apart? Not the average guy, not Mr. Normal . . . surely that would never be me. I've always valued originality, odd visions, and unusual, even eccentric, people.

What would becoming a man do, if anything, to my writing? One friend told me that the change would ignite my "brilliance." Those were generous words, and I hoped that any inspiration I had could be set ablaze.

"Weird guy," "brilliant," "nice, sensitive man"—I don't know if any of these will ring true or not, but I already feel the gates shaking, the jambs of the doors loosening and pulling free. A wild joy is sparking inside my bones. A low, angular, electrical charge that runs along the length of my body, from foot to crown, awakening dreams and longings, igniting possibilities as the testosterone works on me and my perceptions alter.

The world has tipped; in degrees it turns upside down. The joker, the agent provocateur is loose, opening doors and closing them.

PART TWO
BEFORE TESTOSTERONE

We are what we imagine. Our very existence consists
in our imagination of ourselves....
The greatest tragedy that can befall us is to go unimagined.

—N. Scott Momaday

CHAPTER 2:
GET MORE CIGARETTES

Get More Cigarettes '82—Crawford
—Graffiti scrawl on the wall at Hotel Hell

'm watching my image retreat in the rearview mirror of my girl-friend Roxanne's beat-up Ford. I feel gangly; dyed black hair straight up, spiked, and drenched with Tres Flores brilliantine over Black & White pomade. The old-fashioned gunk that's thick, white, and waxy, with a faint scent reminding me of drive-in movie theaters, or long airless stretches of highway amplified by still night darkness between intermittent lights of rest stops and gas stations. I wear a long, heavy chain over the shoulder of my black leather jacket, spikes on the collar, and leather studded gloves without fingers. White, pointy Joe Jackson shoes—"winkle pickers" is what they're called in England—and tight stovepipe black pants.

The guys out on Mission Street stay clear of me: When I walk down the street, they say, "Watch out for her, man, she looks mean. . . ."

I'm living at a place on Mission Street called Mission–A, or Hotel Hell. It's next door to a cramped beauty-supply store; an "A" painted in red with a circle around it graces the glass of the front door. Once inside, a long, narrow stairway starts at a sharp angle—steep and straight up. From the top, it's a long way down. The place has two stories and I share it with seven or eight other people, all "young professionals," a roommate quips. Once, I spied a rat sitting at the top of those stairs, a large, tawny-colored rat the size of a small cat, upright on his two hind legs, sniffing the air. I passed the creature on my way up the stairs. He hissed, feral eyes and a long, cordlike tail slipping close to my ankles. Then he plummeted down the stairs, *clumpety-clump* to the bottom and into an opening in the wall, swallowing darkness as he entered.

Red spray paint marks the wall the animal disappeared into: WILD WOMEN OF BORNEO—WILD, WILD. Huge red graffiti scrawls line the walls down the long flight of stairs. Mornings, I get up and gingerly make my way to the kitchen through a hallway and living room littered with beer cans, wine bottles, half-eaten pizza on paper plates, empty record sleeves, wads of odd and assorted trash. We're an eclectic group—punk rock musicians, a filmmaker, a speed dealer considering law school, a German art student with a brassy, high-strung American wife. We've had members of punk bands—Bad Posture, Verbal Abuse, the drummer of the Dead Kennedys, and, of course, the Wild Women of Borneo—who can barely tune their instruments but are full of spit and fury nonetheless. Bad Posture practices downstairs on a regular basis, sometimes after midnight, making a din I somehow manage to sleep through. Their lineup is a study in contrasts. The lead singer is close to seven feet tall with a Mohawk and a long, wiry torso; the guitar and bass players are barely five feet five—two Chicano guys from Texas who came to San

Francisco to play hardcore punk music, drink beer, and flee the threat of suburban strip malls forever more. Slit the navel of the American Dream with an open vein, a hot, white drug, and an adolescent guitar chord.

Parties spring up spontaneously like dirt devils after shows at the On Broadway. We'll be in our rooms, doors shut, and then downstairs the front door will burst open. Voices at the bottom shout up the stairs: "There's a party here, we heard there's a party here!"

Roxanne is sassy, witty, and sexy with her bracelets and bangles, raccoon makeup (the calligraphy of tropical birds that she draws in, tipsy, from eyelid to temple), her droll observations, her tequila and brandy, the euphoric shimmer of coke or speed in her eyes. We hang out with a small, tight circle of dyke friends and go to see punk bands: X, The Exploited, Flipper, Wilma, The Contractions, The Varve, Black Flag, the Mutants, and the Dead Kennedys. There's an energy in the air raw with joy and discovery. My life is one long party with a black-leather nimbus, an energy that is endless. There's Felix and Selene, who are madly in love and given to drama; Raven, a handsome and intense leather dyke; Pam, a wayward though determined medical student, and her girlfriend, Mona, who dances with the most absolute abandon and concentration; and Johnette, a sparkling extrovert in go-go boots who was once a Marxist. We imagine ourselves a "girl gang," we complain about the stick-in-the-mud attitudes of most of the lesbian world, get high, have long, arduous, and revealing discussions into the night about our lives. Go out. See and be seen. With a paroxysm of abandonment. *Fun.*

The Tool and Die, On Broadway, the Mab, even Amelia's are fun with this group of friends. Amelia's is the dyke bar where we all originally met, spotting each other across the long room with the Holiday Inn lounge decor. Despite the bad disco music, the dull crowds, the hours of waiting around for an excitement that never came, we had managed to collide.

In Roxanne, the excitement's there. We make love all night for hours on end, high and delirious. Each time we dare each other to go a little further, stretch at the edges of one more taboo, lacerate one more wound. Roxanne whispers a suggestion into my ear. I can barely hear it, then I realize what she's saying. I've never been talked to in bed like this before. She says it again, moans and twists under me. "Force me . . ." I stop for a moment, stunned, then go at it, harder than before. She's never been penetrated. I start with one finger at a time, gently, then slide in, deeper. One more finger each time I fuck her, stretching her, until I can almost put in my entire hand. Eventually we graduate to silicone cocks. We are afraid. We stop and laugh and wonder what this could mean.

In 1982, these acts feel forbidden in the lesbian world. We're afraid to talk to other dykes about how we are having sex. When we go out shopping at Good Vibrations for a suitable dildo, we're careful to pick one that doesn't look too realistic—no swollen head or pulsing veins. A large purple dildo with a wavy shape is what we choose and secret home.

I don't use a strap-on at first, but hold this object in my hand and guide it like a missile inside her, stabbing her with it, in and out in prolonged combat. New feelings rise up in me, a sticky dark lust, an image of myself as nearly, *almost* male. I can almost see it, hear it, inhale the mute, tense odors, feel the way my male self moves, but the complete image, the idea of myself as a man, is hidden. It occurs to me that I have never had a clear idea of myself as anything or anyone when I have sex. My form is a vague presence, although I am always active, aggressive.

Roxanne asks me to rape her, break her open. I smile, shake my head, and keep on, fucking her until I can't fuck her anymore. I blindfold and handcuff her, watch as she teeters in black Parisian high heels, briskly spank her ass. Sometimes I can't believe we're doing these things, and neither can she. One night, I take the wavy-shaped silicone dick and strap it on. Attached to my torso, it's not nearly as abstract a presence. As I stand with that thing jutting out from my body and look at it bobbing up and down as I walk I feel a new, strange excitement. And fear.

I don't understand what this could mean. If anything, for most dykes who strap it on, it means nothing more than sex play, an exploration of gender roles or power and sexuality, or just plain hot sex. For me, the feelings are more conflicted and complex. I'm drawn back into an earlier, deeper dream of myself.

CHAPTER 3:
ADOLESCENT SPHINX

I ponder a monster figurine I've retrieved during a Christmas visit to my parents' house, peer at it in perplexed wonder, trying to draw out an answer, as though petitioning an adolescent sphinx to answer an intimate, absurd riddle. This Ed "Big Daddy" Roth monster is identical to the kind I drew in second and third grades. Its lingering fascination provides a clue. I study this blue-green monster wearing its lightning-streaked helmet, caught at the moment of impact as he steers or brakes into a delirious crash, wild-eyed. I know this monster is the real thing.

Roxanne thinks this little toy remarkable for a singular reason. "It's so phallic," she smiles. This embarrasses me. I'm not supposed to like "phallic" things or relate to them in any primary way. I mean, I am a lesbian. Lesbians imagine themselves outside of the phallic male world, which juts out all around, ubiquitous, a facade of raw impulses welded into a landscape of skyscrapers, porno magazines, action movies, corporate structures like power-drunk circus tents. We are indifferent. Or so we think. *But am I really indifferent?*

Looking into the maniac figure of the monster, I'm not even sure that I know what Roxanne is talking about. I stare at the monster, attempting to remember a place and a time saturated with dreaming, unselfconscious impulses. Why had I loved that monster so much when I was a child? Why had I drawn him, and others like him, over and over? I know that some secret is encoded in the monster's slender form. I've studied him for years, carried him reverently as I moved from place to place. In time, his form became more distinct.

I begin to see with a vivid eye the resonant details composing his small, explosive visage. I see all at once, with a hook of recognition and joy, his primal, anarchic male qualities: his long, bloodshot eyes bulging out, the haphazard tongue hanging down in a sneer or a defiant leer, his wild racing in an oblong car with big wheels, oblivious to danger, cranked on adrenaline, smashing with an affront of force and willfulness—the sheer artful adventure of virility. The long stick shift jammed up into his tiny hands like a kamikaze erection! He is a messenger. *This is my male self!*

Drawing was my first artistic discovery, before writing. I'd continued over the years, trying out various subjects but always returning to monsters, alien faces, archaic-looking demonic or slashing forms with sensual alliteration, an agenda of crime.

I feel like that—reckless, wicked, and male.

CHAPTER 4:
DRESSES, WRESTLING, AND BARBIES

One of my earliest memories is of my mother saying that someday I might be crowned Miss America. I am outraged. The feelings linger, stronger in my mind than the actual sequence of events, drawn in static black and white, like the television shows of that time, the early sixties. It's past my bedtime. I've crept out of bed, into the living room where Mom sits watching the Miss America pageant on the flickering black-and-white TV screen. A loud, important-sounding voice. The announcer bellows a song, "There she is, Miss Americaaa . . ." as the winner turns and waves at the audience watching her royal promenade. Waves a tiny, gloved hand, cheeks streaming with tears, an eclipse of agonized joy on her face, mouth quivering. This bizarre spectacle has absolutely no appeal to me whatsoever. At this young age, around three, my ambition is to be a soldier, like my father, a career-enlisted army man. I've told my mother this, which is why my shock and outrage is deep and nearly unspeakable. After all, I'm not really a girl, and this is all weird girl stuff. It's inconceivable to me that night as the lights flicker across the TV screen that I will ever grow up to become a woman.

I'm becoming aware of a fundamental problem. It has to do with my internal dialogue, my ongoing sense of who I am. If the people around me could hear the way I think of myself, they would be shocked. The person I see in the mirror is not the same person they see.

The fact that my mother perceives me, naturally, as a little girl is a source of great pain for me. When I try to correct her, I feel as though I'm talking to a wall. This is the strongest of our conflicts and will endure, in various guises, throughout the remainder of my childhood, on into adolescence, and finally into my adult life.

When I grow up and move to San Francisco, my mother will keep sending me panty hose every year at Christmas. She'll make long, dramatic speeches to me from time to time about how I have to "compromise" and wear dresses. "That's the only way you'll ever get anywhere in life. You have to compromise, Anita. You don't have to advertise the way you are."

I was an anomaly from birth, born with blue eyes and wisps of blond hair on my otherwise bald head. Since both my parents have dark hair and eyes, my lightness was a surprise. My father, Steve, is a "Manito," or Hispano from Ranchos de Taos, New Mexico, and my mother, Margo, is Blackfoot Indian from the Blood or Kainah Reserve in Alberta, Canada. In their youth, my parents were extremely slender, attractive people who looked as though the wind could easily blow them over. Dad's first language was Spanish, my mother's Blackfoot; neither learned English until they went to elementary school. Steve was a career army man for twenty years and we lived all over the United States and in Europe, usually moving every year and a half.

My mother is an intriguing, unpredictable combination of stage mother and adoring sycophant, of raging, haranguing critic and overprotective parent, and we have had a relationship that is complex and extreme in intensity. Without a doubt, I saw her as the dominant force in the family, a turbulent and charismatic person with some barely contained and mysterious inner force. She saw me as both god and devil and very little in between. Her ambitions for me were always great, as was her overall assessment of her own background and life. Although she mostly went to the punitive Catholic boarding schools for Native children that were mandatory for the Indians of her generation, she has never seemed to see herself as a victim. I never had the impression that her people on the reserve wanted for anything, even in the days before they had running water or telephones (the sixties). Her family had land, cattle, and influence.

My mother is an artist at heart, a fantastic pianist who plays classical music, boogie-woogie, show tunes, nearly everything she hears, by ear and by memory. She had dreamed of going to Juilliard but gave it up to get married, like many women of her time. I grew up listening to her hammer out tunes on the piano, drenched in music. Mom also had a good drawing hand in her youth, and encouraged my interest in music and art. Mom also bred Siamese cats throughout my childhood and would walk them outside on a leash.

Dad is a gentle, easygoing man with a fantastic sense of humor. My relationship to him is simpler and less ambivalent. I could generally count on his acceptance if he was pressed to give it. He is fun, amiable, and comforting, and he has often surprised me with his open mind and generous support. When my mother and aunt opposed my becoming a poet, it was my father who championed my cause, agreeing with me that the poets of Latin America and Spain are known for their visionary political involvement. He even gave his support for my being a lesbian after I told him that I would never change. Steve enjoys fishing, doing research on his family tree, reading, going camping, and, now, his grandchildren. There is something of the stargazer and the romantic in him. The only person in his large family to finish high school, my father joined the army since it offered him "a warm bed, meals, and a steady job," not to mention the opportunity to see the world. He enjoyed the military life and was upset when the army base at the Presidio in San Francisco, where we had once lived, was closed down and given over to "civilians." Yet, for all my father's involvement in the regimentation and pageantry of the military, he would occasionally say, wistfully, "I wish I was a hobo."

Will once made the joking observation that, being what many would consider a "shiftless" poet and writer, I was actually fulfilling my father's secret dream.

My father's people lived for hundreds of years as farmers and sheepherders high up in the Sangre de Cristo Mountains of northern New Mexico. A few, like my grandfather Francisco (Frank), were Penitentes. When I visited Taos, I watched hummingbirds with my grandmother Jesusita on the porch. She loved to point them out hovering above her flowers, wings flapping so fast they were a blur. The Virgin of Guadalupe decorated her walls, as did old family portraits—her father, Cristóbal, an intense man with blue eyes, and many other relatives and ancestors from the 1800s into the 1940s and '50s—handsome men and striking women with bedroom eyes, wavy dark hair, and sweet features. I visited my cousins and played the Ouija board, caught trout with my hands in the small streams, and walked all over the dirt roads. There were houses where *brujas* were rumored to live and we'd always walk past them quickly, scared yet enthralled, looking up at their adobe facades for a sign, a glimpse of the powerful, secretive witch. In Ranchos de Taos, the spirit world lived in quick proximity to the world of the living. When I got bronchitis one summer on a long visit, my grandmother slid through the house in her bedroom slippers to my bedside to rub holy water on my chest. The Blessed Virgin was close, somewhere nearby listening to prayers, lowering her eyes and bowing her head to hear us beseech her, lit with tenderness and resignation for our suffering. Just as the houses of the *brujas* were mysterious with close evil, whispers that settled in the air, misting over your face like a shroud as you walked near them on the dirt road to the old adobe church. The devil was rumored to have chased many a wandering husband home or to have appeared at some dance disguised as a handsome, svelte man who whisked an unsuspecting girl away. Now, if you had stopped and looked closely, it was said, you could've seen his cloven hooves, tapping on the dance floor as he held a virginal woman close, breathing into her ear some intoxicating lyric. La Llorona was heard weeping for her lost children, near a small stream or river in the mountains. Weeping with agony, a mother crying for her dead babies. The *moradas* of the Penitentes were closed and dark; it was forbidden to look at them too acutely. When we went by them, my grandmother would quickly point out the squat adobe buildings and whispers softly with awe and respect for the secret rites enacted within.

Recently, I've learned of a strong Sephardic Jewish ancestral connection on my father's side of the family. A number of my direct ancestors, including Francisco and Francisca Gomez Robledo and Bartolome Romero, were tried in Inquisitional tribunals for Judaizing—practicing Judaism secretly, behind a Catholic facade. I remember how my grandmother would bless me by placing her hand on top of my head. Every afternoon during Holy Week, a special meal was eaten that bore a resemblance to the Passover seder. Looking at our family tree, I've discovered that certain families intermarried repeatedly over generations, often with cousins marrying each other in arranged marriages. And though my father was the son of a Penitente, he didn't know what the Trinity was when I interviewed him recently about his family's beliefs and customs.

"What Trinity?" he asked. "There is one God."

I was given the Blackfoot name Apoyakee, which means fair or light-haired woman. Growing up, my fair coloring was one of the most significant things about me. Both of my younger brothers and sister have black hair, dark eyes, and darker complexions than I. And there I was, the "white person" in the family, always standing out in family pictures or gatherings. I overhead people ask my brothers and sister, "Is that really your sister? Is she adopted?" Indians would ask me, "Are you *really* Indian? Why do you look so white?"

I wanted to have that black hair more than anything on earth. It seemed to me to be the most beautiful hair in the world—shining black like a raven's wing. And the fairness of my skin, as light as a white person's, made me feel even less Indian, like a sham or a fake. As a teenager I sunned myself for hours each day to get as dark as I possibly could, eventually turning a darker shade of brown. But it was such a stupendous effort, requiring hours of tanning in the highest heat and daily upkeep in order for my skin not to lighten, not to fade with obstinate certainty to my original light color, that I finally gave up, exhausted and pickled. I was doomed to be a paleface. As I grew, it became clear that my facial features and body type are more Plains Indian than anything else. Even so, because of my light eyes, complexion, and hair, I felt like an outsider from the beginning, different in an essential, unmistakable way from the people that I was supposed to belong to. It was my first recognizable deviation in what was to turn out to be a lifelong and escalating estrangement from family, culture, and accepted normalcy. At every turn, I was to defy expectations.

In time, it became clear that I was left-handed, a discovery that didn't please my mother as much as my light hair. "That left hand is terrible," she would exclaim, threatening to train me to use my right hand. Although, like many left-handed people, I had developed a sense of clumsiness in the execution of what to most people are routine physical tasks, such as cutting with scissors or folding paper, I never understood what the fuss was about. To this day, I hate to use scissors, and resist any task that seems too involved with measuring, tying, folding, or cutting.

I take pride in my left-handedness now, having discovered its link to an entire array of behaviors, including transsexuality and homosexuality, as well as creative ability and antiauthoritarian tendencies. Having that sinistral tendency, that slightly sinister preference from the beginning of life, has been the target of suspicion in many countries and cultures.

Although I had an ongoing, escalating sense of difference as a child, not everything about me was clothed in a sense of alienation. I was born in Heidelberg, Germany, in February 1957, an Aquarius. I was my parents' firstborn and my mother tells the story of how she would go to my crib each morning and peer down into it; there I'd be, smiling up at her. Worried that all this smiling might mean something bad, she took me to a doctor who examined me and reassured her that nothing was wrong; in fact, I was beaming with joy. "Mrs. Valerio, you have a very happy baby."

Will, with his perennial wisdom and wit, muses that I probably was smiling so much because I was already planning all the ways in which I would torture my parents once I got older, like having a sex change and eventually writing a book to tell the entire world all about it.

The year I spent on my mother's reserve was one of the best in my life. I was five. My mother decided to take my sister and me there while my father was away on duty in Korea. We lived at the north end in a spacious valley close to a river where my grandfather had a house. He was a prosperous rancher who owned a great deal of land, horses, and cattle. We'd watch him round the cattle up on horseback, herd them into a corral, and brand each one, wrestling the steers and calves to the ground. Sizzling hot metal brands on their hides, flailing hooves and horns, legs all over the air. Then set loose, wobbling up, running off, tails switching.

Grandpa Chris adored me. Partly because of my light hair, then light blondish red, like his had been when he was a kid. He was a half-breed, brought up on the reserve by his Indian mother and Indian step-father, who adopted him in his youth. His white father was a whiskey trader and pharmacist at Fort McCloud, Alberta, and a sheriff and troublemaker in Montana. He'd left my grandfather and his brother behind on the reserve when his marriage to my great-grandmother, a Blackfoot woman named Reverse Walking Woman, ended. Grandpa Chris would die never knowing what type of white man his father had been. As it turned out, his father was mostly Dutch and German, and an American, not a Canadian, who had French Huguenot forebears who'd fought in the Revolutionary War. Others had been abolitionists with the Dutch Reformed Church, or had fought for the Union in the Civil War. This errant, colorful ancestor, Fred Kanous, was a crucial ingredient in the enigma of my lightness, the northern European great-grandfather, the link of recessive genes from my mother's side, which, when combined with certain criollo (Spanish born in the New World) ancestry, conspired to form my vexing, distinctive coloring.

Grandpa Chris was a shining force, a legendary figure to me. Larger than life. I remember him singing Indian joke songs, beating on a drum late at night under a deep, bright moon . . . *"Even if you're married, I will get you honey babe yahah ya ah ya."* Killing rattlesnakes that crept too close to the house with a long, crooked stick. Hanging them up on a fence post, a wild banner to retribution and valor. He'd go deer hunting and bring the animals back to skin and clean for venison. I'd peer into the deer's guts as its belly was being slit, queasy, awed with a tight excitement.

That year on the reserve was charmed, framed in enchantment, the sweet songs of the elements: river and wind, bright, hanging sunshine, dust from the roads, the smells and sounds of horses. I was surrounded not only by loving grandparents but also by the whole extended family. Like many American Indians, I have always had a strong bond with my aunts, uncles, and cousins. For me, family was always more than just the nuclear unit. I got a great deal of attention all around, went fishing a lot, horseback riding, and berry picking. Deer would come up close to the house, and we drew water from the Old Man River nearby.

I play mostly with little boys at this age, feeling at ease with them. Overall, they seem to accept me as one of them. I become an ardent wrestler and can beat up just about any kid on the block. By age six, I've gotten scrappy, and am out to prove my strength to all. I fight the "other boys" in contests of skill, speed, and nerve, often coming out the victor.

Another time, a boy throws a rock at me that hits square on my forehead, creating a huge lump. I run home crying. My mother isn't sympathetic. She applies a damp cloth to my forehead, then scowls at my tears, telling me, "Don't come crying to me; just go back out there and beat him up." I am astonished by her lack of coddling or sympathy. She's distant in the kitchen as I rest, nursing the large bump on my forehead. But my mother is adamant, repeating that I should just go back out there and beat this boy up. "Don't be scared, just do it, don't come crying to me." So I rouse myself, dry my tears, and go back out there to find the rock thrower—and beat him up.

I'm not treated like a typical little girl. In many respects, my courage, independence, and physical vigor are encouraged. Perhaps my parents perceive my masculine nature, my intrepid, adventurous spirit. I'm an imp, willful with a sunny disposition and, having been the first child, and the only child for four years, I'm used to being the center of attention. I have a stubborn streak and great tantrums are ignited if I don't get what I want. My mother sending me back out there to go and fight back for myself is one of many incidents of my youth that will develop my pluck and self-reliance.

Any significance of my reluctance to wear dresses is lost on my parents. On Sundays I have to wear a white dress to go to church, as well as little white anklets, Mary Janes, and, to top it off, a lace doily on my head! One Sunday morning I'm so upset by this charade that I'm in tears, and refuse to go out to the car in that dress. I feel absurd, embarrassed, like a weird French poodle wearing this outfit. What if one of my little buddies, one of the "other boys" in the neighborhood that I hang out with, battle and explore with, sees me? It'll ruin my reputation for sure. But I have to wear this weird dress, and I run to the car, shaking with tears and humiliation. My parents think this scene is hilarious and film it on their home-movie camera. They play it over and over to guests, pointing out what they find to be cute, silly, and completely illogical behavior. Given the times, the early sixties, I guess you can't expect them to take seriously or even understand my feelings.

My father never seems to care one way or the other; he is always good to me, no matter what. As an adult, he'll give me his old army boots when I ask for them, much to my mother's chagrin. I enjoy the time that we spend together, fishing or watching the stars at night. I love listening to his jokes, making faces, and being silly with him.

"Anita is a real tomboy," my mother announces to people regularly by the time I am eight. She is amused, not overly alarmed. My parents, aunts, and uncles all think that I will grow out of this "tomboy phase" and magically become the feminine young lady that they envision me to be deep down. Somewhere, beneath that surface, that subterfuge of riotous boy play and tough boy talk, is a real, genuine girl. I'm told over and over that it's a "phase." "Don't worry," my aunt Florence says, "you'll change your mind about getting married." I'm not worried, and this unsolicited reassurance irritates me. To back up these claims, my mother and aunt declare that they too were tomboys, as many Indian girls are—riding horses, barrel racing, ice skating—active, athletic, free-spirited. Even as I hear them talk about their childhoods, I know without being able to articulate it that my feelings are different in dimension, in texture, in meaning. I know, somehow, deep down, that I will never grow out of *it*, and furthermore, I don't want to.

In these early years, I have a very difficult time relating to girls. I'm teased and tormented by a group of girls because I'm unable to play house to their expectations. They try to get me to play their girl games, sweeping floors and wearing fake curlers. I refuse and the girls get angry. In my memory, their faces blur through a film of tears and frustration. Perhaps I'd told them that I was a boy or wanted to play a male role. In any case, my homemaker skills are all wrong. They reward me with laughter and scorn.

Like most of my encounters with little girls, the one with Laura, the daughter of one of my parents' friends, feels strained and off-kilter. She wants to play Barbies; I give in to be a good sport. Her Barbie world is complex, a finely honed landscape of costumes, tightly entwined interpersonal relationships, tiny, sweetly detailed interior decorations. Looking into her Barbie house, I am drawn into another world. It strikes me how different we really are. I always want to torture Barbie just a little. Without knowing how to talk about it, I'm already beginning to sense the sexuality she displays in her miniature heels and tight outfits, her long blond hair wrapped up on top of her head like an erotic beacon or falling in a long wave down her back, shimmering. I identify with Ken a little, but more with G.I. Joe. Ken is too tame, an adjunct for Barbie's theatricality. He's a New Age, sensitive kind of guy. G.I. Joe is completely, unapologetically male, in a male universe of danger and conquest. When I give in and play Barbies with Laura, I'm at a loss; it's foreign territory. I try and liven things up with theatrics between Barbie and Ken, a child's theater of sexual tension masquerading as conflict, or pursuit and capture. I introduce strategy, danger, a whispered, secret, and treacherous adventure. Get an invasion going from outer space. Action! I watch Laura take the dolls through a panorama of psychological rituals, barely able to stifle my restlessness. My initial begrudging curiosity, a fascination with an exotic otherness— Laura's intricate, quiet Barbie universe—eventually wears thin. Soon, I take her up to a low section on the roof of the house and dare her to jump off. Laura is scared and won't do it. I jump, falling through the air in joy and bouncing to the ground on my feet.

CHAPTER 5:
KAMIKAZE NIGHT WALKING

984. My muses are on the ascension, hoodlumlike, flirtatious, ambivalent, and musical. Menacing with an ironic and dark presence, auspicious, out for the kill. I'm living out my high school dreams of visions, extreme states, and angular, lanky bohemia. Working at odd jobs, hardly eating, taking speed and other drugs, staying up all night talking with my friend and roommate David. Our conversations are long, detailed, breathless. My childhood and his—horseback riding, military moving, both of us having suffered allergies, glasses, left-handedness, the awkwardness of being the "smart kid" in class. We spend timeless hours on less personal areas, going into detailed explanations and roaming discussions about Mayan hieroglyphics, Blake, William Burroughs,

Language poetry, and drugs. David gets into all the nuances and flavors of each and everything we take, and we take a lot of different things. Mostly speed, but there is a little heroin, cocaine, acid, Dilaudid. He brings in morphine, which produces a spray of sharp, warm particles in my chest that sparkle up to my throat.

After being up on speed for two or three days, reality begins to shift. We sit together at a big picture window in my room and watch elves dancing on rooftops, nuns walking in a bunch, their long black habits lifting up in the night wind. "Look at that, do you see those nuns?" I'm able to suggest an image to David and he will see it, too. Kamikaze visions, night-walking minds.

Roxanne and I have broken up. Most relationships appear to have allotted life spans and we have hit the limit of ours. The breakup feels confounded and sudden, but also inevitable, having something to do with her maintenance-style drinking, my not getting a job, and both of us doing too much speed. I had moved out of Hotel Hell to live with her, and now, on my own again, I search for a new living situation. After a brief stint as the unlikely roommate of a glitzy woman from Beverly Hills who's just been released from a cocaine farm for wayward corporate wives, I move in with David, an old friend. He's a poet and runs a weekly reading series at a local photography gallery. We met at my first featured reading at the Intersection for the Arts in 1979, where David was also a featured poet. I was twenty-two, and he'd told me that I was the most confident "kid reader" he'd ever seen. The admiration was mutual. His writing was quirky, funny, and sharply observant. We became fast friends.

David knows Roxanne and since she is still a speed dealer, he gets most of our speed from her. From time to time he lets me in on news of her life.

Before we'd broken up, we'd tried heroin for the first time. I wasn't too impressed. Mainly I threw up a lot and had to remain motionless throughout the night, holding myself in a rigid position on the bed in order to not feel a clutching burning at the root of my belly. Later, when I did junk again, the experience was smoother. There's no doubt that junk is relaxing and soporific, a sweet dream with a mechanical aftertaste. When I closed my eyes, odd visions slid across my eyelids, mostly mechanical shapes and blinking dials, clocks or—once—clowns in polka-dot outfits beating each other with huge sticks. This was good for a few laughs, a smile into and from the daft unconscious that concocted these cartoons. But I never liked these relaxing and odd dreams enough to dedicate my life to them; junk wasn't *that* good. And I never liked feeling that distant from my raw feelings for too long. I wanted to live with all my faculties intact, and so I resisted. Or maybe I just got lucky: *There but for the grace of God, go I.* In any case, I made sure that my heroin use was never more than occasional, and eventually, I phased the cool-faced lizard drug out of my life for good.

Roxanne, however, is pulled in. She is getting more and more junked out, a necrotic robot. Her eyes are vacant, her expression null. There is a wooden quality to her movements, as if she has been voided from her life. I'm saddened and haunted by this outcome.

Roxanne takes up with a man, the first she's been with in her life. Although relatively unforeseen, this event doesn't completely surprise me. I always imagined that my girlfriends might secretly harbor heterosexual feelings. From time to time I would find myself tortured with illogical, crazed, jealous fantasies about them with men. In my confusion it *feels* like this: *since they were attracted to me, they could be attracted to a man.* On the other hand, they claim to be lesbians, and I know that I am not actually in a male form. Like all heated jealousies, there is a strong element of sexual arousal in it. It turns me on. I battle this contradiction, not understanding why I find this painful fantasy so compelling, so vivid, and such a turn-on.

Whenever I'd brought up these suspicions, Roxanne had denied any possibility with a shocked outrage. *"No way,* you are crazy! I am a dyke! I don't want to get poked like some milking cow!" I would sheepishly apologize. After such a vehement denial I felt intensely ashamed even to have suggested such a possibility. After all, Roxanne had been a lesbian her whole adult life, and any goddess-fearing lesbian would feel insulted by such an accusation.

Strangely, after I hear about her new boyfriend, an odd idea occurs to me: I am really the first man that Roxanne was sexual with. Somehow, I opened her up to this experience. This feeling, apparently illogical, persists, a secret thought that I rarely voice to others.

I don't understand what lesbians do in bed. This incongruous realization occurs to me one day. I just don't get it. Deep down, I don't take lesbian sex seriously. It is vacuous to me, absent.

Is this simply a symptom of my being taken in by patriarchal thinking, an unwieldy phallocentric attitude that I can undo with proper consciousness-raising?

If it is, I should have gotten over it by now. I've been in dyke boot camp for some time.

I get horny looking at condom ads in magazines, almost allowing myself to imagine a woman unrolling a condom and carefully holding my erection, sliding the long latex sheath over it.

When I confided this fantasy to Roxanne, she said, "You're hardcore."

When she realized two women together didn't arouse me, she declared, "You're terrible."

I surmise that it must be simply a matter of "butch and femme," a need for me to reclaim roles with an erotic power dynamic, a sexy play of differences communicated and translated through female flesh.

But then I realize perhaps my situation is not that simple. These feelings are anchored deep, in the dream the flesh has of itself. I mean, here I am, ostensibly a lesbian discovering that, on some level, I don't identify with lesbian sexuality. There is no charge. The fact that what I do in bed looks like what two women do together simply because I'm in a woman's body does not feel authentic. *Is the kind of sex I have really lesbian sex?*

I realize at the same time that I'd better never let any other dykes know that I have these feelings and fantasies. This is way *too much,* it's blasphemy.

Masks appear in kinetic patterns on the walls of my room as I lie down to sleep after being up on speed for three nights straight. Surreal totemic masks float near the doorway of my room, flash circuslike at my window, changing shape as I watch, sleepless. Circles to cones to triangles with elongated bases flaring at their edges with purple light. Darth Vader slides into Mickey Mouse, then Frank Sinatra. Headless forms stagger, sprouting tiny knob-shaped heads that balloon into iridescent laughing faces, heretical and childlike. I *know* I am seeing things. These forms are phantoms. They drift into vapor or vanish in a snap into dark air. The ragged, long coming down from methamphetamine. Hard to endure. Terrifying at any minute. I stare up at these shapes and attempt to control their incandescent mutations. Other times, these visions are fascinating to watch. I wonder what part of my mind these hallucinations are coming from. Steps in the hallway, doors closing, someone coming in or going out. I startle and am up, in bed, wondering who it could be, and realize right away, no one. Grit my teeth, lie back down in the dark. Feel a cold and painful spot in my chest, my feelings rubbed raw. Roxanne, losing her, drugs, the rent, work, where and how. My fantasies of Roxanne making love to a man. I see the image and feel it in this pitch black room, stifled and hot. I slide my cock inside her, in and out between her wide-open legs. Slower, then faster and deeper as she holds onto me, gasping. I want her to feel how hard my dick is. Hard and thick, I fuck her, feeling a tense, wild excitement.

How can I think these things? Do I want to be a man? Do I feel male inside? I turn over and watch patterns of light ignite the floor.

I am becoming aware that I don't want my body to be touched during sex. Although I wouldn't have articulated it like that, an absolute statement that feels like a fiat.

I begin to think of myself as "butch." A word that is just beginning to come back into vogue in lesbian circles in 1983. Women are reviving and experimenting with erotic role-playing. I figure I'm into "gender play." I read the (then) lesbian sex writer Pat Califia and become interested in the idea of people who are essentially attracted by differences in their partners as opposed to sameness. Some, of course, are attracted to both. To my knowledge, Califia was the first writer to elucidate this. (Now, Pat has transitioned to Patrick Califia, but at that time, he was still a dyke and quite likely the most dangerous and controversial dyke writer on these topics—way ahead of the curve, and fearless.) Califia's brilliant and innovative concept of "heterosexual homosexuals" and "homosexual homosexuals" intrigues me. There is a "heterosexual" element to my sexual imagination, after all. I'm attracted to "femme" women. Femme as in feminine, and for me, petite. Dressed in high heels and skirts, lacy anklets, the dazzling smell and texture of feminine beauty, its vulnerability and controlling seductive power. I'd gaze at Roxanne's clothes with a tight longing. These pieces of clothing are the way she telegraphs her need to be taken. The notion of "femininity," once only a nuisance of oppression, a cookie-cutter outline that women bought into for acceptance and love, is becoming a plaything, an expansive, alluring, erotic toy. I speculate that one could take off and put on butch and femme gender and sex roles at will, to arouse pleasure, to have fun. These ideas are liberating. I'm becoming comfortable with a new unfolding story about desire. But will it be enough?

I am never a woman in any of my fantasies. I am a man. I *feel* like a man. That feeling . . . walking into a roomful of women talking about men and feeling as though they are talking about me. Reading books about men describing their fantasies about women and feeling as though I share exactly the same fantasies. Feeling included in those books, as though they were not *like* me but somehow *about* me. I'm beginning to become aware of a faint memory of another way of naming myself, hanging at the back of my head.

Is "butch" the correct term for me? In some ways, I'm not that butch. I don't work on cars. I don't watch football. I am a poet, a "sensitive" type. Roxanne used to laugh at me as I walked up to flowers and touched their petals all the while dripping with chains and black leather, hair spiking out over my head like a nettle bush. I have never wanted to join a softball league or build a shelf. I would rather read or listen to music. I am "in my head," though always avidly sexual with a streak of hedonism. Could my feeling of being male really be the same as being butch?

At this time there is also the idea of "woman-identified woman." This is an idea older than the butch-femme renaissance, older than Samois (the first lesbian S/M public organization that devoted itself to lesbian sadomasochism and the exploration of fringe sexual practices and experiences). This clunky-sounding identifier, woman-identified woman, had originally appeared in an essay, "The Woman-Identified Woman," by the Radicalesbians in 1970. A woman could be any way that a woman wished to be and she would still be a woman; in fact, she would be more of the essence of what woman is since she would not be relying on patriarchal definitions of womanhood. She had no reason to constrain herself, to contain her actions or choices within a tightly-defined arena called "feminine" or even "female." Any piece of clothing a woman wore, even a man's suit jacket and tie, was a piece of "woman's" clothing because she was wearing it. This helped all kinds of women try on traditionally masculine roles and not feel as though they were "trying to be men." It took the sting out of that old insult, often used to keep women in line. For many years, I felt freed by this concept. Over time, however, the relief wore thin. Something was wrong.

I talk to David about my feelings. I feel male, somehow, *male* . . .

I tell a lot of people about these feelings, actually. But ask David now and he would tell you that I was nowhere near thinking of getting a sex change, and he would be right. "You would have been horrified if I had suggested that. You thought you were a lesbian, you were very adamant about that."

I am sure that's how it seemed to him, and it was definitely true at the time. But I didn't know anything else. I was a dyke and proud. That had been my identity since adolescence, a way for me to identify and understand the fact that I was attracted to women and had been ever since I could remember—from childhood on to a time when I felt a need to put a name to my desire.

I'm eight years old. I lie on the floor, listening to the radio play as my mother cleans house. It's "King of the Road" or "Abilene," then "These Boots Are Made for Walkin'," in which Nancy Sinatra struts around in those white go-go boots. Stretched out on the floor lying on my back, staring at the ceiling, I'm a long ways off, drifting through rainy southern towns, or daydreaming of the reserve, the long, flat plains and my grandfather's house in the valley, or feeling the stirring of strange excitement as I daydream of girls' faces. An electric quality clings to their forms, there's a rapid pressure in my chest. I am the man on the radio singing "Almost Persuaded" . . . by an unfamiliar woman with "ruby red lips" and "coal black hair and eyes that would tempt any man." Or listening to Hank Williams, his lean yodel and stark images, plaintive love songs. I envision some lonesome velvet night watching my sweetheart walk out the door. Disappearing into her "loveless mansion on the hill." I am the man, living these songs, playing all the parts, feeling tenderness and longing for the spectral soul of a woman slipping away.

It's third grade. I rush into the bathroom, steal a quick look in the mirror, go into the stall, lock the door, and close my eyes tight for a few seconds. I smile, take a quick glance at the small rectangular window opening up a portal into the blue sky. I'm getting into my Superman mode. I transform into Superman and fly away; Lois Lane sees me flying in the blue sky high above skyscrapers and feels a yearning, an ache in her chest. I tell my friend Lee, a boy I like to toss football with after school, about being Superman, really secretly.

My legs feel long and muscular, I'm tall and awkward. My bangs are cut way too high up in a sharp line across my forehead. Every few weeks my mother chops them back, a stiff stripe of hair. My brown hair is shoulder length, bowl-like. I feel like a geek. My navy blue sweater stretches too tight across my shoulders. I scrape my knees playing soccer with the boys out on the big field, I'm the only girl who plays. I hang upside down from the monkey bars in defiance, with my shorts showing beneath a plaid shift.

"Anita loves Paula! Anita loves Paula!" the girls' singsong voices slip around me. I'm in Oklahoma City. We're near the gray entrance to the back of the school, out near the playground. It's recess. The afternoon light filters a soft blend of images. The girls surround me in a half circle. Their young voices mesh into a net, a nubile chorus. I'm embarrassed and amazed that they can tell. I do love Paula. I've never felt this feeling before, the tight aching concentrated in my chest. Bright, ardent, a flame. This must be the feeling you have when you want to marry somebody. I definitely want to marry Paula. I stare at her picture in the elementary school yearbook and contemplate this strange new feeling. I am a third grader, and she is in second grade. Paula has long, dark hair, large brown eyes radiant with a gleam, fringed with long lashes. She's missing one of her front teeth. She's the most beautiful girl in the world, with mysterious charm, a suggestion of some unknowable, titillating mischief.

I talk tough and use a fake southern accent to impress these Oklahoma City girls—telling jokes, squinching my face into wild contortions.

Many of the girls are impressed by my drawings of monsters and other cartoon characters. They watch me draw and request copies. I draw Paula a dragon eating popcorn, I set his smile at just the right angle, color his scales green and blue, give him a long, curling tail. Smoke puffs from his nostrils; wisps of flame halo his head, he's impertinent and gallant. The kind of guy to inflame women with an aura of nonchalance, a hint of danger.

Paula returns the dragon to me the next day. "Why?" I ask. I peer into her dark eyes. "My parents told me to give it back to you. They don't want me to keep it." I sense she's being dutiful. Mechanically, Paula places the picture in my hand without any further explanation. I don't think she really understands, either. Yet, perhaps both of us do, in some way that we don't have words for yet. Somehow it is not right . . . I shouldn't be acting the way I act or feeling the way I feel. What did she tell her parents about the drawing? I wonder, uneasy, feeling sick. Sometimes we walk together at recess and I put my arm around her. What did her parents say to her? I feel dirty. Puzzled. Hurt. Increasingly, I want to grow up right away. Childhood, once unselfconscious, charmed, effervescent with fantasy and discovery, begins to drape oppressively, a prolonged state of dependency, physical insubstantiality.

I'm increasingly aware of the allure of women. We move to Germany and my fourth-grade math teacher, Miss Klee, wears miniskirts and a huge, puffed-up, perfectly round beehive—spectacular—a living salon hair dryer that she carries on her head, along with dark eyeliner and go-go boots. Sharp perfume wafts from her. I'm entranced, enamored of her Shindig! *sixties style. I visualize her doing the jerk, strutting in her go-go boots like Nancy Sinatra— cool, seductive, and deadly.*

I still don't know anything concrete about sex, except that it has something to do with kissing or the faintly repulsive animal grappling that I've glimpsed adults doing on television or in parked cars. Even so, I'm drawn into vague daydreams about Miss Klee, something similar to how I felt about Paula. Kids spread rumors about being able to see her underwear when she bends over in her miniskirt to take a drink at the fountain. One girl reports that she saw her taking a little pill once. We all think it might be one of those birth control pills.

It happens. One evening I'm taking a bath. My mother walks in, gazes at me for a long moment, and smiles. My chest hurts, a tenderness around the nipples. I have no idea what's going on. My nipples are swollen, poking out into small tents. When I wear a T-shirt these two tiny tents are visible, vulnerable underneath the thin layer of cotton. A month earlier, my mother had asked, "Do you need a bra?"

My reaction was disbelief. "Oh, no, I don't think so!" Ya gotta be kidding, *I thought.*

Now she looks beatific. I'm soaking in the bubbles and hot water.

*Pleased, happy for some reason, she makes it official: "You're developing!"
Her excitement is palpable, a delight at discovering something precious. With
a mild horror, I watch her glee. I don't know what to say. I'm still not completely sure what she's talking about . . . developing . . .
     This word haunts me. I realize moments after she's left what she must be
saying. I still don't understand why this event would make her so delighted.
Developing . . . oh god. Something is happening to my body, it's starting to
swell here and there, a bit of hair is coming out in my pubic area, there's an
all-over feeling of a climatic change gathering momentum.
     I've been transported into this realm, slowly, by degrees. This realm of
intense feeling, longing, a growing introspection that feels nearly sensate, a
shifting awareness of myself that's connected to my senses, to my perceptions
of the shape and contours of my body. My body is swelling up like a water
balloon. More and more around the chest and then at the hips. I'm growing
taller. I've always been tall, but now I'm not the tallest kid anymore. I look
around at the older kids; some of the boys are stretching out taller than me.
     I'm told that I'm beginning to look a little bit like Linda Ronstadt or
Carly Simon, but in my secret seventh-grade mind, I envision Jim Morrison.
Not that I look like him, of course. I don't. But I feel that my persona is more
related to his. Male rock stars become my role models now, instead of superheroes. Flamboyant males with edge, danger, poetic hair, and lots of colorful
clothing, red and black, neon jackets, tight pants, cool shades.
     At night, I get up out of bed and grab a flashlight. Take books into the
light by the half-open door. Lie on the floor and read. Poetry: Sylvia Plath,
Langston Hughes, Yeats. Sylvia Plath is my favorite. Her humid visions, stifling in their lucidity. Incandescent poems hurtling to suicide. I read by the
thin light long after I'm supposed to be asleep. Then go to bed and turn on
the radio, tune my transistor in the dark to a station out of Little Rock, Arkansas, that plays all the music that most of the radio stations won't play. I
listen for hours, tune in to Wolfman Jack in Mexico. More rock and blues,
James Brown's "Cold Sweat" and "Sex Machine."
     I'm beginning to write poetry, with a shaking hand in the light by the*

door. I scribble the lines down; I don't know why it makes my hand shake, but it does. Some power overtaking me, some need and burning compulsion.

I've begun filling a notebook with my poems. My mother comes in once and finds me poring over them. I close the book fast as she walks in. She says, "Don't write anything down. Don't ever write anything down that other people might see." I think she's nuts. Why not? I have to write. These poems have a force of their own.

I'm thirteen, in the girls' restroom at school. It's 1970 now, Fort Riley, Kansas, junior high. Something's happening, I knew that it would. In fact, I was waiting. My underwear has brown stains, a thick brown goo. Is this it? The goo appears for seven days, and then finally there's blood, real indisputable blood, red and dark. Then, a sharp ache in my lower back, a throbbing, inflamed sensations shoot in tendrils down the entire area. The cramps pass within a day or two, the blood continues for another two days. It's all weird in the beginning, irregular, sometimes it goes on for seven days, sometimes much less. I try and ignore these new feelings. A part of me inside, that I've thought about, is coming alive. I've got no choice. Against my will I'm transforming.

I feel a disconnect, an uncomfortable, awkward relationship with my femaleness that translates into a denial. There will be a point in high school, later, when I have to remind myself not to slip and refer to myself as "he" while telling stories where I talk about myself in the third person.

"Don't do it, Anita. Hormones are very powerful substances, and you could just end up without a sex." David is lying on his bed, stretched out, hands behind head, feet folded at the ankles. The light shines on his blond hair. Behind glasses, his eyes are intense and expressive. There's a nasal tone to his voice. He's gentle, even refined. I hadn't thought that David was straight at first. This was my own stereotyping, yet David is different, many people agree. A good poet, he is sensitive to a fault. He watches my face with an unwavering gaze. I wince. It must be true. I know what he is really saying. He is declaring that the sex-changed body is neuter.

"Well, I guess they have surgeries. They can make some kind of penis. . . ." I speculate out loud. I figure this is true, but the idea is vague in my mind.

"Oh, those are butcher jobs. It's not the same thing, Anita."

The next morning as he cooks breakfast, he says it again. "Let me tell you, as a man, it's not the same thing."

I am quiet, scraping at my eggs.

"The skin of the penis is a very particular kind; it's erectile. You can't get that kind of skin from another part of the body. And it won't get hard. It is very difficult . . . no, not just difficult but impossible to reproduce the skin and function, the erectile function, of the human penis."

"I see. . . ." I'm sad. I want to rail against what he is saying. I have never been fixated on penises as such, at least not obsessively, although I certainly yearn to penetrate a woman with one. The penis is an important part of the package—it's the prize. Without it, how can I attain manhood?

At this moment sex change seems like an alien solution, science fiction, far away, a little *too* extreme to consider seriously. "Don't worry, I wouldn't go that far," I say. "It's too much. But, who knows, maybe the surgeries will get better." I shrug, depressed by the topic, suddenly embarrassed and uncomfortable. It occurs to me that I am allowing David to see a part of myself I probably shouldn't. An older idea of myself that I've learned to keep hidden.

CHAPTER 6:
CRIME, POETRY, DUNGEONS, AND PSYCHIC FORCES

Lost in a world where it's a crime to leave
a crime to love, a crime to breathe
now I'm searching for my brain for the crime that frees
a crime to share a crime to please
Lookin' for a new crime
I want a new crime, a crime of passion . . .
—The Feederz, "(Looking for a) New Crime"

985. Selene introduces me to Frank Discussion as one of her "male friends."

I'm surprised by this notable introduction and don't quite know how to react. I feel recognized, seen. I wonder, *Should I feel insulted?* So many lesbians or feminist women I know don't even like to be called "guys" in casual conversations, as in, "Do you guys want to go and see a movie after the Women's Liberation Steering Committee meeting?"

"I don't see any guys here," they'd bark with severe, angry expressions.

I'm secretly thrilled by Selene's introduction and feel an illicit stab of pride. This one night, I'll go along with it. A playful admission of a sub-liminal subtext, a closer truth. I say the forbidden words out loud, grinning like an escaping devil, "Yes, I am a man."

Selene often tells me that she perceives a man in me as part of a shifting panoply of characters. Holding one of my photographs that her ex, Felix, has taken of me, she explains, "Every time I look at you I see someone different: an anarchic punk, a librarian, a striking woman elegant and leggy, a strong dyke/Amazon woman, a writer concentrat-ing on an inner world. And the male sides: There's a truck driver who enjoys listening to the jukebox in greasy spoons while chain-smoking and drinking cup after cup of watery coffee, there's a priest, a swivel-ing, ardent gigolo." Selene tilts the photo and squints into my face in the picture, "And from this angle, I see a young, confident man with a halo of cryptic dreams, it's hard to see him, he's a glimpse sparking in and out of focus. . . ."

Selene met Frank Discussion one night at the dungeon in Berkeley where she works as a dominatrix. A mutual friend brought Frank over af-ter a party to see firsthand the palatial dimensions of the place, tour the red-carpeted high heel room, where foot fetishists adored a wide assort-ment of ladies' shoes, investigate the surgery room, where Selene played doctor with more than a few attorneys and stockbrokers who could af-ford her high hourly rates. I'd heard of Frank. He was the founding member of the Feederz, a seminal late seventies punk band. Their album *Ever Feel Like Killing Your Boss?* was already a classic by the mid-eighties. Frank's short and muscular, with a shaved head and a devilish expression emanating from big eyes and a goofy, menacing grin. He refuses to tell anyone his chronological age, his birth name, any background informa-tion at all. Frank claims that this secrecy allows him the freedom to reinvent himself, to be freed completely from his biological family and life history. He and Selene hit it off with a thunderclap.

They move in together and, by extension, in with me. For the next year and a half, I live with Frank and Selene in San Francisco's Mission District in a large, rambling two-bedroom apartment. My life with Frank and Selene is nearly idyllic. Although they squabble occasionally, with Frank striding out the door or Selene crying copious scalding tears, the times are expansive. Selene, a member of my close-knit "gang" of punk dykes, has been a close friend since 1982. She was a lesbian but recently crossed over to dating men. She is a great believer in my work as a performer, poet, and writer, and her friendship has been one of my greatest sources of inspiration. One of the most compassionate people I've ever met, always there for her friends, she's tall and striking, with dyed black hair cut straight at her shoulders and a pouty expression. Selene possesses a purity, a wholesomeness to her beauty, that is intriguing and soothing. A combination of Bettie Page, Madame Blavatsky, and Neal Cassady, she's a tender-hearted, winsome adventurer.

Selene gives rambling tarot card readings or improvises subterranean psychic information with a glance at a person's astrological chart. She tells me about spirit forms in my room—a man who comes to the entrance and plays strange tricks. Removing his head then putting it back on, he talks in a stream of consciousness, plays an accordion or a banjo. "You've got a female spirit in there, too. She's got golden skin and slanted eyes. She floats. I can only see her face. She's just a head floating above your bed smiling with her eyes closed. Golden Flying Girl, I call her. When I see her, I figure you are going to be doing some writing."

I'm not sure what to make of Selene's psychic readings, but I know that if I listen attentively I'll hear a thread of insight running through many of her observations. She declares, "Neptune in the first house of your natal chart means that crazy people love you—they think you're psychedelic." I have since thought a great deal about that idea.

Like me, Selene has a voracious appetite for the dark side, the submerged and taboo, even though she has that wholesome quality, defiant in its stubborn purity. She couples penetrating intuition with a cartoonish sensibility that sometimes feels absurdly pop, even lightweight. Once when we compared notes on nightmares, she spoke of having awakened screaming from one about dancing Q-tips.

Selene's job as a dominatrix allows her to give miniature one-on-one performances that showcase her imagination and playfulness. She celebrates her clients' bizarre fetishes, their accomplished sexual imaginations. It is not outrageous to suggest that Selene takes her occupation into the realm of shamanism since she works with people's souls, their most intimate and charged feelings. She enables them to work through layers of pain or anger, and often brings her clients into altered states of consciousness. To her, being a professional dominant is also just a really offbeat and interesting job, fun and lucrative. She enjoys hearing investment bankers and eye surgeons beg for spankings while wearing baby bonnets or pig masks, and we enjoy hearing about it.

Frank writes music, works odd jobs, and does voracious research on various spiritual traditions. Recently, he has decided to teach himself an Amazonian Indian dialect in order to dissect Native shamanic traditions. Together we do performances, all-night psychic readings, and have intense, sometimes speed-fueled discussions on shamanism, situationism, and sexual politics. Frank composes the songs to the second Feederz album, *Teachers in Space,* in the living room on a four-track. We have house slaves who come in once or twice a week to clean the kitchen or common rooms. These are clients of Selene's who can't afford her rates. She trades beatings for their cleaning services. Sometimes I join Selene in the green room and help give these house slaves their weekly spanking. One man in his sixties, George, loves to be spanked briskly with a small paddle while Selene scolds him for having sexual fantasies about Donny and Marie Osmond. "Oh, Donny, oh, Marie!" he cries out as Selene and I paddle his sagging bottom. Afterward, George bends down reverently to kiss my red Converse high-top sneakers.

I've just entered the latter part of a productive period of writing and performing my work. I'm stretching my capacity to visualize. Many poems created during this period, the mid-eighties, appear to exceed all I've written in the past.

The audiences appear mesmerized. We do a number of shows, packed with responsive, attentive people at Martin Weber Gallery and the Valencia Tool and Die. Frank is resplendent in a black nurse's outfit, wobbly on red high heels. He's strapped a knife to his thigh. Looking slightly maniacal, bald as Mr. Clean, he plays bass as I incant my poetry.

We also do performances with Kristine Ambrosia and Timothy O'Neill. Tim is one of my collaborators and performs with me and Frank, playing synthesizer to some of my longer poems. Kristine does grandly staged thematic performances with many participants. She goes into trance states, hanging upside down and swinging from scaffolding while wearing antlers or a gas mask. These performances have many elements, depending on the theme, and may include drag, ritual piercing, genital torture, snake dancing, trance painting, and various kinds of musical accompaniment, including cellos, large drums, and electronic tape loops.

The celebration that is to become Burning Man is one of the many events that our small, extended crowd of performers, artists, and iconoclasts will invent and take part in. As I remember it, the first Burning Man was simply about burning a large wicker "man" at the beach, and we all were asked to put in a wish. Certainly, no one expected this ritual to become the amazing annual event that it is now.

Living with Frank and Selene is a never-ending adventure, hilarious and colorful. Selene nurtures me by providing a pillow for my writing chair, giving me rambling advice on lovers and herbal potions, encouraging me to pay more attention to my immediate environment with small, tender gestures. I've always been somewhat oblivious to my surroundings. Selene convinces me that I should get a pet, a grounding agent of love. Together we go to the SPCA and find a wide-eyed cat who reminds me of Selene. She is beautiful and supernatural. I call her Zoa, after William Blake's four Zoas, and one March evening I find her in my closet nursing five mewing kittens. One of these kittens, Pluto, will be a cat I cherish for many years. For a moment, time seems to nearly stand still, poised with an equilibrium that is absolutely alive.

The next phase of my life will be war.

CHAPTER 7:
FUN HOUSE

When Tama calls I feel anxiety, agitation, a corrupt passion. Her voice is unmistakable. A whiskey-drenched escalation of vowels. Fire and brass: She sounds tender, mean, nasty, and cunning all at once.

We met through writing. She'd read my poetry chapbook *Animal Magnetism* and called me one afternoon sounding spaced, woozy with some ongoing internal dialogue. I had no idea who she was, but she left a message with Frank. "Tell her Tama called," as if we'd known each other for a long time.

When we did finally speak on the phone, Tama was familiar in an odd way, although I knew we'd never actually met. She was impressed with my writing and wanted me to submit a poem to the next issue of her literary magazine and to read at an upcoming benefit for its publication. We went back and forth about the logistics of the performance, the microphone, the stage, the lighting. Her answers were vague, non sequiturs. She kept calling back with a rotating arrangement of details. Yet the conversations slanted into intriguing areas. We talked writing; I told her I had a new piece called "Virus" and she said that was interesting because she had recently been writing about parasites.

This woman is a nut, but she does know writing, I thought. This fact alone was a treasure. My last hardcore writing buddy was David. He helped me put together the poems that would make up *Animal Magnetism.* In those first ambling phone conversations I found out that Tama loved Kathy Acker and thought Barrett Watten's poetry was funny— abbreviated with an aphoristic surrealism. She listened to X and Joy Division. She loved cats. It turned out we had a lot in common.

For the benefit at CoLab, a local art space, Frank plays bass in accompaniment to my poems dressed in a light blue catsuit that has the texture of terry cloth. Jayed Scotti, the Feederz drummer and a visual artist who worked with the punk collage artist Winston Smith creating symbols and album covers for many bands, including the Dead Kennedys, plays drums, backing us up with a net of percussion. We've composed a score for each poem, texturing the words with an expansive, alluring array of sounds. I read a portion and Frank gets an idea in his head—"That sounds like Japanese robots"—and plays it. We do the long, hypnotic "Slumber of the Christ Child." Long, dirgelike bass notes . . . singular, sustained. Trills like a strange bird on the bass. A spray of sharp drum sounds. Then the lengthy, nearly symphonic "The Profile," as well as the shorter, tighter "Painted Lips/Masticated X's." There's a rustling in the audience, a shiver. We're pushing them toward a barely contained hysteria.

Tama tells me later that she overheard people in the audience saying things like, "Can you believe what she's saying?" "Did you hear *that?*" Oddly enough, it wasn't just the poetry but the catsuit Frank was wearing that provoked outrage. The audience was composed generally of poets and literati, not folks with community or political agendas. I'm surprised by their reaction.

What was so disturbing about what I was performing, half singing, half chanting? Perhaps the section about the priest who wore "the primary sexual organs of fur-enclosed life around his neck to remind himself of the constancy and lure of the physical urges"; maybe the glimpse in "The Profile" of a "conspirator's white face, bloated jowls press into the window, tearing the vaginal opening . . ." Perhaps it was something totally different, some odd configuration of visual and verbal imagery that tugged at their guts. Made them shift in their seats. You never know what will work its way under people's skin and why.

Poetry is a wonderful way to meet.

It's July 1986. I'm twenty-nine years old and working sporadically in telephone market research after finishing up a sweaty stint the year before as a bike messenger downtown. I have a Mohawk. Tall and slender, I wear torn-up T-shirts with an array of designs—a row of smiling nuns with shotguns, a U.S. Marines logo, Mona Lisa with a Mohawk and a safety pin through her cheek, James Dean. I wear a purple sweatshirt with Bugs Bunny in drag. Sometimes I wear a dog chain around my neck, and, of course, always my black leather jacket and Converse high-top sneakers.

Tama is eight years older than I, slender with dark eyes and a mass of curly hair that reminds me of electricity. Tama has a gleam in her eyes, mischievous and seductive. I love her writing, which is flatly textured, acerbic, oddly humorous. It gives the impression of having a tensile networking structured beneath cerebral twists and shoots. There's edge to her prose poems—edge and a twisted sensibility. Tama's mind is strong, with a rigor and an aimlessness to its logic. This is one of the reasons I'll endure our tempests, because she has a perceptive mind and an original, incisive ear. Her writing gives me hope and inspires my own. It is related to the more inspired forces of her personality, working off the darker forces, transforming and capturing their insoluble potency. The stuff that holds together radiant dreams as well as nightmares.

Tama has a stuttering, edgy wit, absurd and without warning: "Did you know that Bloomingdale's in Westchester County was once an insane asylum for women?"

"Really?" I ask, unsure of what to say.

"Yes, I remember from my childhood. My mother used to point it out to me from the freeway, she'd say, 'Tama, look, Bloomingdale's, it's an insane asylum for women!'"

Tama, a carnivorous chain-smoker, always has a cigarette in her hand, which she uses to great dramatic effect. She is a natural comic, making funny faces while on the phone or stretching in the morning. Her face contorts into a hundred configurations in seconds: strange stretched-out shapes, squinching, brow kneading, neck cracking, jaw clenching, eyelids fluttering open and closed. She tells me that people often suggest to her that she go on the Jewish comedy circuit back East.

The best thing about her humor is, as with many outrageously funny people, that very little of it is deliberate. Tama is always surprised that people find her so funny, and never completely understands why.

Tama appears manic, possessed of a whole range of personalities. She tells me about each of these in rapt detail: There's the mischievous little girl; the older woman, cold and logical; the demonic sides to herself that she calls the "beasts." I don't think she has multiple personality disorder in the clinical sense, yet there is something discontinuous, abruptly unsettling, about this florid, highly discursive range of personae. There's a quality of hallucination to her speech.

And can she talk! Constantly. Never-ending. Story piled upon story. Her whole life laid out for me: her defunct marriage, her affairs, the warfare and obsession of it all, the betrayals. Men who would threaten her, steal from her, go into long sieges of silence and not rise from the bed for days. How some would stare up into her window for hours from the ground below after having been kicked out, or call and hang up, and she would call and hang up every day, every hour on the hour, back and forth, and how another boyfriend tied her up, leaving her alone in an abandoned toolshed for hours, coming back and threatening her with a gun, taking her out to an isolated industrial area and leaving her to find her way back on foot swearing and cursing him all the while, and the time she was kidnapped by strangers, stuffed bound and gagged in the trunk of a car, and the time she slept with a different man every single night for an entire year. How she was homeless with one of her boyfriends, living in motels, and they would have sex on speed and if he couldn't get it up or if he tired, then she would stand half-dressed on a table close to an open window and threaten to rush out into the street in the night and find someone, anyone, to fuck her.

I've never met anyone with such massive surges of energy. When we sit and watch television together I feel as though I'm sitting next to a blasting furnace. Tama claims that she sets off electric doors when she walks past them. That people try and "suck" her energy out of her. She declares that the man in the upstairs apartment is moving furniture because she's moving around the room. She screams at the ceiling, trying to get him to stop, to leave her "energy" alone. Hearing these stories, I decide, with a sinking feeling in my stomach, that she could very likely be mad.

And Tama drinks, going to bars at odd hours. The Bubble Club, the 500 Club, the Mirage, and the Chatterbox, the black-leather rock bar down the street. Yukon Jack in the mornings, martinis in the afternoons. Calling me from these bars with a growling and loose voice, all throat, all whiskey and confusion. I remember with a start of humorous recognition how when we'd met she'd shown me her business card. It had on it a drawing of a large black funnel cloud menacing a tiny house. She had said, "This is me." She meant the funnel cloud. *It always pays to listen closely when people tell you things about themselves.*

We argue. For hours, from the afternoon into the middle of the night, in strange tongues, odd dialogues. I attempt to catalog and analyze her different personalities and imagine ways to calm her, distract her. I become, in time, like all her other lovers—obsessed, drained, overwhelmed. Nearly inert from continual combat.

The first year we fight nonstop, breaking up at short intervals. I cut it off, then go back when she calls. Always knowing it's the wrong thing to do, but unable somehow to do otherwise, entranced with anticipation and dread.

We shoot speed and have sex. Stay up all night listening to music: Diamanda Galás, X-Ray Spex, Lydia Lunch, The Birthday Party, Iggy Pop, the Ramones, and especially, Joy Division and X. Now, whenever I hear the moody ambience of Joy Division, I'm brought back to that time. Into a dark tunnel where fragments of conversation—human sounds—recede without location in time or space. A pensive landscape, ambivalent, stark.

With Tama it's easy to be male when we have sex. She'd been exclusively heterosexual up until we met. We go on for seven or eight hours, sometimes in the same position, until my hand is cramped up into a claw from being inside her for so long. I take it out slowly and grimace in pain, stretching my fingers out. "No," she protests. "Don't stop, *don't stop. Whatever you do, don't stop!*"

"But I have to get a drink of water, just a little drink."

"No—no—don't stop!"

"But I really have to get a drink, Tama, I'll be right back, okay? See?" I run across the room down the hall to the kitchen for a glass of water or a swig on a beer. "See, just a little drink."

Then we burst out laughing as I look at my shriveled, pained hand and shake it to get the cricks out. And then I go right back at it, as intense as ever, for another two to three hours.

Tama talks nonstop, high, telling me stories about fucking carpenters or lanky gas station attendants as we carry on. She describes my fingers as a cock, a young hard cock inside her and I pump her as fast as I can with unflagging intensity. Only once, in the beginning, did she want to enter me with her fingers. I allowed her to, not knowing quite what to do about this request. I figured it was only fair. But I know that I don't like to be penetrated. I want to be with a partner who will ignore my female parts. I've come to the realization that I have to be seen as male with a woman in bed in order to be aroused. Feel any rising heat. So it's perfect to be with a heterosexual woman like Tama who's not really all that interested in women's bodies. Someone I can be a man with in bed, who will not try and make me into a woman by groping my breasts or cunt. Who will talk to me in bed as though I am a man, physically, with all the right parts.

Nevertheless, the fact that I don't like my body to be touched very much sets off a conflict between us. This conflict is subtle, running beneath the surface of our relationship. We hardly ever talk about it. I want to deny a problem exists. Perhaps she does, too. I don't know. Mostly, what we do together sexually works. And since we prefer sex high out of our minds on speed, it doesn't matter. Sexuality becomes for us a gateway into the realm of near hallucination that methamphetamine ushers people into. We're whacked out of our brains when we're doing it, so what does it matter? I'm able to be male with someone who accepts this as natural, sexy. And it's great fun, a crazed, passionate sport.

I don't realize how much it disturbs her, even hurts her, not to be able to touch me freely. She wonders if there might be something wrong, if perhaps my reluctance to be touched means that I don't really love or trust her.

By the age of twenty-nine, my sexuality has become fixed into a paradoxical pattern. One formed over a long, perilous struggle of many years. Since it's expected, I take my clothes off in the initial phase of a relationship. As I become more comfortable in the relationship, I slowly drop the pretense of enjoying this revealing and gradually begin keeping more and more clothes on, even during sex. For me, comfort equals clothed.

Once, she gets it right. Lying down together on a Sunday night, at the end of a long, sex-crazed, speed-filled weekend, we begin to have another senseless fight. I can't remember how it began, but suddenly Tama glares at me and spits out a long, detailed invective. It's different from her usual endless character assassinations that are circuitous and vacuous rants, tipsy with illogic. This time she has something real to say. Tama points out how I keep my clothes on almost every time we have sex, how I didn't do this in the beginning. She blasts me: "You have gender problems!" Shoots up from the bed and strides off, leaving me speechless, unable to answer, found out.

No one before Tama had ever pointed it out so clearly and with such damning insight.

CHAPTER 8: THEATER OF FATE

ama and I move in together, an ill-advised move that feels le-
thal. It's her idea; I give in only after a series of long, drawn-out,
dramatic discussions. She lays out her case with defiant persistence, mesmerizing me with stories about commitment and obsession.
She waxes poetic, holding up one of my computer drawings: the words
THEATER OF FATE tilt at me from the page, suddenly ominous.

We paint our flat together, black floors and white walls; one tiny
room is a dark blue. Tama criticizes my painting and uses it as an opportunity to free-associate, going on long diatribes about the meaning and
subtle symbolism leaking out from my paintbrush as it glides over the
walls. She is angry that I fail to criticize her efforts with the same gusto,

taking this as a lack of caring. Tama keeps me up late into the night talking with a wild energy about how we are not really a couple. Increasingly, I feel hopeless. I need to end this, but I can't. What should be so easy is suddenly so difficult.

Tama regales me with stories of how she flirts with other people, usually guys, and describes their bodies in minute detail, dropping hints about how she might be meeting them later. It's usually a bluff; nothing happens. But it gets me. Against my better judgment, my rancor is aroused. I vent my jealousy, anger, pain, and confusion until I'm exhausted.

Tama's also jealous and gets angry with me if I talk to other people at a club or a restaurant, getting up and leaving in a fury. It doesn't matter who they are or what sexual preferences they have: gay man, straight man, lesbian, or straight woman, her jealousy is equal opportunity.

She'll suddenly turn on me and rave. This might go on for hours; Tama interrogates me in that impersonal, brutal way I associate with her "older authoritative" personality. She insults me and rages with an unstoppable venom, ruthless. These rages I associate with the energies she calls her "beasts," and sometimes she does look demonic—eyes pinched and gleaming, nostrils flaring. The force of her fury astounds me and I try to figure out a way to get her simply to stop. At some point, the raging has lost any connection to the original, disruptive event. We're off, straining through an endless loop, out of control, intoxicated, hammering at a series of hit-and-run tangents. Often, I can't even remember what the fight was about to begin with.

In time, after I run out of ideas, when I'm baffled, unable to make any more (futile) efforts to calm or distract her, I learn how to turn the tables, to interrogate Tama in return, to throw her off balance. This tactic doesn't bring peace or resolve any issues, but at least it gives me a sense that I am fighting back. This approach is not wasted on Tama. At one point she abruptly halts our run-on verbal dueling and declares, suddenly sober-faced, no longer caught up in her demonic mode, "That's good, you're learning, you'll find these skills come in handy, they are *very* useful." I sit stunned by this sudden, unforeseen praise. It appears Tama is admitting it is all a hurtling farce designed to put me through my paces and force me to endure. To focus all my previously scattered energies on survival, on cultivating barely sensed strategic talents and a ruthless, fighting heart. As though I am being beaten, broken down and toughened up as a kind of preparation for some unknown future mission.

Obviously, this is not a "healthy relationship." I am determined to get out, but it's not as easy as it should be. Some nearly hypnotic force always brings me back for another round. This is the type of relationship that will drive anyone to a therapist, or to a sudden religious conversion.

Eventually, the relationship blows up. Tama leaves for the East Coast. We talk long-distance constantly. I make a couple of pilgrimages for rollercoaster visits. It isn't completely over between us, yet I know it has to be.

CHAPTER 9:
FIRST SIGN

The wildness, the frenzied explorations of my twenties, have begun to quiet down. For a while, my life settles into more conventional patterns. I'm thirty, freelancing as a technical writer and database programmer in the South Bay. Working a full-time job and hammering away at my writing in my free time.

After our initial breakup, with Tama now in New York, a young lesbian by the name of Naomi will move in for a while. She will be my first "real" dyke roommate in years. Deep down, I hope that by having an incontrovertible lesbian as a roommate, I might connect more completely with the dyke community, and therefore with my own shaky sense of lesbian identity. Having a genuine lesbian around might help me to stop feeling like a fake lesbian, a sham. And, if I can connect to being a dyke, I can continue somehow to live as a woman. It will make it real, or at least bearable.

Naomi's young, only twenty-two. She's just graduated from an Ivy League university and moved out to California with her lover, Sandra. Sandra's always visiting. Perceptive and ironic, short, buxom, and Jewish, they are charming, extremely bright, and seem irremediably wholesome. Even so, Sandra and Naomi are not overly politically correct. Naomi even stipulated that she didn't want to be roommates with a lesbian who played "that horrible women's music." This was a good sign, and we become fast friends. Their soothing companionship helps me to heal from the painful, lingering aftereffects of my searing relationship with Tama.

Around this time, I decide to stop taking drugs entirely, and gradually I completely phase them out. My drug use had been intermittent since the mid-eighties, when I lived with David, and now I find that I have outgrown these cranky potions and am losing interest entirely. I'm lucky that I'm able to accomplish this without too much melodrama, and only two visits to a twelve-step meeting. Not that there's anything wrong with twelve-stepping; for many it has been invaluable. But at least you won't have to read through a text about me being in rehab and having a breakdown. No long-drawn-out confessions of my wasted youth and eventual tearful culmination of an overwrought salvation, like an episode of *Behind the Music*. Over time, I'm able to phase my usage out entirely, and I am glad of it—thankful. That party is over, and it's time for another stage of my life to begin.

Frank and Selene are breaking up, a startling but not completely unexpected development. Toward the end of my time living there, which coincided with my meeting Tama, their fights had become more frequent and the idyll of our time together had become fragmented. Once I left to live with Tama, their relationship seemed to unhinge and deteriorate rapidly. Almost as though I had buoyed them with my presence. Perhaps it had been easier to stay together when someone else had been there to keep the balance. When I go back to the old flat to visit them, Selene and Frank appear to live in another world, a claustrophobic place that feels airless and strangely detached from anything outside it.

Selene tells me about a psychic flash she's experienced since my leaving. When she was painting what had been my room, to convert it into a dungeon, she heard voices screaming. I can tell that the memory is disturbing; her eyes dart around the room as though she's searching for the source of the sounds.

"What were they screaming?" I ask, taken in by the sudden image. I feel a plunging in my stomach.

"Oh," Selene scans the room, nervous, as though she suddenly doesn't want to tell me. "They were saying, I mean, the voice was screaming about how it couldn't be a beautiful woman, and it wasn't a man. I mean, something like it wanted to be a man, or felt more like a man but . . ." Selene looks troubled by this, as though she has been allowed to hear something that she shouldn't. She looks at me and attempts a smile.

"What?" I can't believe this. I feel a chill.

"There was some painful issue with gender, with being a man or a woman. . . ." Selene trails off again and grimaces at the air as though she can still hear the screaming. She laughs at me nervously.

An empty, expectant brightness hangs in the air. I lie on my bed, watch the white ceiling for long stretches of time.

I've not written many poems in either first or third person for many years; I begin to now. Most of my writing is nonnarrative and without a definitive voice that can be located as a person in time or. space. It is abstract, like a film or a densely energetic painting that is alive. For the first time in many years, I begin to introduce a tentative narrative thread; in some of my new poems, a more personal voice is on the tip of emergence.

The first sign comes on a gray November day, chilly and damp. I'm going out for coffee, down Valencia Street past Kentucky Fried Chicken, farther on past the Sports Palace where power lifters train, squeezing their faces into contorted red expressions. Past windows of stores with basketball and baseball coffee mugs on display, past rental agencies, bicycle shops, Chinese restaurants, arcane bookstores.

I habitually browse bookstores, drawn by a magnetic force. In the Modern Times Bookstore window I see it, like a map to a faintly imagined and hoped-for place. In a stack of remaindered books, *Female-to-Male Transsexualism,* by Leslie Lothstein, MD, only $2.50. A bargain. I look through the store window at the book jacket for a long moment, startled. *What is this? A book about—female to male transsexuals? What if . . .* I hesitate inside . . . *I am a transsexual?* Transfixed by the book, I'm gripped by a fascinated, queasy excitement. A relentless curiosity. *There's no way. Being a transsexual is the worst thing to be. The most difficult, the most absolutely shameful, difficult path.*

I'd never once in my entire life seen anything in book form about female to male transsexuals. I'd read a couple of articles in the local papers years back concerning a female gym teacher who became a man and got fired from his job in the process. Entranced, I'd gazed at his scratchy indistinct photo in the paper—its edges blur in my memory. The process of changing from woman to man seemed inscrutable. Yet the weirdest thing was the excitement. It tingled in my chest, restless and intelligent. I faintly remembered where it came from, my long-lost childhood dreams, yet it felt unfamiliar, threatening.

Alongside the excitement was a feeling of incredulous awe. I also felt horror. The awe and horror one feels when a cherished belief has been subverted. The belief that biological sex is immutable.

I was beginning to enter the crossroads—a place of raw, unmitigated energy.

The process struck me as an odd series of medical events that only desperate, gruesome-looking women undertake as a last resort. I surmised that these women must have looked like men to begin with. I figured you had to have hair growing in odd places on your face and body, possess brutish mannish features and thick, muscular limbs, perhaps even have some certifiable endocrinal abnormality. I didn't think I would qualify. Although I was sometimes mistaken for a guy when I walked down the street or entered a store, once people got a good look at me, or once I opened my mouth and said more than a couple of words, it became clear that I was not a man. I am tall and thin, nearly five feet nine inches, and I weigh 130 pounds. I have slender hips for a woman and a cocky walk. The fact that I wear mostly men's clothing creates a strong impression of androgyny. However, when all is said and done, I decidedly do not look like a man.

Thoughts and memories accelerate as I stare through the plate glass of the store window. *Find out what this book is about. Or maybe just forget it. Forget this craziness. Too weird.* I go on my way. Walk down the street, get coffee.

On my way back, I think of that book again. Blazing with portent. I go back and forth in my head about it. Have to look at it, at least glance into the pages, get an idea of what it's about. *Dare I?*

I walk into the store, scared. What if someone here sees me looking at this book about female to male transsexuals? *They will know.* Quick thoughts: *It's surely weird for a self-respecting dyke to be seen reading such a book. About confused women who want to be men, women so maligned and self-hating, so unevolved as to think that they are men. Unsophisticated, not exposed to feminism. Poor, old-fashioned, twisted-up bull daggers from some small town in pigfart nowhere who can't face the fact that they're actually dykes.* Isn't that what I'd always thought about this?

I buy it. The woman at the counter doesn't seem to notice anything strange. Bored and distant, she rings up the sale. I run home in a blur, stash the forbidden book away.

CHAPTER 10:
PSYCHIATRIST'S TABLOID TALES—FEMINIST PARANOIA

I feel ashamed to be reading this book. In the late eighties, transsexuality feels like a shameful subject, held in suspicion or contempt by both conservatives and radicals. Besides the scratchy newspaper photo of the gym teacher, Steve Dain, I have never met or seen a female to male transsexual in my life. Not even on television.

Lothstein's book is damning. He paints the transsexual men he works with as psychopathic, borderline, fractured, pathetic. He feels that most of them are mistaken in asking for sex reassignment. The few who are so poorly adjusted as to need it do so as a treatment of last resort. They are in for a series of painful, mutilating, and nearly fruitless medical procedures. The hormone treatment leaves them frail looking, only slightly more masculine in appearance than before. Their voices barely change. Dr. Lothstein describes the mastectomy as a horrific procedure, evoking images of breast tissue being spooned out, not to mention massive, unsightly scarring. His descriptions of both clients and treatments make me feel creepy. It's a patronizing, damning psychological study, seductive in its authoritative posturing. I sense it's off base, but I also don't know enough about the subject to know just how wrong the book is.

Even so, in spite of my suspicions, the book scares me off. If this is what female to male transsexuals are like, I don't think I'm one! If the change from woman to man is so blatantly ineffectual, so unconvincing, why bother? May as well stay a dyke. I have been told that I have looks, I know I have health, and some say I have a certain type of androgynous appeal. Why give that up . . . if the alternative is to become a man who looks like a woman pretending to be a man?

I feel distaste for Lothstein's case studies, a mild revulsion at the medical procedures he describes and their unattractive results. Even so, I suspect that his data is skewed and unreliable. As an adolescent, I'd read psychiatrists' damning research of lesbians and gay men. Many psychiatrists have a way of making ordinary troubled people sound totally disturbed. They sometimes refer to case studies of individuals who are inordinately maladjusted and use these as examples of the typical psychological profile for that entire group. *Female-to-Male Transsexualism* is highly reminiscent of those psychological studies, which had attempted to posit homosexuality as a psychiatric illness.

Although psychology has illuminated and reinvented the human psyche—artfully translating our machinations, motivations, and passions into a language that can clarify and focus energies, often enabling us to transcend limitations—I'm also skeptical of its obdurate authority. Psychiatry does have a tendency to uphold the status quo morality, the consensus of the mass mind. It has taken the place of God and religious convention, or just day-to-day unquestioned social and moral convention. Conformity: a complacency of imagination masquerading as scientific insight.

My other official point of reference for transsexuality is equally bleak. Janice Raymond, a well-known lesbian feminist academic, wrote a book in the seventies called *The Transsexual Empire* that basically set the tone of feminist discourse about sex change for many years to come. Raymond postulated that all transsexuals were dupes of the patriarchy, "mutilating" their bodies in order to live out stereotyped sex roles instead of changing those roles through a rigorously applied program of radical feminism. She focused most of her book on male to female transsexual women (MTFs), with female to male transsexual men (FTMs) thrown in as an afterthought. FTMs were basically the brainwashed tokens of the "transsexual empire." Sexless, wan imitations of men, they required only a couple of pages in order to be dismissed. The threat of MTFs loomed in apocalyptic tones. They were being engineered by the male medical establishment to eventually replace natal biological/genetic women, a bionic Barbie race tailored to male specifications that would satisfy a man's every whim. Or, even more insidiously, MTFs were out to infiltrate and weaken the feminist movement by declaring themselves to be lesbians, joining feminist women's organizations, and slipping like a rapidly spreading virus into "women's space," slowly taking over from within. Raymond was dead serious, and she was taken seriously. She stated that transsexuality should be "morally mandated out of existence," and began the task of making this happen, working with the Reagan administration to eliminate Medicare payments for both sex-change surgery and hormones for poor transsexuals in Minnesota.

Between these two extremes, which were actually very much the same, I sought the truth.

CHAPTER 11:
MANHATTAN JULY

B y the summer of 1988, Tama is living in New York City on the Lower East Side in a large studio with white walls and track lighting. I bring Tama a model of Frankenstein from San Francisco and place him in the window next to her boom box with an Iggy Pop tape inside. That humid, hot July in Manhattan, I stay with Tama for three weeks and we fight and cry and carry on as we had when she'd lived in San Francisco. There are thunderstorms and I walk through the Village into the Bowery in the warm rain, soaked through my clothes, in wonder at this intersection of nature and concrete. When I get back from walking in the rain, I discover that a sly set of hands has cut through the screen on her window, reached past the bars, and stolen both the Frankenstein and the boom box from the ledge.

I fight with Tama in Chinatown, and she leaves me to find my way back alone. Which is better than the last visit, when we fought in Grand Central Station and she walked away, leaving me to get back to her place by train. We fight loudly at four in the morning outside a Lower East Side rock-and-roll bar. She screams in my face and waves her umbrella menacingly. I snap it in two while she smashes on a trashcan with a two-by-four and yells. People hang out of windows screaming at us to shut up. Nothing has changed.

By then I know with great certainty that nothing ever would. Nothing between us. But I would change.

I had been Tama's only lesbian lover, although somehow I never felt that I was bringing her a "real" lesbian experience. I felt like an impostor.

On the third night of my visit, Tama stays out late. I wait in the apartment, barely able to sleep, with only sheets and a fan on in the dank heat. *Where is she?*

"She wants to feel snapping pussy."

Wanda said that. The counselor. She's Tama's shrink. Tama arranges for us to see her in search of some kind of insight. Wanda has stringy bleached-blond hair and wears a halter top in the wild heat. She's an impressive sight—large, with a startling beaklike nose and small, dark eyes that pin you down. She looks as though she cackles, like the Egg Lady in John Waters's *Female Trouble*. And Wanda is sharp-tongued, never even bothering to pretend to withhold her opinions in any posture of professional "objectivity." She reveals things that Tama has never said to me directly, subtextual thoughts and feelings that I've feared . . . *"She wants to feel snapping pussy."*

The night I spend alone is long, sweaty, restless. I turn in the white sheets, unable to dream, resting lightly with my eyes shut. When Tama finally returns, late the next morning, I find out she's spent the night with a dyke friend, Anne. When I ask her if they've slept together, she says yes. She protests it doesn't mean anything and will never happen again and she's sorry. I tell her that this is the last straw, the final, faintly catastrophic act. She's finally pulled it off, and I am done with her.

Tama describes Anne to me as a tall, strapping butch, an ex-firefighter who carries a switchblade and drinks Jack Daniels straight. Anne punches guys out in bars, does lots of coke. She's been hot for Tama for some time. Until my visit, Tama has resisted her advances. Now, some impulse, some combination of circumstance and feeling—revenge, anger toward me distilled and sweetened to a raw pitch after one of our long fights, a moody curiosity, perhaps booze—prompts her to finally give in. More than anything it's the timing that gets me. After all, I'm here visiting her.

Tama admits she wanted revenge. This admission softens my anger. On one level, after all the insane raging fights, I'm beyond caring; on another, it is the final outrage, the last insult. She's committed a final, irreconcilably rotten act. Somehow, I'm not surprised.

"She wants to feel snapping pussy."

We go to see Wanda together for a couples' counseling session the next night. Wanda defends Tama's right to sleep with someone else while I'm visiting in New York. I explain that we'd agreed before I came to visit that this was wrong. Wanda goes on, unperturbed. To her it's simply a matter of my being possessive, unreasonable. I'm shocked and in great pain. I cry, feeling cornered by both of them. I've come seeking help, insight, but instead have gotten this strange, unexpected defense of Tama's bad behavior. I can't believe it.

Nothing is resolved. We fight a little in Wanda's office, then calm down and go back to Tama's place. I'm stunned by Wanda's lack of sympathy. The therapy session feels like an act of collusion against me.

Later, Tama and I lie on her couch and talk about her therapy group. She tells me that a woman there told her that one night, when Tama got up and went into the bathroom, she came out looking entirely different.

The woman was amazed, exclaiming, "It's amazing, it's like you are suddenly twelve years old, your entire face has changed!"

I say, "That's incredible."

I don't quite know what else to say. Neither does Tama. She tells me these stories with as much astonishment as I feel when I hear them. Tama witnesses her own personality shifts and is helpless to completely fathom or control the changes.

Perhaps it was, in part, this interminable and deep puzzle that had attached itself to her soul that kept me with her. As much as her fits of spectacular generosity, her sweet, imaginative domesticity, her humor, her New Yorker's edge, our common interest in writing and music, and, of course, the fact that I could be a man with her sexually in my head and she didn't seem to want to interfere.

In some way, I could be her boyfriend. I certainly felt as though that's what I was. Selene had said, "She treats you like a man." This had offended Selene quite a bit. I was intrigued by this observation and didn't know whether to deny or confirm it. I felt, in my heart of hearts, like saying, *Well, what's wrong with that? I want her to treat me like a man. What else is she going to treat me as? I like it.* However, this observation brought up some kind of shame in me, some old, confused shame.

For my thirtieth birthday, Tama had gone all out. Tama loved birthdays and celebration was something she honed and fanned to a flaming pitch. First there was a small black cupcake with a candle in the center, which she brought to the bed from the kitchen singing "Happy Birthday," smiling, lit up. She gave me a card that said, "Welcome to the big 3-0, these are the best," and then she retrieved a small box. "I've got your present," she told me. Beaming, she watched me open it. It was beautiful: Two dragons faced each other on a jeweled surface, a sword and a crown scattered beside them on the ground they did battle upon.

"This is me, the female, and this is you, the male." Tama pointed at each dragon. The female was leaning back and holding a paw, or hand, out to the male to simultaneously ward him off and bring him closer.

"See, she's teasing and her legs are spread . . . she's got that crystal ball, *the secret.*" The female dragon held a small crystal ball in one hand, raised, just out of reach of the male, who looked as though he were trying to get to it. "See, he's being very male, pushing through." The male dragon, who was supposed to symbolize me, was poised with one hand up, as if to push at an invisible barrier between himself and the female dragon. He looked determined, heedless of danger. Unstoppable, but possibly not too attuned to his surroundings or to her internal workings. "She's smiling," Tama noted, gleeful, pointing out the details of their entangled pursuit and battle. And so she was: The female dragon was smiling, holding up the small crystal ball, tantalizing, teasing, leaning back, in control of the situation with her acumen and knowledge. Possessing the crystal ball gave her control over the situation; she had the power, and the male was in pursuit of this secret, sweet jewel with a relentless determination that made her smile even more. "This is us, happy birthday."

So Tama and I lived out our relationship pushing against and inside the borders of male/female. It felt natural. Yet, underneath there was a tension running through the relationship, strung like a wire. The tension had to do with the male/female configuration, which we simultaneously enjoyed and felt ashamed and uneasy about.

Later, I go back to Wanda's alone. I meet with her and she lays it on the line with me. "I once was a stone butch, and I thought about getting a change. But I decided against it." I have been thinking about it, but I didn't realize that this might be so obvious to someone else. At this early moment, I am nowhere near the point where I would talk to Tama, or to anyone, about the possibility of sex change. But it seems nearly a moot point with Wanda that I have "gender issues." She shows me a photo of herself dressed in a huge blue tux getting married to another woman. Her hair is cropped, dark, but she has the same eagle nose, the same piercing eyes. Her bride is petite and feminine in a white lacy bridal gown—beaming with demure grace.

"That's *interesting,*" I finally reply, peering into the photos.

It is out. Tama has actually spoken to Wanda about the fact that I am so uncomfortable being touched. This pains me beyond almost anything that has ever happened between us. But it is different from the other pain. It is pain that engenders truth. Truth hidden for years under an ongoing pattern of longing, frustration, confusion, and denial.

"She wants to feel snapping pussy."

I laugh remembering this. Was it really true that Tama wanted to feel the inside of a woman's vagina? Put her fingers inside and savor the sweet rushing contractions of female orgasm? Perhaps she just wanted to feel as though there was nothing about my body that was off-limits to her. On the other hand, I guess it shouldn't have surprised me that she might wish to experience a woman's body, to have a genuine, incontrovertible lesbian sexual episode. The problem was that the woman's body in question was mine. And I couldn't conceive of *my* body as *really* being a woman's body. I knew it was, technically, but this fact had no basis in reality for me emotionally.

Well, Wanda, she ain't going to get any "snapping pussy" from me, I think with a rising defiance. *I* don't think of myself as someone who has a "snapping pussy." The image is nauseating, incongruous. How can anyone think of me in those terms? And yet, I have to admit, of course they could. I do have female parts, although the reality that they are female is incomprehensible to me. *What is wrong?*

The night before I leave New York, in bed with Tama, the TV screen flicker lights my body gently. Prone, I look down at my breasts. For once, I am naked, my skin moist in the humid night air. My entire torso shines softly, taut, a resilient, elastic stretch of flesh. My slender arms rest parallel to Tama's. Nude, our bodies seem congruent. Contextualized in erotic closeness, I become hyperaware of my physicality. The way my body is motivated through its flesh. I yearn to embody a physical presence that feels more tangibly other. Stronger, larger. My arms feel too slim, almost fragile, my skin too soft. I want my body to sharply contrast hers, to be muscular, firm, hard. And it isn't simply a matter of becoming well muscled, of getting the sculpted physique of a female bodybuilder. I yearn for my body to have the density, smell, and look of a man's body. To possess a physicality I don't completely comprehend but, at that moment, instinctively know is male.

Perhaps I'm not really a lesbian after all.

CHAPTER 12:
IMAGINATION AND BODY

Frankfurt, Germany, 1966–1968. *I get pale blue cat's-eye glasses. I'm Clark Kent now instead of Superman. My male self is cloaked, I keep it close to my chest, locked up inside.*

In Germany we live on base, and I go to American schools. I make friends with Martin, a fantastic singer with an operatic voice, featured in Amahl and the Night Visitors *at Christmas. In English and history, we tip our chairs back as far as we can without tipping them over and pretend to fart.*

In lieu of TV, we American kids entertain ourselves with comic books. Trading door to door, lugging boxes full of Marvel, DC, or Archie comics up the long stairwells from one set of government quarters to the next, ringing doorbells, pounding on doors, standing on the doorstep where the German beer man leaves huge brown bottles of beer instead of milk. Even in this popular hobby, I feel singular. The girls trade mostly Archie and Veronica comics while the boys, like me, are into the superhero Marvel and DC comics. (I'm sure there was some girl somewhere who was trading Thor, Fantastic Four, The X-Men, Spiderman, *and* The Incredible Hulk, *but I never met her. Even if I had, chances are she probably didn't want to look like Spiderman, The Flash, or the red-suited, nattily horned Daredevil.)*

I want to look like these superheroes—muscular, svelte, great in tights and a synthetic bodysuit! I spend hours drawing their perfect, well-muscled forms, contemplating with awe what it would be like to possess their agility, speed, fantastic legs, and great biceps. It's the same excitement that I'll feel overtake me when I run across ads in magazines where a confident, brawny muscleman tells all the ninety-nine-pound weaklings of the world that they too can get great bodies and wow the chicks. How could I have that? There must be a way. I want it so much I could burst.

As I look and dream, counting up my allowance in my head so that I can send away for one of those muscle-building manuals, I'm not completely aware that I'm in actuality —a little girl. A girl with long, thin legs and cat's-eye glasses, transforming herself into a muscleman in her imagination. The possibility feels so real, I barely realize I'm imagining it.

My parents are gone and I'm in the bathroom peering into the mirror. I comb my hair back and to the side, male hairstyles. It doesn't look right, I know, but I can almost see it, if I look long and hard enough. An instant, a flash where I look like a boy or the grown man I feel I should become. It frustrates me that I can't make it more real. One afternoon, my father sees me doing this and takes the small black comb from my hand, and, doing what I always do, parts my hair to one side, then tries combing it straight back. Together, we gaze into the mirror. He laughs at my reflection. Does he know what I'm doing? Why is he laughing? Embarrassed and puzzled, I wonder how aware my parents might be of the conflicts and feelings going on inside me.

Blake believed that the imagination was the voice, the agency of God. To imagine is to be one with divine forces. Looking back I realize that I spent hours of time alone honing that imaginative faculty, reconfiguring my basic physical reality.

Out on the playground at recess I play with a magnifying glass, using it to focus the rays of the sun onto a small area. Flames burst up out of dense strands of sunlight. I show Susie, transfixed. She and I have the same birthday. Beginning around the age of eight or nine, as part of an attempt to accept my birth sex, I try and become more acquainted with girls my age, to understand them. To fit in. Susie is one of the first girls my age that I bond with. In time, I'll learn to talk on the phone with them and share complex intuitions—gossip, as well as my own far-flung ideas. Susie also wears cat's-eye glasses and is in my advanced math classes. We're both awed by the miracle of the magnifying glass. Again and again, using the small lens, I transform sunlight into flames, transfixed by this effortless mutation of elemental states. Vision and fire, light and heat, the concentration of a gaze lit into a searing, expanding circumference.

CHAPTER 13: CAUTIONARY TALES

G ene finds me. He's an old friend, a visual artist and a fellow struggling bohemian. We share a passion for punk rock, quirky art, and wild parties. I've known Gene since 1983 when we met at a party at the Strand Theater. Androgynous, with shoulder-length blond hair, he has an impish charm. Our friendship has grown closer over the years, and he's kept in touch, writing regularly from Seattle after his marriage and the birth of his son. Now, he's moved back to San Francisco and is going through a painful separation from his wife. So that summer, the summer of 1988, Gene and I hang out at night drinking beer and listening to Iggy Pop, X, the Dead Milkmen, the Ramones, and The Liars. I sit at one end of the table, he at the other—strumming a guitar, a languid smile on his face. His long, straggly blond hair creates a rakish curtain over his eyes. We crank up the stereo, Iggy Pop's *Metallic KO* album blasts an explosive whine, white-hot. With unflinching, deliberate honesty, I begin to tell Gene how I feel about my gender identity. I don't censor myself, I tell him things I've never really told anyone before, groping toward some kind of truth.

When I first met Gene he'd been going through the process of sex change. On estrogen, he transformed slowly, by degrees, into she. She grew breasts, her skin became softer, her body more curvaceous. She began a long course of electrolysis to remove the facial hair she'd had as male.

As a woman, Gene identified primarily as a lesbian. It had been tough. Many were not accepting. Feeling isolated and lonely, she struggled with shame, the intolerance of family and friends.

Like many transsexuals who fight the urge to change their sex, Gene had hoped that having a family would effect a kind of "cure." So she stopped taking estrogen and reverted to the male identity, met a woman, married, had a son. But kept yearning, even as a married man, for a female life. Now, separated from his young son and reviled by his wife, who had called him a "drag queen" and had taken to marching up and down the hall in the morning screaming this epithet out, Gene told me that he'd lie awake at night realizing he still had breasts and be overcome with a sense of relief and hope. He could still go back and reclaim life as a woman.

Gene was my first real transsexual friend.

"So, do you think you're going to do it?" he asks.

I peer across the table at him. Grab at the beer in front of me, pull at the label on the bottle. I realize I'm avoiding Gene's question.

"You're *really* thinking about this? Becoming a *guy?*" He's looking right at me, a strong look of disapproval skirting across his features. *How can Gene disapprove,* I think, *since he once tried to transition?*

"I don't know yet." I grimace. This is hard to talk about. "I'm thinking about . . . things."

"Well, I wouldn't do it if I were you. I mean, what would you want to be a *guy* for?"

I peer up from my view of the beer bottle's label, head tilted. I don't answer. My stomach's beginning to knot.

"A guy?" Gene strums his guitar absently. Gazing off in space away from my vexed expression. X's *Wild Gift* album plays; John Doe and Exene's voices slide in a scrimmage of harmonies, dissonant, tense, pulled to extreme angles of energetic collage. Exene shrieking over an amphetamine beat: *We're desperate/get used to it.*

Gene doesn't understand the appeal of being a guy. Since he hasn't made peace with his own gender conflicts, he hasn't come to an objective acceptance and understanding of maleness. He can't understand how someone would want to be a man, or feel like one. After all, he tried to become a woman at one time, and a lesbian at that. I am perfection in his mind, a terrific Amazon, a lesbian with style, strength, and graceful rebellion. I symbolize a dream to Gene.

I know, half-consciously, that when I became close friends with Gene and accepted him initially as female, he'd felt closer to that dream himself. In order to accept me as a man, he will have to let go of this cherished notion of me. Something he does not want to do.

I know what guys are to Gene. They are the lowest human life forms. For each and every guy that we know, Gene analyzes his personality flaws dead on, summarizing them with withering acumen. Ed is a nice guy, but his stolidity is hard to take, he is too rigid, like a sweet bull with blinders on. John is a cuddly, pop-eyed, baby-faced boy who is passive, ineffectual, conceited. Phil is a self-centered, egocentric has-been who's bound to get potbellied and shrill as he ages. Drake's a good-looking, svelte guy with a sinewy body and a smooth-talking low voice, cool and hard as a shiny metal weapon; he's also an abusive, cunning womanizer, possibly a pathological liar and con man.

These antimale values aren't only Gene's. They're also part of my armored ethical code, my radical feminist arsenal. I've stated for years that, with a few startling exceptions, men are lower life forms. And even if I hadn't always genuinely felt that extreme about it, I'd known, as a lesbian feminist of some unspecified variety, that men were to be seen, by and large, as pugnacious, counterintuitive, violent, self-centered. They took up too much space and didn't even realize it. They were ugly, they talked too loud, they raped and plundered. And if they didn't do those things, they were effete Milquetoasts, searching for a sensitivity that didn't really exist. Guys were the excrement of the goddess. Even so, I couldn't help but identify.

Gene had a low opinion of most men, although he had chosen to go back to being one. But how long would that last? Inside him, the battle still raged. The pull of Gene's female self was too hard to resist, a siren call inside his soul, a hypnotic song amplified by the bodily changes he'd endured as his physical form shifted back from female to male: as her shoulders broadened, her waist expanded, and her hips shrank; as her skin became harder, the muscles in her arms began to thicken, and she became he again, resigned and weary, barely able to cope. I remember feeling surprised when I saw Gene the first time after he'd gone off the estrogen. He really did look different. He pretended that it was okay, but told me in anguished moments that it really wasn't. In fact, he could barely stand the way his body had shifted back to maleness so sharply, the veering away from his dream.

In tears, he'd tell me how his estranged wife was threatening to take his son away forever if he should begin transition again. And Gene wanted more than anything to have this boy be a part of his life. The love he felt for his son was larger than any love he had ever experienced. But now it was all unraveling and they were separating.

"You know, when women do this, when they become men, they are really, really . . . Oh, how can I describe it?" He pauses and looks off again into space for dramatic effect. There's something calculated about Gene's persona, a quality that makes me feel as though I'm watching a staged performance. This irritates me. But since my sense of this is elusive, I can't really complain about it.

He continues, "Well, they are really phony." Gene grasps an invisible hand as if to shake it too firmly in a macho grip, he lowers his voice into a macho tone, "I mean, like a stereotype, a jerky stereotype." He glances at me from his pantomime, shoots a stabbing look across the table.

"Really?" I ask. I don't know if this is true or not. I figure Gene knows. After all, he's tried this; he was a transsexual. "Did you ever know any transsexual men?"

Gene keeps singing to himself softly. He brushes the hair out of his face with one hand, takes another swig from his beer. Finally, after what seems like a long time, he answers. "Well, I knew one. I mean, I saw one, once."

"What was he like?" I'm acutely interested.

"Well, like I said, he seemed just like a cartoon character. He seemed like a windup toy." Gene looks at me hard. I'm listening anxiously, balanced on a slim margin of hope that maybe there will be *something* in what he says that will open the door for me. Is it really that bad? Are all transsexual men posers—brittle, bitter cartoons? "I mean, this guy would just act like one of those really horrible macho guys, stiff and all. Really unattractive." Gene doesn't say anything else; he doesn't have to. He just continues to absently strum his guitar.

"Oh, well, that's a drag," I reply. I yank the beer up to my mouth. Maybe it isn't such a good idea to try the change after all. Maybe I should just forget it.

"Why bother, then," I say. It's a statement, not a question. "I could never be that way."

"Yeah, they have to lower their voice in this real fake way," Gene continues.

"Really. Like pretend?" My stomach is sinking.

"Yes. Like, 'Hi, I'm Joe.'" He does the creepy imitation again. Then shoots out a staccato laugh, puncturing the air between us. Gene's portrait of a transsexual man is unremittingly bleak; there's a chill behind his every word.

"Anyway, you're so great as a woman, why would you want to spoil that? *You'd lose your charm.*"

This backhanded compliment pulls at my gut. Could it be true? A part of me whispers *No.* I feel this damning phrase is a curse, yet underneath and inside, the words also contain a subliminal dare: "You'd . . . lose . . . your . . . charm. . . ." *Not me.* I rebel. The fighter in me flares. I won't lose my charm! Still, I'm confused. What if it's true? What if I do end up looking like an odd version of Julie Andrews on steroids with a paste-on mustache? Well, maybe Gene is exaggerating a bit to scare me. . . .

"Let's listen to the Ramones!" I exclaim, breaking the pensive mood.

Gene gets up and puts on the record, grabs another beer out of the fridge, and picks up the guitar again. He begins to strum again with that same faraway look.

That night Gene will inscribe HEY HO LETS GO! on his leg with black ink. He gouges it into his skin in a warding-off ritual, exclaiming, "That'll keep me from wearing panty hose again!"

I think about all the weird stuff Gene has said about transsexual guys. Well, what is the use? If FTMs are like that, if the change is so ineffectual, so strained, why bother?

A few nights later Gene tells me that the surgery scars from the mastectomy FTMs undergo are gruesome. "They look like monkey tails, swirling around and around right to the center." His index finger traces a spiral in the air. He grimaces with distaste.

"Really?" I ask, distressed. "It's that bad?"

"Yeah, it's that bad. I saw this guy once, he was standing in a parking lot with his shirt off, and he had those weird, monkey-tail scars. I thought to myself, that must be a transsexual guy."

I lean forward to hear this disturbing story. "You're *sure* he was a transsexual?"

"What else could he be?" Gene responds calmly. He yanks open a can of beer. We're listening to "Slip It In." The sound of Black Flag's pillaging is raw ecstasy in my ears.

I nod quietly. I don't completely believe this story. Why would some random guy be a transsexual just because he has weird scars on his chest? Yet Gene is insistent. I don't say anything else. It is too painful to talk about.

The anecdotes that Gene relates to me are withering. Discouraging, yet at the same time, strangely reassuring. The part of me that is afraid of transition wants to hear *something, anything* to turn me back; that part feels relieved. If it's this bad, then I won't have to do it. I can resist.

CHAPTER 14:
THE HORMONES REALLY WORK

When I meet Lou Sullivan, I'm shocked.

Lou Sullivan runs the group FTM, an information and support group for female to male transsexuals and/or female to male cross-dressers. He founded FTM in 1986 and, with Kevin Horwitz, began publishing a newsletter.

After I get over Gene's horror stories, my curiosity gets the better of me. For a couple of years, I've seen a small strange ad in the back pages of *On Our Backs,* the lesbian sex magazine, for a mysterious organization called FTM. The idea of an organization for female-born people who wish to wear male clothing in order to take on a male identity, or who actually become men, is completely bizarre. It is beyond politically incorrect. I write asking for the *FTM Newsletter,* and when it arrives I rip open the envelope with nervous, eager fingers. "Genetic Men Have Big Feet" are the first words to snap out at my eyes. The article is about buying guys' shoes if your feet are smaller than average. This is amazing. I can't believe there are people out there thinking these thoughts and writing these articles! I order and read Lou's booklet about FTM history and the female to male process entitled *Information for the Female to Male Cross Dresser and Transsexual.*

That long, easy summer I must have read that small gray booklet five hundred times, over and over, the same words, till my eyes blurred. How to bind, how to pad your crotch, the histories of women who had lived as and passed as men in various countries and centuries, the startling effects of testosterone and the details of various surgical sex-change procedures. And when I was done with the booklet, I'd read that little newsletter a half-dozen times till it was tattered and smudged, and then I'd hide both of these seditious materials under my bed in an unlabeled shoebox. *Worrying* that someone might find them and *know. Worrying . . .* realizing it was silly, but worrying anyway. No one should catch me with that material, which felt so seductive and so terrifying.

As I sift through my memories, I focus. Stretched out on the bed, I watch the ceiling. A tree bends outside my window. It's quiet, late afternoon, time moves sluggishly toward evening. I'm in a world of shifting time, reflection. Memory animated by a sense of discovery.

Childhood feelings elongate into adolescence, feeling male inside my body, standing and screaming "I'm not a girl!" at the age of three, over, over, and over again. "I am not a girl!" In tears, desperate for someone to believe me. My mother has told me I'd stand, cry, and scream my lungs out. Where did those feelings go? Thinking back now as an adult—thirty-one—I feel a chill as I remember their ferocity, clairvoyant and lucid. Sometimes, that voice returns. "I am not a woman!" This voice isn't disembodied, it's not anyone else. It's a part of myself, barely articulate yet breaking out into awareness.

I wake up in the mornings with fear clutching at my chest. This is the scariest act I've ever contemplated, the most absolute and extreme. Strong emotions come to the surface. Fear, then shame, tremendous shame rolling up in waves, scarlet and sticky. Being a transsexual, embarking on a sex change, feels like the most shameful and loneliest thing. Yet the prospect of doing this unspeakable act, which many see as mutilation and monstrosity, fills me with hope.

I feel shame not only about being transsexual, but about having a male gender identity. An identity I have tried to deny. First as a child in order to survive in the world, to adjust. Second as an adult, as a lesbian feminist, in order to fit in, again to adjust. Not that I am the world's greatest lesbian feminist. I have always been on the outside, uncomfortable. I ornament the edges of that world. Still, I have my friends, I know the language. Susie Bright says that lesbianism is a language you learn. I know the language of that country, its nuances.

It didn't occur to me that my male identity was deep, rooted in my body. That finally, like all transsexuals, the body is the issue, not the role. Lou writes in his booklet that as long as men and women have different bodies, there will be transsexuals.

One day I get my courage up. I call Lou one bright afternoon in early September 1988. Lou is listed in the phone book, so I just pick up the phone, take a deep breath, and dial.

His voice is deep; it's a man's voice, no doubt. Not a trace of ambiguity. Lou's friendly in an immediate kind of way, warm, down-to-earth. There's nothing pretentious about this man, nothing calculated or affected. I like him immediately and trust him, which is crucial. He says I should come to an FTM meeting. "It's amazing to see these guys," he tells me. "They start out female, but each and every time you see them they look more and more male." Finally, he exclaims how hard it is to believe they were ever women. Some of them even look like lumberjacks, burly, with beards. He pauses, declaring with a mild astonishment that clearly hasn't worn out with time, "*The hormones really work.*"

"You can be as weird as you want," Lou declares.

"Yeah?"

"Yes. I'm a gay man," he states, matter-of-fact and proud, as though it's an accomplishment.

"Really?" I'm amazed. Although I know that many transsexual women are lesbians, it's never occurred to me that a transsexual man could be gay. I like the idea. This elegant twist of identity shines a clarifying penumbra, a sparkle of sheer freedom. One could explore. Possibilities multiply.

"That's great," I say, turning this idea over in my mind. I start to consider that Lou's being a gay man *is* an accomplishment. I learned later that Lou had been denied hormones several times by different gender clinics simply because he did not want to become a heterosexual man. Lou worked very hard as an activist to change this rule, and he won. Now, no transmen are denied testosterone simply because they are attracted to men. This important change is one of his greatest and most hard-won accomplishments.

Lou tells me that before I go to an FTM meeting and meet a whole roomful of transmen, I can and should first meet him. I set out to see him in early September on a brisk San Francisco night. Searching for his apartment number in the dark, looking for the iron gate on Albion Street, his motorcycle parked outside, I wonder, slightly anxious, what he looks like. *What will he think of me?*

When he meets me at the door, I am amazed. Lou has light brown hair and glasses. His build is just slight of medium; he stands around five feet seven inches. He has sharp features and a pleasant quality to his face, a roundness at his cheeks. There is nothing out of the ordinary about him.

We walk into the kitchen through a long hall. Sit down at a table. I face him at an angle. I can tell he's peering at me, scrutinizing me. I return the scrutiny, looking at him with growing amazement from across the kitchen table. Searching his face, his shoulders, his hands, his legs, his chest for a mark, a distinguishing feminine characteristic. There is nothing visibly female about him that I can detect. He is a guy. No different from any man I've seen on the street anywhere at any time. I tell him so: "I can't tell."

Lou smiles. He's used to this response and says it again, "Yes, the hormones really work."

The hormones . . . I'd read about testosterone and its dramatic effects in his booklet, but I had never in my wildest dreams imagined that it could be this good. This transformation is a miracle.

We walk out into the night and have dinner. He speaks at length about the process, about himself. Lou is generous, genuine. We warm to each other. He has on a tank top and I notice his arms. He isn't burly, but he has muscles. "I couldn't have gotten these without the hormones," he tells me. "I mean, I never work out, and even when I worked out before, I couldn't have gotten this kind of muscle." Something about him reminds me a bit of Popeye.

I can feel Lou sizing me up. When I stroll up to pay the check, he watches me walk from behind. I have on a white jean jacket and tight black jeans. When I get back to where he's sitting, Lou gives me his seal of approval. "You could do this, you have broad shoulders."

I don't think I have broad shoulders. But I am narrow overall, my hips are trim. My silhouette is slender, long. Nonetheless, regardless of its inaccuracy, his observation makes me proud.

Lou tells me that he is happy with his chest ("top") surgery and that he's about to get "bottom" surgery.

"No," he says after I inquire about the scarring. "The top surgery scars aren't like monkey tails. Whoever told you that was way off."

I tell Lou I've read the Lothstein book, and he exclaims, "Oh, god! I read that. It put me off the change for a while. That book is horrible!"

He makes a sour face. "Throw that thing away!" We both laugh. Already I feel my head is beginning to clear.

We have drinks at the Albion. Lou drinks rum and Coke. He watches guys wrestling on a television screen over the bar and makes comments about the wrestlers' bodies. Then his voice takes on a sober tone, and he looks into my eyes intently. "You might decide you're like me and that's great, or you might decide you're not like me and that's okay, too." Then Lou turns and looks down into his drink, perhaps remembering the remote time when he faced the decision I'm about to make. He's happier now, he says. There is a way. The change can be done.

Lou continues to watch the wrestlers on TV, drawn in with a fascinated look. "You know, I always got turned on by the idea of men together. It just made sense to me, erotically, in my body. I identified." I tell him how the idea of lesbian sex has never done anything for me. Lou gives me a knowing look. "That's because there's nothing for you to identify with."

I fantasize about being a man and having sex with a lesbian. It's her first time in a long time. She's not a virgin with men, but she hasn't had one in years.

I'm strong and my chest is hard and smooth. This lesbian needs a dick and I am just the guy to give it to her. Hard, good, long strokes in and out, then I lift her up, tilt her hips back, and slam my cock in deeper. Tease the lips of her pussy with the large head.

She's ashamed at her strange, overwhelming feelings. She likes it so much more than she ever thought she would.

I convert her to heterosexuality.

This fantasy is intermittent. It comes and goes, but there's a persistent intoxicating lure. I struggle with what it might or might not mean. After all, I knew already by the early eighties that a person can have any number of sexual fantasies without being bound to embody them, explain them, live them out, or even understand them.

Even so, this doesn't feel like just a fantasy.

CHAPTER 15:
EPIPHANIES

As I take a bath, the air streams in, webbed with sunlight. I gaze at my naked body in the water. Memories rush and coalesce. I can nearly touch them—they feel tangible, filtering the air. Sensations, feelings, images of my life from childhood to puberty to adulthood—a film running through my head.

I see a woman's body, long smooth legs stretched out, slender arms. I lift my head and look toward the window, which opens out into the sky. It occurs to me, as I sit still in the quiet water, that I've always had this feeling.

Looking straight ahead, I have another of what is to be a series of realizations that summer, some small, others overwhelming. . . . In the cloister of the bathroom, where the afternoon light provides a kind of mirror, I'm entranced. It occurs to me in that silence that I'm actually a man looking out from the eyes of a woman, looking out of the body of a woman, which I see in front of me. . . . The moving backdrop of my life, a feeling of being male—not so much a man *in* a woman's body as a man *with* a woman's body. When I was a child I could feel my boy self peering out of my eyes, knowing that other people were seeing a little girl.

I know. At that moment I know, with the sun streaming in and the air bright with some kind of hope, some shining clarity. I understand so much about my life in that moment. No wonder I've always wanted to relate to women as a man. No wonder I have always had that ineffable feeling in the background of my life, of my daily activities. A feeling of maleness, that somehow I was male, strong inside my core, my center. *I am transsexual.*

I thought I was a lesbian. I begin to smile. *All those years I thought I was a lesbian.* Fourteen years of believing I was a dyke, and here I was a straight man all along!

I laugh out loud. This is great! The truth and the absurdity! The paradox. What will I tell my friends? Especially my lesbian friends. Oh boy, I am in for it now. And then my parents . . . and sister and brothers, everyone, so many people to talk to, to explain this to. Where will I begin? What will they say? I keep laughing! I don't care. *All those years, I used lesbian feminism as a cover-up.*

Although this defies reason, it feels like the abiding truth of my life. I will vacillate, I will wonder and worry. There will be times I almost lose courage. But from that moment on, I know. Past, present, and future converge—an explosion in my head.

It's when we're outside that first night and the street is damp. I remember Lou stepping on wet pavement, the streetlights swirling down on him, a rainbow splitting on his moving shape. *The hormones really work.*

Standing in front of me is someone who has done it. I glimpse a flash: my childhood dream realized. Here is someone who had once been a little girl wishing and praying to become a boy, the boy he knew he was inside, and who had now become a man. Taken a magical potion and transformed. I know then, as we talk and cross the street to dinner. . . . I know, looking at Lou, that I will do this. If the physical transformation is so complete and so convincing, it is irresistible. This incredible and nearly absurd act, this act that feels so illogical, so defiant, so completely wondrous. I will take on the risks, the rejections, the possible pain, the long-drawn-out changing of the physical form. And I know I can make it work. The idea makes me so excited I could burst. If this transformation is possible, I know I will not settle for anything else.

CHAPTER 16:
BEARDS, HOUSEWIVES, AND EX–LESBIAN SEPARATISTS

In October, a month after meeting Lou for the first time, I attend my first FTM meeting. Slicking my hair back, wearing my black leather jacket and tight black jeans, putting on a brave front as I climb into the taxicab that'll whisk me to Chez Mollet, where the quarterly meetings are held, I'm scared, but I strain to put on an air of nonchalant confidence.

Everyone at the meeting looks closed, self-contained, distant. I definitely feel as though I'm in a roomful of men. In fact, as I walk in, I feel as though I'm being submerged in a tank packed tight with masculine energy. And I immediately feel alone. I'm one of the only people in the room who has an intact female biology. Most of the transsexual men around me have been taking testosterone for at least a year, many for much longer than that. As I'll discover, many have had sex-change surgery—top and sometimes bottom.

As I peer around the room, searching for a place to sit, I can barely keep myself from gawking. What's strange, nearly unbelievable, is not that these guys look bizarre or freakish, but that they look so *completely normal.* Average guys. There's nothing unusual, or even noteworthy, about them, except that they're mostly shorter than average men. A convention of short men, some husky, others thin, many with beards. In fact, that's the only other distinctive feature about this otherwise unremarkable roomful of men—there are more beards here than you would see on average elsewhere. It's as though the men here are inordinately aware of and proud of their facial hair. There's a wide range of styles: wispy adolescent chin beards, muttonchops, devilish goatees, Paul Bunyan lumberjack beards, Abe Lincoln beards. Some of the men are bushy like Fidel Castro, with complementary eyebrows thick and grown together, with matted dark hair sprouting from arms and shoulders.

A few of the men have thinning hair, or are completely bald. Some are boyish and have a youthful energy, awkward and barely contained. Others are bookish, professorial in glasses and tweed jackets. One guy smokes a long pipe. A couple look like Old Testament prophets with long, curling beards and bald heads. At least four wear tractor-pull hats, like good old boys. Others are dapper, with a hint of elegance in a carefully chosen tie, a crisp pleat in the slacks. A few wear Izod polo shirts. Some have beer guts, others hard, muscular bodies. A couple have long hair pulled back from receding hairlines and tied into ponytails. There's an Italian guy sitting in the corner who looks a bit like a young Al Pacino, sporting a tattoo of a busty woman with long legs on his arm, a leather jacket draped over his chair. But mostly it's a clean-cut group. No one looks like a woman, and the energy in the room feels nothing like the energy in a roomful of even the butchest lesbians. I'm surrounded by men, a group of rather short, rather conservative-looking *men.*

Most meetings that I'd attend in the future would have more transmen just starting hormones who still looked like women, as well as a large
scattering of people in between, slowly changing from one state to the
other, looking as yet nearly indefinable. In time, I'll be able to track the
phases of development: the voice dropping, cracking, and deepening; the
jaw becoming wider and stronger; the hair on the face, arms, and, sometimes, chest cropping up; the personality changes; the struggle many will
face as they try and get the large sums of money they'll need for surgery;
the elation after surgery. Just observing their beards sprout and their shoulders broaden—the delight as well as the insecurity and confusion.

I ask if there are any men here who used to be lesbians. I want to
know, how can I leave behind such a heavy identity, such a completely
defined worldview? How much will it hurt? It's like asking how much it
would cost to remove an extra limb. And how long does it take to heal?
How can I transition from a world so indifferent to, or openly hostile
to, maleness into the world of men? I want to ask, How did you become
"the enemy" and survive? Do any of your old dyke friends talk to you
anymore? How did they react initially to the news? Are guys really the
assholes we were told they were by all those lesbian feminist journals on
ethics? My questions fall on stone ears. Everyone seems put off by them.
I go from table to table and ask the same thing, "Uh, were you, uh, did
you used to be a lesbian? I mean, a dyke?" Kind of like, "Are you now
or were you ever a member of the Communist Party?" The guys snort at
me; they turn their faces away. Or they answer resolutely, "No!"

I'm astonished! What the hell were these men if not lesbians? Housewives from San Jose?

As it turns out, some had been exactly that. Like Brian, who actually *was* a housewife living in San Jose and then in Los Angeles. He is
mild and eager to begin transition, and we start around the same time,
comparing notes along the way. And there will be others. There is no
predicting where transmen have come from or how they lived their
lives before transition.

Finally, after walking the length of the two rooms that make up the meeting area, I meet someone who says, "I was. I was a lesbian separatist for ten years."

Meeting this transman is illuminating. *A lesbian separatist for ten years* . . . Later, when I meet Will, he will tell me a similar story—of being a lesbian separatist, a lesbian who did not tolerate or encourage contact with men, even as friends; a lesbian who did not read books by men or listen to music made by men. Who was committed only to women and their political struggle and who changed over time, realizing—both before transition and after—how so many of his old beliefs were a subterfuge for a hidden male identity. Fanaticism and extremism as camouflage, an inventive and stubborn attempt to make sense of a body and an internal identity that don't match.

I'd known many lesbian separatists who'd gotten disillusioned with the "movement," or "community," and become heterosexual women, or at least bisexual. The separatists' passion regarding men knit their emotional lives together. It was so entirely defining of their worldview that it translated, after a long struggle, or perhaps with a scalding explosion, into physical heat. Their obsession with men could stem from either love or hate, but it was passionate. I would never have considered that becoming a man would be a possible outcome to leaving a lesbian separatist existence! Some separatists become men, and some of them become straight women. "Lesbian separatism is where the men and the women get together," Will quips.

Of course, I had never really been a lesbian separatist. Not for more than a month anyway, when I was twenty and trying on different feminist political stripes with a searching confusion. I couldn't feel it. Although I did have a strong resentment of men that surfaced from time to time, and I did want to destroy the "patriarchy" like any self-respecting dyke, I just couldn't cut myself off decisively from half the human race. However, although I was never actually a separatist, I did absorb many of their attitudes. Many lesbian separatist attitudes and ideals are foundational to lesbian feminism, although very few women actually live them out in full and fanatic glory. Lesbian separatists are like cloistered nuns—the most extreme and completely dedicated group of dykes around. They spend their entire lives immersed in the unwavering practice of a belief system that is rigorous and pure in its intentions, though ultimately closed in its beliefs and expectations.

I conclude that if people have been able to come out of a phase of lesbian feminist existence so extreme, so intolerant and narrow, then I can slip out of the dyke world and right into manhood.

I plan out my change step by step. Overwhelmed yet completely lucid. I find it hard to concentrate on anything. I have so much to think about. Even so, I navigate the journey with a strategic intuition, a tight willpower emerging from my deepest imagination of myself.

The man in me wants out, a life freed from the female form.

CHAPTER 17:
BIRTHDAY PARTY

It's my thirty-second birthday. Alexander, Sandra, and Naomi are going to stop by later tonight, and Gene is helping me clean the place up. I have to tell Sandra and Naomi what I'm going to do. Alexander already knows. This inexorable machine, I've discovered, has a drive of its own.

I've been telling people little by little. One by one. I need to be strategic.

Gene appears to be accepting. He's gotten over his resistance, or so it seems. He was rattled for awhile, but at least we have been able to maintain communication.

But he's still uneasy. I sense it, but decide to ignore the tension between us for now. We clean up the kitchen and vacuum, mop the bathroom, arrange the papers on my desk into a semi-intelligible pile, tilt the loose and crooked lampshades to respectable angles, make the place sparkle for guests. Buy beer.

We put out all the snacks and begin the wait. I'm nervous. How do you tell people something like this? We've drunk a couple of beers by the time Sandra and Naomi are supposed to have arrived, and they haven't yet. I'm feeling woozy; a soft euphoria has settled over my perceptions. I play over in my mind a number of possible reactions to my announcement. Each and every person I know will have to be told with painstaking efficiency, patience—a nod and a smile at the right moment. I have to find the best time for each one—when they are able to take it in and when I have the wherewithal to handle their reactions.

You can't have a sex change and not tell people.

Do they already suspect?

When I called to invite Naomi and Sandra, I told them I had something important to tell them.

"I have something important to tell you guys. . . ."

"Oh . . ." It's Sandra on the phone.

"Ah, don't worry, it's not bad. I just think it would be better if I told you in person." I'm wondering how I can possibly ever tell them news like this.

"What is it? Any hints?" Sandra is playful on the other end of the line.

"She's going to be made chief of her tribe!" Naomi yells in the background.

I laugh. "No."

"She's pregnant!" Naomi yells again.

"Are you having an affair with a man?" Sandra asks point-blank.

"No, it's even worse than that!"

"It's worse?" Sandra is genuinely puzzled now.

Sandra and Naomi arrive late. Gene and I have already had one too many beers. I'm nervous, but I want to get it over with. Part of me is eager to see their reaction. Part of me is worried that it will be too intense.

"*What is it?*" they both ask at the same time upon walking in.

"You'd better sit down." I'm smiling, but getting increasingly nervous. I bring out two metal folding chairs and place them awkwardly near the center of the room. The light is on bright; there's something barren about the entire setting. I feel as though I'm interrogating them in a vacant room with a bare yellow bulb in the center of the ceiling. My intrepid guests sit down. I pace in front of them, offer them both a beer. "No, we can't stay long," Sandra says. She is beginning to look concerned. Sandra is wearing a flowery blouse. She has nearly matronly taste with a dash of feminist inscrutability, a nearly forced ordinariness.

Naomi wants a beer and I hand it to her. "*What is it?*" Naomi has a sweet face, a devilish, alert wit. "*What is it?*" she repeats, impatient.

The room becomes tight with compacted attention. Slippery with fantasy.

Naomi is laughing on and off. She has been since she came in, giggling in fits and starts. "I know!" she exclaims. "You are going to become a prostitute!"

"Uh, no." I'm smiling, or trying to, stretching my lips over my teeth. Trying to pick the right moment to drop the bomb.

"You're going to have a sex change!"

I look at Naomi for a split second with stopwatch eyes. "Yes, yes, that's it."

Suddenly, Naomi is sober. "You're going to have a sex change?" She repeats what to her must seem like an announcement that I'm actually a gray alien.

"Yes, I am. I'm going to have a sex change," I declare with a force of will. Still standing up, awkward, I force a wan smile.

Sandra's looking at me with nearly the same expression as before my announcement. She is so hard to read. Her head tilts to the side; she's gazing sideways up at me. "They'll take you out of *This Bridge Called My Back*!"

Already the great feminist "they" are erasing me from existence.

"No, they won't!" I say, although I can't be sure. As the words settle in the air between us, I don't quite know what else to say.

Naomi looks freaked out. Her eyes are no longer playful. Shock hits her face in waves. As if someone has hit her in the face, lightly, but a blow. It's in her eyes.

I have never seen that look on her face before.

I make an attempt to fill in the space, crush the gap widening between us. "I know it sounds intense. I've been going through a lot of thinking. At some point I realized, in some basic way, I've always felt more male than female." There is a gaping silence. "It's a big change, I know, but . . ."

Naomi and Sandra continue to gaze at me in odd stages of shock. "I can't believe it, you guessed!" I laugh. "She guessed!" I turn to Gene.

"I was just kidding," Naomi notes.

"Pretty smart," I continue. I'm smiling broadly now. "Preeetty smart!" I try and puncture the discomfort, waving my hands in the air and trying to look casual.

I know Naomi was kidding, yet for some reason I want to keep exclaiming this phrase almost like a mantra. A nullifying declaration. To keep the heat off me and what I have just announced, distract her and Sandra with a little flattery. I keep laughing with pointed, shining eyes. "So smart!"

We are waiting for Alexander now. I tell Naomi and Sandra that he already knows. In fact, by now a small sprinkling of my friends know. Kate was initially aghast at my decision, but she has grown reconciled, if not enthused. She's reversed an earlier determination to end our friendship. Or, possibly, since I haven't begun the change yet, she is waiting to see what I actually do.

Marilyn is gorgeous, with dyed jet black hair and sexy, intelligent features. A free-spirited Capricorn with a tinge of electricity around her. She gushes, "You're going to be a really cute guy, Anita."

Zoon, another longtime woman friend, says I've managed to kiss my elbow.

Sarah, a lover I had when I was twenty and first arrived in San Francisco, who was one of my first and most passionate loves, weeps. We are sitting in my basement studio in the afternoon. She holds her face in her hands and whispers over and over, "The woman I loved." Eventually, she'll tell me that she likes me better as a man. That I'm less defensive, calmer, and happier overall.

Tama screams long-distance from New York, "Oh my god! Oh my god!" Then takes a long breath and declares, "I knew it."

Roxanne, who by heroic effort has managed to come clean of heroin and other drugs, still sweetly gorgeous and witty, guesses what I am going to say before I tell her. "I knew you had those feelings," she muses.

I tell Selene and Frank separately, and they have distinct reactions. Frank is supportive and doesn't appear shocked. He speaks about transsexuality in matter-of-fact and accepting terms, making it clear he considers it a genuine and legible expression of human possibility. Selene appears to be accepting, although I can see that somehow she is troubled by the idea. She has always perceived my gender conflicts and manifestations of masculine energy, but I know that she also considers me to be a "beautiful woman." Her reaction feels at once more startled and ambivalent than Frank's. Possibly, Selene has been more attached to the idea of me as a woman, as a rebellious and agile female spirit, than I have realized.

Bella, a gifted musician and visual artist, who was one of my first close punk artist friends, declares, "You'll always be *more* than a man."

Now Sandra and Naomi are beginning to mull the ramifications of a male version of Anita in my living room over beers.

"Why didn't you tell us?" Sandra sounds hurt.

"Well, I had to be sure. I'm being careful. I didn't want too many opinions about whether or not I should do this clogging up my head. I wanted to make a clear decision on my own, basically. Without too much outside pressure. And, well, I know how it can be with lesbians. . . . They think it's the worst thing I could possibly do and, of course, I understand if you feel that way." I'm feeling defensive. I didn't realize that they might be hurt because I waited to tell them.

"We're not like that," Sandra protests. She shifts a bit, sulking at the corners of her mouth, and declares in a baby voice, "Lesbians are icky."

"What do you mean, 'Lesbians are icky'?" Naomi asks, mildly alarmed.

"They are. They're icky." Sandra and Naomi are looking at each other with absorbed faces. I don't know what to say.

"Are you going to be a sexist man?" Sandra asks, breaking the impasse. What can I say to that? How can I possibly answer that yes, I will be a sexist man? "Uh, I don't think so . . ." I'm taken aback. Better not appear unsure ". . . I mean, of course not!" I declare, emphatic this time.

"Good." This declaration appears to reassure Sandra.

Gene has left during this exchange. He comes back in and begins to eat chips. Distracted, caught up in his own internal musings, he watches with a serious face.

Alexander arrives. He walks in and waves his arms around lightly in greeting. Alexander has an otherworldly quality, looking almost as though he could ascend to heaven at any moment. I'm happy to see him, relieved.

Alexander and I are hanging out a lot. He's gay and a number of years younger than me. Handsome, with dark blond hair and pale skin, Alexander is ethereal, soft-spoken, with a penetrating intelligence and dreamy manner. I met him through Naomi and Sandra; they'd all gone to university together. It is clear early on in my decision that Alexander will be the person I know most likely to provide a nonjudgmental supportive ear. Unlike many of my dyke friends, or even Gene, he loves men, and although he's not always completely comfortable with just any heterosexual man, he's had some straight male friends. Certainly, he understands that as I change my biology and life into a male form, I won't automatically become a lesser life form. In his mind, it might even be an improvement.

It turns out that my early intuition was not misplaced. Alexander is the neutral ear that I need; he listens and nods sagely. Encouraging me to do whatever it is that I need to. "Think about it, make sure, but if this is what you want to do, you should *just do it*. Who cares what people think." I am relieved, happy to finally find a friend who is not going to try and change my mind in a deathly panic. Alexander's support will turn out to be a wonderful gift, indispensable, and one for which I am eternally thankful.

"You already know!" Naomi and Sandra chime to him. I guess they really do feel a little slighted by my not having told them earlier.

Gene takes Alexander aside as I entertain Naomi and Sandra. When I go out for more beer, I hear the two of them conversing in heated yet measured tones. Later, Alexander will recount his conversation with Gene to me.

"You've got to stop her!" Gene had exclaimed.

"Why, if that's what she wants to do?" Alexander had countered.

"Anita is just into fads. First it was punk rock, now this. She must not do this!" Gene was sounding frantic.

"I really don't think that having a sex change is a fad." As usual, Alexander remained calm.

"Well, I think you have to stop her. I can't believe that Anita really is a transsexual! Someone has got to stop her!" Gene was exerting an increasing, spasmodic pressure. That was when I made my way toward their corner of the room. Gene cut off, embarrassed; he grinned and offered me a beer.

Naomi has followed me to the other side of the room. She looks me straight in the eyes, starting a smile, warming to this new concept. . . . Perhaps it could become a form of mischief—something she enjoys.

"What are you going to call yourself?" she asks playfully.

"I . . . I don't know yet," I answer, groping after a concept of who I will become. We all look at each other bewildered at that moment; the ground is shifting. Everything about my identity feels unknowable and tipsy with potential. I open my beer and offer another to all of my stupefied guests.

CHAPTER 18:
GETTING MY NAME

I got my name, Maximilian, on St. Patrick's Day over a pint of Guinness stout at McCarthy's, a brightly lit Irish pub in the Mission District. McCarthy's is a surreal island of booze and reddened, whiskey-tinted flesh. Almost everyone who comes in is over sixty-five and looks as though they've been drinking heavily for at least thirty years. Women sit in hair curlers and rouge the veins and mottled skin on their noses and cheeks, pouting into handheld mirrors. Thick old men with long ears and whiskey faces stare into shot glasses of Bushmills and pints of stout. Sometimes, there's singing, with harmonica and guitar—Carter Family songs or Hank Williams. Then the place is alive, nearly redeemed by stringy, yodeling, silver-haired singers with heartfelt catches in their voices.

McCarthy's is huge and mostly empty, with a long, circular green Formica bar. All the lights are always up full blast, even at night. So you catch the full effect of the crowd's faces—puffy jowls, sagging eyelids, and toothless lipstick-reddened mouths, each and every blood vessel on each and every alcohol-wizened face wobbling and flouncing on scratchy turkey-gizzard necks. A few younger people from the neighborhood occasionally saunter in and sit on the other side of the bar, directly across from the regulars. We look in wonder at the old drunks, who talk and gesticulate into the air at old, long-dead drinking buddies, family members, or sweethearts before suddenly flopping facedown onto the counter, out cold on their barstools. Once, I watched a woman wearing a frayed terry cloth bathrobe and pink slippers come storming in brandishing a rolling pin. She screamed and raved at her drunken husband to come home. Andy Capp, and the tenacious rot of drink. You figure, over time, people move from the youthful end of the bar to the older burnt-out drunk end.

On St. Patrick's Day, McCarthy's is alive with the entire neighborhood and more. There's free corn beef and cabbage, Irish jigs; green paper ribbons festoon the air. I am amused when I see Oliver, the boyfriend of an old roommate of mine, on stage warbling "My Way" with a shaky tenor, followed by "Moon River," sliding off key, waving his arms in the air in a thin, tight gray suit with buttons missing. I didn't realize he still lived in the neighborhood.

I've just gotten my hormone letter from Joanne and am slightly crazed with excitement. Frenzied, roller-coaster anticipation. This letter is my "permit" to obtain testosterone, and I've already made an appointment with a doctor. I think back to Naomi's question from the night of my birthday and consider again that I still don't have a male name. I know I can't embark on this journey without a decent name, one that resounds with my truest, most sublime masculine self. That feels like "me"—that hocus-pocus word.

I've already gone through a few names, tried them on, worn them for awhile with a select cadre of friends to see if they turn up any spark.

None did. They were all wrong. I really want an incisive, masculine sound, without being comically macho.

"Demian" came to me one night while I was sweeping the floor. Gene and I were discussing whether or not I would go through with the change. It was dawning on him that this awesome and singular event could actually occur. Wide-eyed he asked, "So, what *are* you going to call yourself?"

The broom was in my hand. I looked up; I smiled slowly. "Demian."

"Well," Gene mused, "your mother is going to have a new son called Demian. And by the way, what are you going to tell your mother?"

We both laughed, pealing wild laughter. *What the hell am I going to tell my mother?* "Hi Mom, I'm a guy now and my name is Demian." *Demian?*

I'd been rereading Hermann Hesse's *Demian* for the first time since high school and found myself identifying with the main character. The name felt Blakean, despotic, wickedly humorous—concretely energetic. It tilted in the right angles to my machine-gun laugh, my turbulent hair.

One night after that initial flash of inspiration, I experimented, trying this name on for size with Sandra and Naomi. I called them on the phone. Sandra picked up, as always. "What would you think if I changed my name to Demian?"

"Demian?" Sandra paused. "Well," she said, contemplating the quixotic name, "I like it!" Her declaration felt hollow. Generally, Sandra is inertly agreeable, even-tempered, except for sudden, sarcastically observant sound bites. I figured she was simply being nice.

I heard a rumble in the background. Naomi and she were discussing the new name. Naomi got on the phone. "Demian! That's a warm and fuzzy name."

"Warm and fuzzy?" I felt mildly embarrassed.

"Yes, warm and fuzzy. Why did you choose that?"

I started to tell her about Hermann Hesse and she interrupted.

"Forget Demian." Naomi was not shy about offering her sincere feelings.

Naomi explained that she had had a cat named Demian. He'd been run over a couple of years back. Perhaps it was a good pet name, but it was not a good human name.

Every male name I've ever heard plays for attention in my head. Brian, Jesse, Woodrow, Mark, Andrew, John, Clyde, Wayne, Bob, Ronald, Eddie . . . They are all wrong! Too common, too regional, too cowboy, too old-fashioned, too obscure. Jacob, Jason, Earl, Raphael . . . Should I try the name of an angel, a god, a machine part, a force of nature? My friend Marilyn recommends a one-syllable name, short and punchy, in order to set off my longer Latin surname. Some names are forever tainted by their association with friends of mine or people I knew growing up. How about Matthew, Luke, Paul? Too Christian. Although I realize many people have New Testament names without giving the least thought to their Christian influence. And what's in a name, anyway? Will the name I take have an ongoing effect on my life, my personality, how others expect me to behave? In some sense, it doesn't matter at all. After all, I've been called Anita all these years, and look what I'm doing now! Even so, now is my chance to make a conscious choice. Which god will I invoke? What type of man am I to become? What type of man am I already? Am I a Bill, an Ezra, a Warner? What does a Bill look like, anyway? Is Ezra too forlorn, is Warner a bloated guy with a bow tie in a plaid jacket?

When I took confirmation vows at age ten, I winced at the inevitability that my confirmation name would be female. I longed to choose the name of a male saint or apostle. At that age, I still believed. I read the Apocalypse and envisioned the four horsemen, the lamb of God, the seven seals of the sacred scroll. I'd gone through a phase of saying the rosary every night and considered each beaded prayer an unwound lyric. Patricia was the name I would take in confirmation. In pained secrecy, I translated it to Patrick. No one ever knew.

So it's a strange synchronicity that St. Patrick's Day turns out to be the day I finally choose the male name I'd longed for in childhood. My friend Alexander and I drink our Guinness stouts and watch the festivities in the brightly lit bar.

"Anthony" is faintly similar to "Anita" and I'm considering it. But being called Tony doesn't feel quite right. I explain this to Alexander. "I'm not sure about Tony," I admit. Alexander considers this name. He says, "It's nice. There's an appealing casualness to the name, a slouchy tough-guy quality, but no, don't take Tony. I don't think you're a Tony. It doesn't feel right. Get a name that feels right. If I could have, I would've chosen to have been called something else, not Alexander."

"Really? Like what?"

"Oh," Alexander gazes into space. The bar's crammed elbow to elbow. Oliver is still warbling on a small stage. "Maybe Xavier."

"Xavier?"

"Yes, Xavier. I once knew a very beautiful young man named Xavier. He seemed strangely detached from his surroundings. He was slender, his skin had a translucent quality. I loved to photograph him." Alexander is fascinated by fragile, beautiful young men who have an unreal quality. It occurs to me that Alexander is a bit like that himself, whimsical and alien.

"Yeah," I say, "Xavier is a good name, but so is Alexander."

"Well, I think that you should have a different name. Tony Valerio is too Italian. You're not Italian. And it's too androgynous."

Androgyny possesses an unmistakable appeal, a lithe magic. No matter what I look like, if people find out my female history, I will take on the luminous ambivalence of androgyny. Since I'll always have some of that charged ambiguity, I decide that there is no need to point it out.

An androgynous name also feels noncommittal, a safety valve, a glib cop-out. After having been a lesbian feminist, becoming a man is something that I feel uneasy, even a bit guilty, about, in spite of knowing better. From the beginning, I want to root out any guilt and apology. I've always been attracted to making bold, relentlessly strong statements; I enjoy polarization and extremes, purity of elements and intentions. Having an unapologetically masculine name is a natural extension of those rigorous impulses. But what could it be? Alexander and I lock heads, pondering.

"How about Ivan?" Alexander suggests.

"Ivan?"

"Yes, it's a Russian name." Alexander continues, "Then your initials will be IV."

I laugh loudly. "Great! IV!" This appeals to my impish side. Yet even I have limits. I try to imagine myself as Ivan. "Ivan is too much like a skinny, weird, pasty guy."

"But it does sound like it would belong to an intelligent person," Alexander replies.

"True." Ivan does evoke images of intelligence—perhaps espionage or chess. Still, I can't shake the idea that Ivan, for me, is a guy who likes to peer through peepholes at women undressing. The real smart guy with greasy hair. "No, it would be too weird. I mean if I were called Ivan it would be too intellectual in the wrong way, the marginal, leering geek way."

Alexander and I get another round and watch the burgeoning crowd. The place is packed, the crush of faces and bodies blurs my eyes. I look at the counter in front of me and concentrate. Somehow, I have to come up with a decent name.

"Maximilian!" Alexander says it, just like that. "You should call yourself Maximilian. Max for short. Maximilian was a decadent Roman emperor. And you're already a Max," he exclaims, looking at me and grinning. *"You're already a Max!"* Alexander repeats it as though he's just discovered something sublime.

"Max? Maximilian?" I conjure it, laughing a little, taken aback. At first it sounds absurd. Maximilian. Then, by degrees, the idea begins to grow on me. It's certainly unique, slightly evil, unabashedly masculine, even warlike, decidedly pre-Christian. Maximilian could be a name from a distant era, yet, especially in its abbreviated form of Max, it feels current, almost as though it might soon come into vogue. A name from the near future. I've always felt both ancient and futuristic. Attracted to traditional, orthodox, spiritual pursuits and simultaneously Uranian, in love with outer space and alien entities, fascinated by extreme technologies. My friend Selene tells me that I am a person from the future.

The next day I wake with a start and laugh gently, thinking of this new name. Max feels like a name with a sense of humor. And although Max could be androgynous, a short form of Maxine, it's distinctive enough that this seems inconsequential. Quirky, relatively uncommon, even punk. I like the fact that it ends in an *x*.

Maximiliano was also the name of my step-grandfather on my father's side, the Hispano side of the family. Max was actually my greatuncle. He had married my grandmother after my grandfather—his brother, Francisco—was killed in an accident while building a highway through the Sangre de Cristo Mountains in the early forties. Although I can't be sure of the entire story, it was often the custom in Ranchos de Taos for a brother to marry his brother's widow. Grandpa Max was a soothing presence. Bald as Picasso, he often wore a gray broad-brimmed hat and had round cheeks, a handlebar mustache, and a calm strength. I remember sitting beside him at meals when we'd visit, listening to him speaking in Spanish with my father about our latest travels. And later, my grandmother mourning his loss at his gravesite after he died, in the late sixties, her long hair whipping back and her loud wails wrapping around the silence without consolation. I remember gazing at the sharp engraving on his large headstone and feeling intrigued and awed by the enigmatic grandeur of his name: "Maximiliano."

A middle name came effortlessly. Wolf. On the American Indian side of my family, many of the names of my male Blackfoot ancestors contained some variation of "wolf": Big Wolf, Wolf Old Man. Big Wolf was my great-great-grandfather, a well-known warrior and the owner of a sacred medicine-pipe bundle. Wolf Old Man was my great-grandfather. One of the last traditional medicine men on the reserve, he'd been a weather dancer in the *Okan,* or sun dance, and a well-known healer. He could hold live coals in his mouth without getting burned. I would honor these ancestors and the Blackfoot side of my family by taking Wolf as my second name. My full name, Maximilian Wolf Valerio, was fit for a king, and could be translated as "the greatest wolf" or "the biggest wolf." Certainly, this gave me pause and made me smile.

CHAPTER 19:
BINDING

The tits are the first thing I have to take care of. Can't go around with those things hanging out, bouncing all over the place like wild rubber balls. They'll definitely put a dent in my male image. So I begin my search for a way to control their erratic impulses, their concupiscent *thingness*. A method to reel my breasts in, tie them down, flatten my chest with the least amount of discomfort.

Lou tells me where to buy the wide stretch of elastic that I'll end up wearing clamped around my chest for almost six years. He tells me about a corset shop on Mission Street that sells this stretchy device, called a "posture belt." This contraption sounds orthopedic, or like a virtual medieval torture tool.

The name of the place is Eva's Corset Emporium. It's tiny, packed with bustiers, merry widows, black lace bras, and, not least of all, the Full Freedom posture belt for folks who need lower back support. All you have to do to bind down a free-swinging set of breasts is wear the thing up around your chest instead of down around the lower back as it's designed to be worn.

Eva's is in the heart of the Mission District, yet it's easy to miss, a discreet store—dark and obscure. The store is tightly squeezed into a dull, brown stretch of space between a portrait studio displaying glossy wedding photos of smiling waxy-looking couples and eerie old people with very white teeth and stiff sprayed hair and a fruit stand that sells papayas, coconuts, and eager red vegetables. In that cramped area is the store with the odd apparatus, the "posture belt," soon to be transformed into a breast binder.

The owner is a middle-aged woman with dark hair, pinched and manic, but friendly. I figure she's Eva. The first time I walk in to buy a posture belt, she seems suspicious. Eva's eyes are flat and compacted in color and expression; she looks me up and down. As she examines me and contemplates my request, her features wind and tighten, her eyelids flutter. I feel an anxious sensation free-floating in my stomach as I watch her watching me.

"You don't look like you got back trouble." Eva looks at me sideways.

"Oh, I do. I really do. I mean, there is a lot of weird pain in that area. I used to do *a lot* of heavy lifting."

"Uh-huh." One eyebrow arches incredulous, a thin arc over a puffy eyelid, sheer nosy nerve. Eva hands me the box with the posture belt inside. "Dressing room's over there. Let me know if you need help."

I slip into the dressing room, pull the flimsy curtain shut. I can barely get it to close. *Great,* I think as I take off my shirt and open up the small box, nervous, perspiring. How will I ever flatten these things? I stare into my reflection in the streaked mirror of the dressing room. There they are, *without a doubt these are genuine breasts, female flesh. . . .* Gazing at the reflection of my upper body at that moment, it's hard to believe that it will ever look like a man's body. Yet I've seen what testosterone can do. My fingers pull at the elastic band and I wrap it tight around my chest, trying to fasten the hooks into the eyelets in order to close the binder. I struggle in the dressing room with only a thin curtain to conceal my flailing. Suddenly, my breasts feel extra springy. They aren't that big, only a modest B cup, but as I twist and gasp for breath they seem much larger, unruly, like huge balloons I'm attempting to submerge in water that keep bobbing up easily, stubbornly, to the surface.

Eva frets on the other side of the curtain. Bustling. Suddenly, unable to contain herself any longer she yanks it open and peers in at me. Pointing feverishly at my lower back she exclaims, "You're not supposed to wear it *up there!* You're supposed to wear it *down there!*"

"Uh, don't worry, I know what I'm doing!" I'm sweating, mildly frantic, yanking the thing around on my upper body, startled. *My god, this lady's crazy, and how do I clasp this thing?* Finally, with a spasm, a sharp intake of breath, I manage to clamp the elastic band shut. It feels like a vise constricting my chest. But I'm flat. Flat as any guy, and once I get my shirt on over it, the contour looks great. I even look like I have a bit of pectoral muscle, curving and solid beneath my shirt.

Strains of rock and roll waft in from a radio on the street, Jerry Lee Lewis's "Great Balls of Fire." I remember a client Selene had when she was a dominatrix. This guy loved that song. He'd always have her play it while he danced around naked and snapped towels at her and the other women who worked in the dungeon.

This guy, Wendell, loved to get his balls tortured while hanging in a leather sling with his legs spread. Afterward, once they'd been tortured to exquisite, radiant levels of pain, he'd do this towel-snapping routine with "Great Balls of Fire" playing full blast, dancing around naked with his large middle-aged potbelly flopping, grinning like a Cheshire cat. He lived in the suburbs, like most of Selene's clients, with a wife and a couple of kids, a station wagon and a tidy rock garden, and worked in San Francisco's Financial District as an investment banker.

Wendell was one of the most extreme and imaginative ball-torture people around. He'd pay big for contests where a string of dominatrices would compete, each one squeezing his balls with a feminine hand in black leather gloves for as long and as hard as she could while he writhed and screamed. Once, he asked Selene to smear his balls with honey and place a jar of bees over them. She obliged. Every session would end with the naked dancing, the towel snapping, and Jerry Lee Lewis pounding on his piano, "Goodness gracious, great balls of fire!"

So here I am at Eva's Corset Emporium, getting tied up, constricted of my own free will. But this isn't for kicks, this is survival. Hopefully it won't be too long before I get my top surgery, a double mastectomy tailored especially for female to male sex change. I've seen what this surgery can do and it's convincing. Lou's chest looks fantastic and I've heard that a local doctor, Dr. Brownstein, does wonderful chest jobs. His work has a beautiful contour, and although there is scarring, the scars are placed in such a way that they blend into the overall shape and appearance of the chest. They fade to white with time.

Scars will be my initiation insignia, the visible signs of a rite of passage to manhood that is unorthodox, perilous, and hard-won. I will have earned them.

Ringing up my purchase, Eva squints at me in disbelief. "You don't look to me like you have back trouble." She sets her mouth in a smirk, folds the posture belt back into its box, puts it into a bag, and staples the bag shut with a crisp finality. Pushes the package at me along the counter: "You sure you don't want any of these?" She turns a fraction and waves her hand at the teeming assortment of corsets and bustiers that hang from the walls of her store. "We could fit you for one, custom fit."

"Uh, no thanks," I smile, lips stretching. They feel dry and cracked. I squelch an impulse to bolt.

"You'd look real good," she sets her eyes on me with a stare that could melt a plastic bag. Hot metal and staccato eyes.

Queasy, nodding, exasperated with embarrassment, I manage to say, "Nah, I'll just take this, thanks."

I dash toward the door; some choir of warbling crooners is finishing up on the oldies station. A Stones song starts: "Jumpin' Jack Flash." Just outside Eva's door, I hold back an urge to break into a sprint, and laugh, *If only she knew.* Tingling inside is a creeping excitement, a sense of celebration; I race down the street and once home, take the binder out and struggle back into it. Putting it on isn't any easier, but maybe I'll get used to this nuisance of a ritual. I'll have to. Who knows how long it will be before I can get together the six thousand some-odd dollars I'll need for top surgery.

A guy at my first FTM support meeting informed me that some people bind for years, *years.* . . . I looked steadily into his face as he made this solemn declaration. Oh god, that can't happen to me. "I don't think it will be that long for me," I had said. I remember reassuring myself over and over in my head as I sat there that somehow, it wouldn't. It will not, cannot, take that long. Not years. *Years and years* . . . To live bound, constricted, waiting for surgery . . . How could anyone endure it? Sometimes, it's better not to know the future.

I've been binding myself flat for six months now. The hormones have made it easier. Testosterone is starting to make my breasts flatter, less springy, more like "soup in a baggy." I watch myself in each mirror I pass with an obsessive, attentive eye. *It's true! I am starting to look like a man!* My neck's beginning to thicken and the smooth contour of my bound chest is convincing.

It feels natural to have a flat chest, although the binding is a tight rubber band across my rib cage. Even so, I don't take it off when I get home. Even alone, I prefer to wear it and do most of my daily activities bound flat.

When I do remove the binding, I feel loose, flabby, with two pendulous growths. Free swinging, wildly moving, indiscreet. When I take my clothes off and look in a mirror, my breasts look more and more out of place as my body changes into male proportions. Thicker, stronger looking, with a treasure trail of pubic hair faintly growing from my navel to my crotch.

When the first binder wears out, losing its elastic snap after five months, I go back to Eva's for a replacement. I wonder if she'll recognize me. It's weird running into people as I transform. Seeing people who don't know what's going on. Like my landlord, or the woman who lives upstairs. They get peculiar looks on their faces, some mixture of shock, alarm, and sheer puzzlement. Eva, however, is oblivious. She looks right through me, and still wants me to try on one of those bustiers hanging on her wall! It's the kind of reaction that undermines my still-fragile confidence in my developing male appearance.

I've told other transsexual men about Eva's. The last time I went in there she said there'd been "a whole bunch of fellows coming in to get these Full Freedom posture belts!"

"One guy is a comedian," she gushes, excitement rushing in her voice as she rings up my purchase. "He told me he's a comedian and he's got these silicone breasts put in, you know, falsies, put into his chest as part of his act. This young, real young guy told me that he has to wear one of these things, these posture belts, around his chest to squish those silicone breasts down, that's because he only needs them to be showing for his act, his comedy routine."

"Oh, really?" I say. I'm not sure how to reply. I think, *Which one of the guys would make up this story?*

"Yeah," Eva continues, manic sounding again, pinching her hair back behind her ears with shivering fingers, "Isn't that something, isn't that just amazing! I'll bet he's very funny on stage. He's a very happy-looking fellow. Yeah, he is . . . very happy looking and he loves these posture belts! Isn't that great that he's gone that far for his career, I mean to put in those silicone breasts, those falsies right *inside* of himself just to further his career?"

"I guess so," I say with a rapid shake of my head, back and forth, back and forth, shaking it no but saying yes.

"Yes, Eva, it is inspiring," I finally proclaim, once more straightening my spine, putting on my most calm, earnest, and sincere face, "It is inspiring, yes it is, how dedicated some folks are to their careers."

CHAPTER 20:
PATRIARCHAL UNDERWEAR CANNIBALS

I had gotten a mania in my head about getting men's underwear soon after I got my first testosterone shot. I'd realized as soon as I bent over, pulled down my panties, and exposed my ass for that initial piercing by the needle that I had on girls' underwear! A pang of embarrassment shot through me, but I figured, *What the hell? So I forgot one teensy-weensy detail* . . . I mean, the doctor knew what I was there for, and he appeared to be way beyond doubting my sincerity.

A few transmen have always worn men's underwear. Brian told me that he had worn them even back when he was a housewife in suburban New Jersey. Even when he had to show up in proper feminine drag at PTA meetings or at neighborhood lawn parties . . . Possibly, he reminisced, he was wearing white Fruit of the Loom briefs or plaid boxer shorts on the night his husband proposed. And he knew for sure that he often wore them at the supermarket, glancing nervously at the neighborhood women, worrying about whether he was saying the right things to get on with the "other" housewives . . . *If only Eileen knew what I was wearing, my hubby's indigo Calvins, his sexiest pair, which I swore I'd lost in the wash.* . . .

Other future transmen, like me, were too embarrassed to go and buy a pair of boxers or briefs. It would have been too piercingly kinky at the time, before "gender transgression" was trendy. Quite possibly it was really just too close to the bone of our conflict, so to speak. If I started wearing boxers, who knows what I would want to do next? Many transsexual men work hard, pretransition, at not opening the Pandora's box of their gender conflicts.

Besides, I was just too spacey to care about such things. Oblivious to many earthly details, I didn't spend much time thinking about my underwear. Still, once I realized that the other transmen were wearing male underwear at the beginning of transition, I had to go and get a few pairs of my own! It was too weird to be a man running around in women's underwear, and in no time flat, that's exactly how I felt.

Wearing panties is fine for some guys, but it isn't my kind of kink.

Going shopping for guys' underwear turns out to be a nightmare. I make the decision to go out on a nocturnal hunt for a pair late one night and can't find them anywhere—none in Walgreens, none in Cala supermarket. It's too late to check anywhere else. I am surprised that Walgreens doesn't offer briefs. After all, I used to pick up panties with running cheetahs on them for just a dollar here.

So, when I find a package of plain white Fruit of the Looms at Safeway, I am relieved. It feels odd to actually purchase them. I am on my third shot, not looking like a man yet. I glance at the checker and then down at the plastic package of men's briefs being transported across the small rubber belt past the cash register. I'm sweating, ready to bolt from the place. I don't yet feel confident in my male appearance. I soothe myself with the thought that I could be buying these as a gift. What does the cashier care, anyway? The next time I buy underwear will be much easier.

Now I'm wearing BVDs, Hanes, Calvins, or Jockeys—whatever is cheapest and most durable without looking like orthopedic underwear. I increasingly enjoy a touch of color, a stripe, camouflage, and, always, basic black. Slipping into a pair of red briefs gives me a secret satanic feeling. I haven't gotten into any of the way-out boxer styles printed with ironic, winking martini glasses, dancing fruit, or bloodshot eyeballs, but I might. I'd love a pair of Everlast boxers that look like boxing trunks. But it's hard to keep a stuffer in a pair of boxers, and supertight briefs work better. I figure I don't have to worry about my sperm count.

I've been stuffing my briefs with a sock, which is what Lou recommends. It works. I safety-pin a large, rolled-up athletic tube sock to the inside of my underwear each morning. Position it so that the bulge looks realistic.

The first time I put the carefully rolled-up sock in my briefs, excitement shoots through me—a new sensation, this fullness in front. I like the weight between my legs, a palpable symbol of potency.

On the street, walking for the first time, I feel self-conscious. Does it look real? Is it too big? Is it too small? What if no one can even see it? Will it move around too much as I walk? I can feel the sock shifting. Is everyone or anyone looking at me weird? *What's that guy looking at? Are that woman's eyes going down there?*

Once, when I go out dancing, the sock shakes loose and slides down my pant leg and onto the dance floor. Luckily, it is pretty crowded and dark, with only a large rotating strobe light in the center of the room. No one notices my alarm and I continue dancing as though nothing's happened, secretly scanning the floor for the errant stuffer. *Where is it? Is that it over there? No, that's a crushed pack of cigarettes; what about that?* All at once I recognize the small bundle next to a woman's green high heel; she's making tiny steps, a postmodern tango, and is just about to step on it. What if she slips? My eyes follow her feet back and forth, back and forth, over and around in a small circular pattern on the slick dance floor. Finally, I spy a gap in the action. Jerking my arm out, I reach down and yank the wandering sock up off the floor. Dash into the men's room and into a stall to stick it back inside my briefs. Return and continue dancing. Smiling.

I have spied men in gay bars licking their lips and peering hungrily at my crotch area. Before it was the breasts; now it's the cock. There are unexpected misperceptions.

Standing across from me on the street one long afternoon, Will discovers that I look as though I have an erection. And he should know; one of Will's pastimes is watching men on the street for signs of an erection. He's always telling me stories of guys getting swift boners when an attractive woman saunters past them, or of men waiting in line for the bus in the morning trying to conceal their morning hard-ons with folded-up newspapers. I tend to think that these sightings are a sign that Will has far too much time on his hands. However, he has pointed out a couple of these men, walking across the street crooked, limping to hide their boners, and I suppose that they did look both embarrassed and aroused. He could be on to something here. . . . Wills tips me off. "Max, you look like you have a huge hard-on, even from across the street. Maybe your pants are too tight."

I decide to switch to a smaller sock. Eventually, I give up socks altogether and fashion a homemade prosthesis instead, using squishy, gummy material—usually various odd little toys—gummy whales, frogs, or rats that I pick up at Walgreens. I wrap these squiggly creatures up in flesh-colored nylon hose and stuff them in my underwear. The hardest part is buying the nylons (could they think I'm a male to female cross-dresser?) but what the hell, all guys have to have a hobby.

In time, there will be relief from this time-consuming and anxiety-provoking ritual. I'll buy stuffers made to order from enterprising FTM friends who sense a new market force emerging from the transsexual ectoplasm of San Francisco. I always stuff big, but I'm careful now that I don't overdo it. People are suspicious of horny men.

PART THREE
AFTER
TESTOSTERONE

Look out honey, 'cause I'm using technology
Ain't got time to make no apology

—Iggy Pop, "Search & Destroy"

CHAPTER 21:
BLOOD RITES

April 17, 1989. My last period. It's skimpy.

A sign. The testosterone is doing its work, suppressing my ovaries, knocking them out with a good left hook!

I enter a new era. With the ovaries down for the count, the testosterone begins to work with greater concentration and expediency. Gathering momentum, surging through my cells, slipping right into the nuclei and rebuilding new flesh, blood, and bone. Blood filled with more red blood cells, less prone to anemia, more prone to heart disease. Thicker bones, less prone to osteoporosis, with denser, stronger muscles. The testosterone is overriding my original genetic encryption of XX, female. As I inject the testosterone biweekly, I watch these changes accumulate.

My body is beginning to "think" it's a male body, and is acting accordingly, building tissue stamped with masculine characteristics. The fact that menstruation is ceasing is a sure sign the hormones are working. In terms of biological sex, our bodies have a genetic sex and an endocrinologic or hormonal sex. We also possess secondary sexual characteristics (breasts, beards, musculature, bone structure, and fat distribution), in addition to genital sex, considered a primary sexual characteristic. Genetic sex has the well-known signatures XX for female and XY for male. There are also anomalous genetic signatures such as: XXY, XXXY, XXX, or X (one X only). Genetic sex determines endocrinologic sex. It instructs the ovaries and testes to secrete appropriate amounts of estrogen and testosterone in order to create and maintain the secondary and primary sexual characteristics. Also at work are hormone receptors; in cases of a rare condition called testicular feminization, an individual can be XY but lack receptors for testosterone. This person will not be able to feel the effects of any amount of testosterone in the body, and will appear to be somatically female, but will lack female reproductive capacity.

Genetic sex cannot be altered. What transsexuals do when we ingest male or female hormones is alter our natural chemistry into that of the biologically genetic opposite sex. Then, since our body "thinks" it is the body of someone of the opposite sex, we transform accordingly.

Endocrinologic sex is determined by the ratio of testosterone to estrogen. The bodies of men and women generate both estrogen and testosterone, so in the strictest sense, estrogen is not exclusively a "female" hormone and testosterone is not exclusively a "male" hormone. It is the *ratio* of estrogen to testosterone in the body that determines whether the person is male or female. Men have a much higher ratio of testosterone to estrogen, and women have a steeply higher ratio of estrogen to testosterone. We're talking about dramatically different amounts here. These differences are not subtle.

The testosterone levels of transmen are generally in the youthful male ranges. High, bright, potent, although not as elevated as the adolescent male ranges of testosterone, a charging blast several times higher than adult levels.

Once we are on testosterone, the estrogen levels of transmen plummet.

I'm beginning to puff up in the face and gain weight. Brian experiences tenderness in his ankles after being on testosterone for a month. We're going through the beginning phases at the same time, and we compare notes on a weekly basis. Although we are having many similar experiences, not everything is exactly the same. I'm spared the ankle tenderness, but I am becoming a puffball. My face is rounder and ridden by acne. The bones disappear into a bloated surface. Testosterone aggravates acne, which is why males tend to have it bad as teenagers.

Fortunately, the bloating is only a temporary phase that the body goes through as it adjusts. The acne will also recede with time, shrinking as I grow up all over again. The first nine months to a year (even up to two years) can be excruciating. Many transmen quit going out, or resort to makeup (sometimes for the first time in their lives) to cover up the livid acne. The worst of this ugly duckling phase is yet to come—I'll gain pounds of water weight from the bloating. It'll be an acne-ridden and water-filled second adolescence. Best to drink lots of water and exercise as much as possible. Only time will really bring relief, so I have to cultivate patience—and optimism. To become a man, I will have to molt.

Since Will went through this phase of acne and bloating a year before me, he tells me not to worry about it too much. In nine months it will begin to noticeably dissipate, and in a year to a year and a half, this initial retention of water will evaporate. The acne follows suit, although some transmen may continue to have some issues with acne for a few more years, depending on their individual genetic predispositions. Hearing the anecdotes and transition stories of the men at the FTM support group gives me perspective, and helps me to cultivate patience. .

When I tell women that I no longer have a menstrual cycle, the usual response is, "God, that must be great!" It's the one aspect of this process that meets with untrammeled enthusiasm.

I no longer have cramps every month, no pain in the lower back, that unrelenting dull ache. Although I'd never had a lot of menstrual pain as female, I usually would have to lie down for an hour or two on the first and heaviest day of my cycle.

Now that I am suddenly free, I realize that guys don't know how easy we've got it. Each month the inevitable struggle with pain and discomfort simply never arrives. It's a smoother, more evenly keeled journey. Men don't go through that periodic, inevitable malaise—no pain of childbirth, no monthly pain from menstruation.

Testosterone does raise a man's red blood cell count, making for vigor, but also creating a tendency toward elevated blood pressure and high cholesterol, increasing the risk of cardiovascular disease.

I read a medical study that indicates that men who give blood periodically have a significantly reduced risk of getting a heart attack. Ritualized bloodletting, practiced on and off in many cultures, and often a part of male initiation ceremonies, has some actual health benefits. Feminists have often characterized these male initiation ceremonies as being rooted in an envy of menstruation.

Knowledge is rooted in the body, without cognition, yet articulate. Not only expressed *on the body* as in self-expression or self-control, but emanating *from the body* itself. An effortless and driven knowing, labeled "instinct" in other species, is, for us, something whose point of origin feels ephemeral. Surfacing in myths, rites, or in chaotic and diffuse expression, intelligible only to the degree that we understand that "body and soul" are not actually separate but are fluent aspects of the same entity. Possibly, it would be more accurate to say that these masculine blood rites are rooted not in envy, but in an instinctual or preverbal impulse toward physical balance.

CHAPTER 22:
SAYING GOODBYE

’m sitting in the dyke bar up the street, Francine’s, the only lesbian bar in the Castro. I’ve started to spend more time here now than ever before, in a furtive, fascinated way.

The experience of sitting, watching, and drinking becomes more and more tedious. Yet I come back. I’m not sure why. I’m looking for something. Waiting for a revelation, a sudden outburst of inspiration. The courage to leave.

I might be saying goodbye.

Bad disco slurs women’s voices.

I watch my reflection in the long mirror directly opposite my bar stool. Every time I come in here, it’s altered slightly. I study the nuances of change and wonder if anyone notices. If so, what rationale would she conjure up to account for this slow shift of gender playing across my face? Women here look at me less and less. I walk in, slightly hesitant, unsure how I'll be perceived. Man or woman? There was a time I remember, just last year, when I could turn most of these women's heads just by striding in. In my black leather jacket and tight black pants, rangy with tomboy insolence, bored. Ready for a long night of standing around, thinking, drinking beer, listening to bad music. Can't say I'm going to miss that. Yet I'm drawn to live this tedium out again, one last long time. I sit at the bar and stare. Linger and gaze into my past as it retreats out from under me. A time tunnel rapidly receding.

Each week I feel more like an outsider, a voyeur.

As I change, the women in the bar appear to change also, incrementally, in linear resonance with my own physical and psychic transformation. Their faces soften, their edges melt into smooth, sweet surfaces. Even women who before appeared to have mottled, rough complexions now seem to have more of a sheen, a glow to their skin. And their voices sound as though they're getting higher, more melodic. I never realized how musical women's voices are! Notes are sprinkled inside the words. I listen in wonder. Entranced.

All the women here seem softer, rounder, more distinctly feminine, prettier than they were before. Even the butch women . . . the women I used to think of as "butch." Sometimes butcher or more masculine than me. They've changed. And I know that they would hate me for thinking this, but I perceive their "womanly" qualities without intending to. Suddenly, their feminine qualities are painfully apparent—in my face. It's an odd surprise. Each time I come here, these changes are more pronounced. Yet I know these women aren't actually changing. My perceptions are. *Can it be I'm beginning to perceive women as men do?*

My neck's thickened. I'm getting more muscular, as though I've been working out a lot. I haven't. I don't feel comfortable enough yet to use the men's locker room, so I have to use my wits. Going to the gym as a man, I sneak into the women's locker room. Stealthily, feeling criminal, I strip down and into my gym shorts, unbind, remove my pants stuffer, then work out as a woman on the weights and the bicycle. Run back into the women's locker room! I shower in a daze. Ignoring the naked women all around me, I steal into a bathroom stall to change quickly into my street clothes, bind down, stuff my pants, then rush out, back into the world as a man!

I won't be able to keep this up much longer. Although it might be my last opportunity to be around so many topless women without being charged for it.

Weird stares poke at me from all corners. I've been on testosterone only a handful of months, but the juice works quickly and the effects become more pronounced with each week. I snatch up the weights so fast! One weight lifter guy stares at me with an odd, puzzled look on his face, some mixture of disbelief and awe. Must be the way I'm moving the weights around, or the fact that I'm getting muscular so quickly— not just muscular, but masculine. My features sharper, my legs hairier, my eyes slanting in virile concentration. *I have so much energy!* And the weights are getting lighter and lighter . . . I yank them up easily, expecting them to be much heavier. Another guy, the one who signed me up for the gym, is wide-eyed, looking at me as though in a trance when I ride the bicycle. Apparently, even though there are women weight lifters here who are seriously strong and pumped, there is something unusual about me. Something off, something not like normal "woman in training." However, since it's practically unheard-of, a science fiction solution that reeks of fantasy, no one will ever guess I'm becoming a man. These guys probably just shake their heads and muse, *"Wow, there's one tough chick!"*

I thought I was a lesbian. Fourteen years of believing that. Two women circle the pool table, trading shots. Intent. One wears tight Levi's and a checkered cowboy shirt. The other wears a red tank top and a leather vest; short, tight blond curls sweeten her neck. They stride and lean into the table to shoot.

I was convinced I was a lesbian. What does that identity mean now? What will it mean to me in years to come? Was there something redeeming in all those years, in spite of the fact that I eventually chose to leave? Or did I waste all those years of my life?

I won't be coming to dyke bars much longer. The choice I've made precludes that. But was it really a choice?

Perhaps my transformation is as much a recognition, an acknowledgment of my abiding male identity, as a choice. Jung said, "Free will is the ability to do gladly that which I must do." Fate, free will, destiny, and choice—points of reference that appear oblique, veiled, as life animates them. As meaning is played out through one's blood. I've been hurtled by a more intractable force than choice toward this moment; it could be revelation.

Transsexual science fiction writer Rachel Pollack has described transsexual identity as an experience of revelation.

I am a voyeur of my own transformation.

I've become an audience to my demise as a woman, as a lesbian. *I want to see it.* I strain my eyes and search the faces of these women to witness my transformation as it registers on their expressions, as it glows in their eyes, an uneasy glimmer. As it twists into their lips a smear, heretical. *Woman to man, the impossible choice.* The worst possible thing in their world, to go from lesbian woman to heterosexual man. I observe and wait; I watch these lesbian women whom I've known and felt an uneasy yet tangible identification with for almost a decade and a half, my entire adult life. We were all in it together and now I'm leaving. A spoiler.

I'm becoming a nonentity. I've discovered that lesbians hardly look at the men in their midst; I am invisible. A faintly outlined shroud misting the air, receding, vanishing as I become more and more a man. Other. Stranger. The weird guy in the dyke bar. They're picking up on the testosterone tuning my cells; it must be male pheromones, an un-conscious attunement to my smell, which has changed. Some subtle yet profound shift in ambience. The mirror and the smoke in the air, bar music driveling on, I sit alone, surrounded by women on all sides. I'm beginning to feel like a fox in a henhouse.

Wolf man with shackles on his feet
Moon-slurring man, angel with two halves, split
down the middle

One night, after being on testosterone for seven months, I return to Francine's. Hardly a soul looks at me. There's an invisible barrier. A glass wall that feels stronger, more impenetrable each time I visit. These women speak in another language, although they are moving their lips in a familiar way. I recognize the words, yet can't quite grasp the meaning. An essential dimension has become hidden. The laughter, the gossip, the exchange of hellos and easy compliments, the camaraderie; I'm not understanding any of these conversations the way I did before.

Why do I still come here? Watching alone, waiting alone. Fascinated with the demise of my female identity. It's like watching a part of myself die. Doesn't anyone in this place remember who I was before? I came here often enough as Anita. Bored then, too—an outsider then as well, but not like this. Not with the glass wall.

I once thought of the woman wearing black engineer boots and a leather jacket as "butch." Was it her hair, shaved short on the sides and back, or her jacket? Was it the way she moves her hands, her walk, or her slightly stiff grin? *What was I seeing* when I was a dyke that made me think that woman was so butch? I stare, trying to solve this newly discovered puzzle. She looks as though she could lift a heavy motorcycle up from the street or lay some pipe in humid weather, walking cat-like inside an underground tunnel. Even so, suddenly, from this new perspective, she seems so much a woman, so female in her hips, her glowing fine skin and small features, her melodic, rich alto. Each time I come to Francine's she looks increasingly curvaceous, a tiny bit more vulnerable, subtly infused with a conventional femininity. It's eerie. She's shifting shape as I do.

And that other woman there, she seemed so "butch" to me before also, rough looking, broad shouldered, hardly "pretty" in a conventional sense, and now, it's startling, I see her softness. She's become "pretty." There's a seductive lilt in her voice, something that might even be construed as maternal about her expression and earthy wide hips. How come I couldn't see these attributes so clearly before, when I was a dyke?

Is this the way men once saw me? I used to think, "Why do they always come on to me, can't these guys tell I'm a dyke?" Now I'm beginning to understand why my butch or male qualities weren't as obvious to men as they were to myself.

I have always preferred feminine women, and actually dated mostly heterosexual or bisexual women from 1984 on, finding many punk and "alternative" bohemian girls to be open to new experiences. It's not that I suddenly find these butch women attractive enough to date; they still have a missing "feminine essence," or look dowdy or plain if not entirely masculine . . . yet they are so much more feminine to me now than they were before. Will has the same experience, and tells me over the phone that after being on testosterone a while he had a hard time telling the dykes from the straight women. It's like we are losing our gaydar. He also said, "Before, 20 percent of the women looked attractive, and now 80 percent of them do."

This change in perception is due to the fact that when you see someone, you unconsciously compare them to yourself. You are your own standard. These women are now more feminine in comparison to my own changing image in the mirror, my own deepening voice, my quickly masculinizing body. It is startling and strange to experience. It's similar to how young people look younger as you age; when you're sixteen, other sixteen-year-olds don't look extremely young, they look normal.

I'm beginning to discover just how many of our "perceptions" are contextual—in contrast to, or grounded in, who we are, relative. *Perception could be as much about the relationship between the observer and the observed as it is about actual definitive observations.* I'm experiencing an odd variant of the Heisenberg Uncertainty Principle firsthand, without recourse to a physics lab.

The other night I sat down at the bar at Francine's, ordered a Bud. A woman leaned over and asked me, genuinely puzzled, "Why do you come in here? Don't you like to go to boys' bars?"

It's almost time to go.

A couple of weeks later, I go to Francine's on a whim and sit befuddled, facing my reflection in the mirror opposite the bar. One beer. It's a slow night, Tuesday, and only four women are here. All talking together. They ignore me as though I'm completely invisible. They order pizza. Each woman has a sumptuous slice with cheese, olives, mushrooms, tomato sauce. One of the women walks to the bar to retrieve her slice and sits right next to me, inching her way toward the bartender with a big smile. She doesn't look at me, or even appear to see me. I watch them eat and realize that I'm no longer welcome. These women will abide my presence, but they will no longer welcome me.

When I get up to leave, no one lifts their eyes to see me out.

One morning in a restaurant, a lesbian waitress strolls over to my table to take my order. I shift in my seat, uneasy, and smile at her as though I'm holding a guilty secret. She's a woman I've seen around for years at lesbian events or clubs. I glance up shyly from the menu, expecting to hear my old name. She looks right at my face, right into it, and without any hesitation calls me "Sir."

I know then that I have gotten through—to the other side.

CHAPTER 23:
THE INCREDIBLE HULK

Naked and alone in the shower, I find it hard to believe that people really are beginning to think I'm a man. From this angle, with water streaming down my torso, my body still looks completely female. The masculine changes I see in the mirror when clothed have vanished from my field of vision. Yet, the longer and more acutely I look, the more I see that my body *is* actually changing.

My toes are sprouting hair at their knuckles. Strange, hair on the feet . . . I'd never considered that before. Being half Indian, I've never been hairy. I remember my mother peeking into the bathroom when I was thirteen and taking a bath and telling me through the half-opened door that I should never shave my legs, an odd female ritual I'd never wanted to do anyway. "We don't have any hair," she said. She made this announcement suddenly and then vanished, closing the door as abruptly as she had opened it. It was true. I'd always had smooth, hairless legs and only the vaguest covering of hair on my arms.

Yet, here is hair sprouting on my toes. And at the ankles, more hair. I figure it will eventually extend up my legs, growing in from the bottom up. Alexander reports that when he was a teenager, his body hair also crept in from the feet up: first the toes, then across the top of the feet. Next, coarse hairs sprinkle in, popping up over my ankles, climbing across and over my calves, up to the tops of bony knees, and over and around the thighs.

And my knees are getting bonier . . . or rather, the fat once concealing their boniness has evaporated. Women have an extra layer of fat on their bodies, the adipose layer, and mine is beginning to disappear. This fat actually makes women's bodies shapelier and softer, covering their knees and other jutting joints or bones with a soft layer. It also covers muscles and even sculpts the shape of the face, making it rounder and, again, softening the features. As my adipose layer becomes thinner, I begin to look more angular in every way.

The bridge of my nose is thickening and getting broader. All these changes are proportionate; each feature of my face is altering in a male direction with a natural ease, a grace commensurate with my growing amazement, delight, and faith.

My muscles feel firmer; there's a hardness to my shoulders and biceps. In the morning, these areas feel sore, as though I've been doing push-ups or pull-ups in my sleep. I have cramping in my calves, sudden knots, as if the muscles are tensing and bundling up in the middle of the night with spectral fixes of energy.

My muscles must be growing.

I like to imagine this body hair growing in the middle of the night, as I sleep. And my muscles becoming tighter, stronger, and larger—basking in shreds of moonlight and neon slipping in through the glass door and onto my sleeping form. A glow, a night shroud of power stretching over me as I sleep, transforming my body. The Incredible Hulk! Bigger, stronger than ever, with a deeper voice, breaking and cracking into strong tones.

I am becoming stronger. I lift objects with ease, shocked at how light they have suddenly become. The whole world is getting lighter, infused with buoyancy. I apply the usual amount of effort to picking something up, a laundry bag or a box, and am surprised. I don't need to try as hard; the bag or box rises up in my arms as though on its own. It's a relief that everyday tasks like taking out the garbage or lugging a heavy bag of laundry down the street have become much easier.

One afternoon I wait for a friend to arrive to help me move my futon frame out to a truck. In the past, I couldn't have moved this bulky frame without help. Tired of waiting, I lift the frame to see how it feels. It flies up and over my shoulders; I carry it down the long, narrow hallway without strain, feeling an expansion of power soaring through my body.

This is a second adolescence, although it's actually bigger than that. A change from one sex to another. And my body goes simply, a natural progression of forms and mesmerizing shapes.

In some ways it's so easy, like walking across the street.

I don't notice these changes as they actually occur, but one day I look, or feel, or hear, and I come to the realization that another part of myself has altered.

I bend over slightly at the waist, reach down, and examine my clitoris . . . my god! Wow . . . it's huge! Before it was very small and pea shaped, like the head of a pin. Now it's shaped like a small yet anatomically correct penis. There is a purple head, and the hood is like a foreskin. I pull it back to further expose the large head. This sight makes me exclaim aloud—shoots of joy and surprise! I was told to expect a surge of clitoral growth, part of what normally happens on testosterone, but to actually see this radical growth so quickly is exhilarating. In time, my clitoris may grow up to three inches from root to head and thicken to an inch or so around. Not the ideal size, certainly, but a great deal better than before. I begin to think of it as a genuine dick. Although it's not my dream eight-inch cock, this small penis has at least a flickering and tangible resemblance to the image I have always held in my mind.

The changes gather momentum. They have a will and force of their own, their own peculiar and unknown schedule.

When I dance, the energy is phenomenal. Power surges through my body. I feel like I can jump through the ceiling! This energy is vigorous—it feels organic, not speedy, as though rooted inside my muscles and bones.

When I go out running, I feel as though an invisible hand is pushing me.

The joy of it! The intensity of it catches me off guard. No wonder men die younger; it's easier to burn out, a rocket flaring and disintegrating. White heat. I travel on a continuum toward a more compact, wiry body, like a piece of twine. Savor the volts flowing under my nerves and skin, torching my glands up a notch higher than before. Sex, rock and roll, metal machines, and screeching electronic shapes. I have more of an appetite than ever for loud music. I've always loved it, but now I can take more in. My capacity is greater than it has ever been. I never thought that would be possible, but it is. Although I generally agreed with Kurt Cobain when he said that the future of rock is going to be made by women, and many of my favorite punk bands or performers have always been female, now that my body is testosterone driven, I understand why so many guys love adrenaline-cranked heavy metal, hardcore punk or thrash, the raw pump of rap. Taking testosterone is like having rock and roll injected into my body.

There is another dimension, a simultaneous aspect that feels *flatter.* A crystallization of space as opposed to a liquid feeling—that drenched fullness on estrogen. I no longer feel the ups and downs, the cyclic mood swings.

Previously, as female, I didn't realize that my emotions were subject to such ups and downs. Now that they have vanished, except for an echo (since I do take my testosterone through biweekly injections), I realize how emotional I actually was. Although I do experience less energy and may feel more emotionally vulnerable as the time between shots stretches out, or get cranky and irritable if I am late for an injection, overall I feel a startling emotional equilibrium. It's a relief not to feel those up-and-down mood swings. My emotions aren't as close to the surface.

I'd always been in some kind of denial about my female biology. Wanting to believe that PMS and hormonal mood swings didn't really happen to *me.* . . . Just as I never paid much attention to many female aspects of my body, I never paid attention to how my breasts got tender and swollen right before my period began. I never acknowledged this fact until I was just about to start testosterone.

It helps that everyone starts out female in the womb. This biological configuration is the little-known secret of female to male sex change. Biological femaleness is the primary, or at least default, human condition, which is why it's so much easier to pick things up from there. Add testosterone, even later in life, and many startling changes will occur that cannot be easily undone. Easier to add on than to do away with, to erase the stain of masculinity.

X is primary. The first variable we tend to imagine when designating a frame of reference such as a variable, or a coordinate, or a point on a grid. X precedes Y, beginning with the alphabet. X is linked to genetic femaleness, the quotidian of human biology, which persists in a recurring and unfolding bloom if left alone.

It's Eve, then Adam.

CHAPTER 24: HUNGER

I'm hungry all the time. Famished. I eat whatever is on my plate with a desperate urge. A howling in the belly. I *have* to eat. The hunger is a sharp ache. It comes on suddenly, taking me by surprise, snatching up my composure. I can't believe the enormity of this impulse to consume—blocks, particles, wedges, ripe wads of food. To snork down, devour! The hunger is a painful craving, bottomless. A hankering life force. It drives.

I eat so much. Everything on my plate and that isn't enough. I want more and more—pile on the food, as much as the plate can hold—bread, potatoes, rice, vegetables, pasta, chicken, beef, and there's room left over! I imagine rich desserts, chocolate tortes, bread and rice puddings, a slice of lemon meringue or banana cream pie, maybe a thick piece of chocolate cake with a shovel of ice cream on the side. I give in. Let these pangs take over.

I'm trying to eat things that are good for me, not too much fat, skimp on the sugar, but mostly I just eat. This hunger is indiscriminate, riveting. A physical rush.

When I report this phenomenal hunger to my therapist, Joanne, she looks at me and states, matter-of-factly, "What did you expect? You're becoming a man."

CHAPTER 25:
SHAVING

It's overcast today, there's a chill in the air. Walking down Valencia Street in the Mission District, I'm aware of the nuances of time and place. Each and every part of this street tilts and swerves with memories.

There are cafés where I sat with Kate for coffee and had long, intense conversations about politics or therapy, the aggravations and intrigues of mutual friends. There's the funky garage where a guy called Batman fixed scooters and had scores of San Francisco mods for clients, the white chalky building that once had been the Tool and Die, a punk club from the early and mid-eighties. I'd performed "The Parking Lot/The Criminal" there and Felix had exhibited her photos—many of the punk dykes of that time, basically all of her friends. Roxanne, Selene, Felix, and I had watched Sister Boom Boom of the Sisters of Perpetual Indulgence give a campaign speech at the Tool and Die when s/he was running for a seat on the board of supervisors of San Francisco, all done up in nun's drag with fake eyelashes. The Varve and Wilma—two all-woman San Francisco new wave/punk bands—had played. Boom Boom was an earnest and articulate prankster on the stage between sets. Black Flag came on later, and Henry Rollins prowled the stage in bare chest and long hair.

Down past Amelia's, the once-premier San Francisco dyke club, had been the San Francisco School for the Deaf, which had featured many of the first punk shows in the city. In the late seventies I saw X there for the first time. They were playing with The Germs. I remember how Exene impressed me with her severe black hair, face lit in dramatic lines, throttling the microphone stand and pushing it down to the ground with a grace adjunct to defiance. And all the kids spilling out onto the sidewalk in the night dressed in safety pins, raccoon makeup on pale faces, black spiked hair, white bleached hair, a few cheeks with chains, torn Levi's and black leather jackets, fishnets, leopard-print miniskirts, high heels from hell. A film lit with grainy light and surreal noir images. One night, walking by, a friend and I saw a girl running down the street with blood streaming out of her mouth. The cops were raiding the place and beating the shit out of everyone, twisting people's arms up behind their backs and slamming them down on the tops of patrol cars. Cops usually came to early punk shows toward the end of the night in order to break things up. Making their presence felt—standing like sentinels near the doors or at the back of the room.

Valencia Street stretches beneath my stride. I watch myself in the mirrored windows on the street as I walk. *What is that on my face?* I stop and look closer, peer into the glass on the side of the building. Is the area under my nose, above my lip, dirty? I gaze more intently. There is a dark area. I go into a restaurant bathroom and try and wash the dark off—rub and rub while I look at my face in the small mirror. It's not dirt! The dark smudge must be hair, fuzzy short facial hairs. . . .

I call up Alexander that night and tell him, "I'm growing a mustache!" It occurs to me that I need to start shaving. Then I realize I don't know how.

It can't be too difficult, but I don't know how to do it.

Brian gives me tips. Like most other transsexual guys, he had to start shaving sooner than I did. It's June, three months into my injections, and I've been watching my face in the mirror for hair. I had begun to think that I wouldn't grow any facial hair. I was nearly ready to give up. "Shave against the growth of the hair, against the direction that the hair grows in," Brian instructs. I try, gazing into the mirror, tenderly scraping at my face. It's foreign to put a razor to my face. I shaved my head once when I had a bleached-blond Mohawk. That was novel, and a lot of work, but this is another category of shaving. I scrape at my cheeks and the area under my lower lip, feeling the strange sensations, the cautious motion of a metal edge so close to my mouth. But my skin is tougher, thicker from testosterone; if it wasn't, the razor might hurt and possibly make me bleed much more from an occasional careless nick.

I wait and wait for more hair. Months go by. Will looks me over from time to time, squinting into my face, asking, "Max, you getting any whiskers yet?" My mustache is still only tiny, sparse fuzzy hairs over my lip, and, alarmingly, two short wisps on the edges of my mouth.

Some transmen get full beards in less than a year. One guy even grew a beard all the way down to his chest in one year, thick and black. He also grew a tangled rug on his chest and hair on his fingers, and his eyebrows began to knit together in the middle. I didn't want to get that hairy, although it impressed me and I was glad an FTM was able to grow hair like that.

It's fun to point out the evidence of what testosterone can do. Facial and body hair sprout in brilliant variety, like an unfurling swatch of brand names, a banner proclaiming each individual's genetic heritage in a sweeping articulation of patterns. Looking at guys at FTM meetings, I see a specially incubated menagerie of genotypes. Some have whiskers directly on the chin; for others the bristling hair covers the area just underneath their chin and creeps along the edges of their jawline; some get a full mustache before any other hair sprouts, and others, a beard but no mustache. Whatever they get, it seems that everyone gets it faster and fuller than me. Mine creeps in, scanty and unimpressive.

Finally, I realize American Indian men don't really grow beards. If you look at pictures of full-bloods from the nineteenth century living out on the plains, you'll see that these men, who didn't have access to electric shavers or razors, had little or no facial hair. Nearly all of them are naturally clean shaven, in contrast to the Caucasian mountain men with huge beards and hairy bodies. Traditionally, Native American men used tweezers to pluck out their scant beards (as have some of my Caucasian girlfriends). In fact, it's likely that the first time American Indians encountered white men they were shocked and dismayed by all that dense, brushlike hair growing on their faces. The movie *Black Robe* captures this moment of shocked discovery between the two races well: Seeing whites with full beards for the first time, one Indian man turns to another and points in shock at their furry faces, exclaiming, "What is wrong with these men? They look like dogs!"

Of course, I am not a full-blood. Although I do identify quite strongly as an Indian, I actually consider myself to be a true half-breed, a hybrid of European/Sephardic and American Indian ancestry. And although I have always felt far too light in complexion, my American Indian heritage kicks in strong when it comes to the beard and body hair. One of my brothers was thirty before he began to grow much facial hair, and neither brother has to shave every day.

Even so, hair continues to creep in, turning up in odd areas of my face—a lone hair appears high up on my cheek, and the wisps at the ends of my lips are beginning to creep upward to meet in the middle, creating a mustache. In fact, my beard is beginning to fill in as time goes on. I've been able to manage a respectable goatee, and I am not sure what the future will bring. Although I now have plenty of hair on my legs, I have a relatively smooth chest. There appears to be no chance that I'll ever have the vexations over a hairy back or shoulders that some do. So although many transsexual men appear obsessed with how much body hair they accumulate, I've come to be proud of not having an abundance of fur. I never wanted to look like a hairy white man.

CHAPTER 26:
BREAKING THE NEWS

There are a few people I haven't yet told about my change, even though I've been on the holy vitamin T for a few months now. They must be told. I announce what I'm doing to my old friend Felix over the phone. The shock in her voice is palpable, a stunned silence. She asks, "When did you decide this?"

When I tell her that I'm already on testosterone, that my face is beginning to change, I hear a sharp intake of breath on the other end. "Your face is changing?" The idea that such an intimate and familiar part of me is altering into god knows what or who is alarming.

I want to reassure Felix that everything is alright. I know that I have embarked upon an arena of uncertainty. There's a quaver in my voice that gives my own fears away. I have no certainty, after only a short time on testosterone, of who or what I will resemble in a few years.

I continue, "And my voice, my voice is starting to crack. Maybe you can hear it."

"A little . . ."

"Well, it takes a while. But my voice is getting some deeper tones in it. It's kinda hard to control. I think it could end up being pretty deep." I'm thrilled. In spite of any fears I may have, when I really get into talking about the changes, my enthusiasm is electric. I talk people's ears off about my changing voice, my shrinking hips, the new hair on my legs.

"Well, you always had a deep voice to begin with," Felix notes.

"Thanks. But not like it will be. Not a guy's voice. . . ." I want her to hear any small change that has occurred. I don't want to hear that my voice had been deep before. Before transition, I would've loved to have heard that my voice was deep, but now I couldn't care less what people thought of my female voice.

"That's true," she replies.

I had been a deep, rich alto with a lot of melodic tones in my voice, contralto in its lowest ranges, but certainly not male. Not only is the testosterone making my voice deeper and more resonant, it's also slowly erasing the notes in my voice at the upper end of the spectrum. There's a relative flatness to men's voices in comparison to women's. As my voice deepens, there are times I feel as though I'm speaking in a monotone. The dips and lilts, the sprinkling of higher notes that I didn't even realize I had, are being erased.

Felix is quiet for a moment. Then she declares, "I would have a *really* deep voice if I did it."

"Yeah, you would." Suddenly Felix is speculating about her own potential for hunkiness. I'm a little surprised, but I continue, "You've got that deep, gravelly voice now . . . it's great, you know."

Felix does have a gravelly cigarette voice, tomboyish, with a hip sneer seductively tucked into the cadence and tone. She speaks with a soft swagger.

Later, once the initial shock wears off and we've seen each other a few times, Felix will stand up straight and flex her arm muscles, cock her head, and point her chin: "I would be a really muscular guy, you know. My dad is."

"Yeah?" I say, incredulous.

"Yeah." Her face is proud. "But I would be really short. I don't think I would do it because I would be so short." She glances at me earnestly. She's around five feet five, average for a woman and therefore average for a transsexual man.

"Well, a lot of the guys are around your height, Felix. In fact, most of them are. They do it. I mean, that's not enough of a reason not to." I stop myself. I'm not sure if I want to encourage her. I decide to be a neutral ear.

From the other room Diviana, her girlfriend, yells, "Don't do it, Felix, don't have a sex change! I can't afford it! It's too much money!"

We walk back into the room where Diviana is getting dressed for a night out clubbing. Searching for her best stockings and leather miniskirt in a small pile of clothes, she mutters to herself and shakes her head, "Just what I need . . . you to have a sex change, we can't afford that, Felix. . . ."

I shrug my shoulders. I've come to expect a wide range of responses to my change. It holds up a mirror in which people examine themselves in unexpected ways.

Some still hoped I could be saved. Susie Bright told me over a cocktail late one afternoon, "You just haven't found the right femme."

One night, Alexander and I go to Klubstitute—a performance club night for the queer community that features a whole luminous array of local performers, including spoken-word poets, gender-fuck drag queen divas, queer rock bands, and a burgeoning group of dykes who do male impersonation—drag kings. I am thinking about doing a reading but I'm not sure how appropriate that would be. Reading here, I know I should do prose. At this point, I've written only very intensely sexual pieces, fueled by my new testosterone-driven sex drive. How would this queer crowd receive my hetersex writing? Even if composed by a transsexual man?

Spike, a strapping butch punk dyke I've known since my days at Hotel Hell, spies me at the bar. She looks at me for a long time across the dance floor. Comes up to me with her big lurching walk, like a cowhand with a skateboard, peers into my face for a closer look, then asks, "Anita?"

"Uh . . . yeah . . ." I manage to sputter. I don't like to respond to my old name, but if someone happens to recognize me before I have told them, there's really no choice.

"I'm doing a sex change. I go by the name Max now," I explain as Spike gazes at me with a look of stunned surprise.

"I see." She glances at me sideways, checking me out. Her hair is bleached out and standing on end. Spike has been around for a long time. She used to live in a building of abandoned beer vats that had been taken over by punks and artists in the eighties. She haunted punk shows back then, too, getting drunk, beating on her chest, gulping beers and belching, wearing metal studs and chains from head to foot, thrashing in the pit. She has a baby face and doe eyes, and in spite of her large frame and road-warrior exterior, Spike reminds me of a *Clockwork Orange* synthesis of Li'l Abner and Daisy Mae.

Spike regards me with a long look. I can't tell what she is thinking. Finally, she reveals, "When I saw you, I thought, 'Is that Anita? Why does she look so much like a man?'"

"Well, now you know." I smile, trying to put a positive face on what is obviously making her uncomfortable. "The hormones work."

She nods, still not smiling, "Yeah, amazing."

I am getting used to these confrontations with old acquaintances. Sooner or later, I know, I'll run into everyone I've known in my past life.

Spike relaxes a bit and takes a sidelong glance toward Alexander. "So, you have a boyfriend now?"

This assumption always takes me by surprise. Many of my lesbian friends appear to want me to become, or assume automatically that I am going to become, a gay man. "No, I'm not gay," I explain patiently. "I'm just here with a friend."

"You mean you're becoming a *straight man?*" Spike looks disturbed, her intent gaze has become a glare.

"Yeah, I guess so. I mean, yes," I stutter.

"Oh." Her face squinches into a mask of disapproval. "Goodbye." Spike turns on her heel, strides into the crowd and away from me.

CHAPTER 27:
SEX FOR SALE

ill tells me how weird it is to have prostitutes start coming on to you. They say, "Hey, sailor" to him. Sure enough, once I'm on the street, they spy me and get a near maniacal look in their eyes. "Hey, baby, need anything?"

I'm walking in Oakland, making my way to Will's apartment. Out here, people party all night, scattering syringes on the steps outside and in the bushes. Prostitutes take their tricks to the Super 8 Motel; these are street hookers on the bottom of the totem pole of sex for sale. As I walk down the sidewalk toward the MacArthur BART station, I see them watching me, trying to catch my eye. It's startling. Before, the hookers would ignore me, look past or around me. There's one small woman who looks really worn, cranked up, who'll walk alongside me and jabber at me, hoping I'll take her up. Can't they see I am poor? Probably doesn't matter much, they go cheap, I'm sure. Strange to be the prey of these women who seem so desperate, so calculating in their contrivance of seduction. I'm a man to them now, a meal ticket, a way to get money and get high. Once a lesbian feminist, now a young man who might put out fifteen bucks for a quick blow job or the chance to get my dick wet.

And I understand the male end of it better now, too, although not even my new over-amped sex drive will make me want to lie down with these scraggly women. But would I, if I could find a young, healthy, and beautiful prostitute, someone with a genuine air of sexy misbehavior? Someone who could at least pretend to want it, like it, as much as I would need it? I can understand now how a man on a slow burn from sexual frustration would want this type of release.

When prostitutes first began to come on to me I was only seven months along, really fresh, with a face full of pimples. Bouncing off the walls with energy and discovery. The first come-ons of street hookers provided a startling marker of my progress.

A nontranssexual friend, Zack, asked me if I wanted to get set up with a call girl. A call girl is distinct from a street hooker, although really it boils down to the same thing in a better wardrobe. "You could have your first experience as a man having sex, Max. It *is* different," he told me. I wasn't sure how different it would be, since I'd always thought of myself as male in the bedroom when I had sex and didn't want people to relate to my female parts. Still, I knew that since my body had masculinized, since its odor, appearance, and texture had changed, these changes were bound to affect how I experienced sex with a partner. I was startled by Zack's offer, coming as it did out of the blue. I hadn't had sex with a woman since starting hormones. Here he was offering to find someone who would be alright with my in-between state physically, the binding and, of course, the lack of a proper set of cock and balls. I considered it, but shook my head. Perhaps this possibility was just too new. No, it seemed too weird. Too impersonal—the exchange of money for sex.

Yet there are moments I'm transfixed. On another street in San Francisco, walking on a silky dark night, I watch a leggy hooker with long hair. My eyes travel along the seam of her stockings from the peaked back of her high heels up to the hem of her black leather miniskirt. I reach up and put my hand on her heart-shaped ass. She turns and eyes me with a long look. It's a fantasy, an idling night dream. I am barely aware I'm having it when she turns to catch my eye. The fantasy bursts. She's smiling and begins a measured, sure walk toward me. Beckoning, hips rolling, a saunter. I deliberately, mechanically redirect my gaze. Cross the street to avoid her.

Other times, I'm completely taken by surprise when a hooker approaches. As I'm walking rapidly down Geary Street on a bright Sunday afternoon, a woman smiles at me with a frantic frozen flash of teeth stretching over cracked lips, "Hi, baby, you want anything?" I'm in a hurry. I blurt out, "No!" At that moment, I'm not even sure what she wants. Is she selling drugs? Then I realize what's happened, but by then, she's down the street, looking a bit hurt and indignant. I feel a little sorry. Sad to refuse her offer of her body so swiftly and bluntly with such a perfunctory tone. Who is this woman and how desperate might her life be? Did she choose to sell sex on the streets because of addictions, street survival, or another hidden, subliminal impulse? Some form of gambling with sex, men, and death—a need to control and survive? Possibly she feels that this is the best alternative to a life of low-paying work. Possibly she's learned to enjoy it. Possibly she always has. She doesn't look hardened to this life. She has a story, a life of struggle and small, hard-won victories.

I am prey in this game. A roving consumer. The prostitutes, strippers, and massage parlor women are saleswomen, a squad of Avon Ladies gone berserk. My FTM friend Charley says that it scares him when women come on to him like that. "What should I do, Max? This woman at work is coming on to me!" Or, "Those hookers are so scary!" He worries out loud, wringing his hands and doing a little nervous dance in place, shuffling his feet from side to side.

I laugh at Charley when he talks like that. I don't understand why flirtatious women and hookers make him so nervous. Yet, I have to admit, I was shocked by my response to a girl in a booth who spied me when I peeked into the Regal Theater on Market Street one afternoon on my way home from work. I peered in the entrance and saw a row of women's heads sticking out over a row of small doors. The women sat waiting in gated booths where they would talk one-on-one with guys from behind a glass partition. I knew about these "See a Live Girl for a Quarter" booths and normally thought of them as hilarious; it seemed absurd to go in and plunk down a quarter just to see a woman naked. From the entrance I could see made-up women's faces nodding at me. A long row of red lips and winking eyes. One girl caught my gaze. In an instant, she transformed into a ferocious, sexual sybarite. A lure lit up with glitter and paint. Her eyes were gleaming, straining at me with a cold seductive glint. She had probably practiced this look before, in a mirror at home and a million times on the men who walked past the theater and stopped to look inside, but in a flash that look, which might have ordinarily seemed phony or even desperate, a mere ploy of artificial lights and Muzak, became obscene, lurid, a serpentine glare. Eve with her fat red apple. Salome ready to have my head cut off and brought to her on a plate. The "male gaze" reflected back from a woman at a man. From the prostitute who wants cold cash to the john, hard yet vulnerable with his naked dick inside her mouth and close to the edges of her teeth. That objectifying gaze swiveled around and thrown back as spawn, a devil girl's claw to tear at the eyes and balls of men. My eyes and the balls that were inside my head instead of between my legs. I was lit with a spreading panic. I looked into the girl's winking come-hither eyes and felt a cold rush of fear. I ran out and away from that place. Shocked at my gut response. I don't know what scared me, but something sure did.

Once outside, I laughed out loud in absurd surprise. When I told Selene about that rush of panic, she appeared to know the parameters of this situation by heart. She named it without hesitation. "Yes, of course you were scared. She was a vampire, a succubus." Intrigued and puzzled, I felt uneasy about Selene's swift pronouncement of judgment on this glass-booth girl. I knew that she wasn't a vampire any more than I was a rapist in training. Yet, the dynamic of the relationship we were enacting in that pornographic theater had the power to pull us both into grotesque, ancient shapes—figments of fear, lust, and greed.

I'm a couple of years into my transition now, beginning to broaden a bit more in the shoulders; I do push-ups and lift a set of dumbbells that Lou Sullivan gave me. I'm maturing; my initial burst of teenagelike acne is finally getting under control. The bloating I experienced in the first phase of hormone treatment has subsided.

In these first couple of years, you change so fast, it's almost like having your face printed on the edges of a flipbook where you animate and alter the face by flipping the pages with your thumb. Or a computer-generated graphic programmed to shift facial features gradually from a female to a male direction. It takes looking at a photo taken even six months earlier for the changes to leap out at me. I'm becoming my own identical twin brother.

I'm coming of age fast, but I'm still mistaken for being eighteen even though I'm thirty-four. Grocers ask for my identification when I buy beer. Their mouths drop open in shock, "You're older than I am!" peering at my birth date. "How do you do it, man, *what are you taking?*" I smile sheepishly and shrug my shoulders. "Man, that's amazing!" The paunchy, thirtyish grocer shakes his head, hands my ID back to me, and I grin and tuck it away. Part of me is delighted and part of me is embarrassed. Doesn't everyone want to look youthful, exuberant, virile—with-it? But then, there's a limit. . . . It is pretty weird to look like you're eighteen when you're thirty-four. It's almost scandalous, *The Picture of Dorian Gray.* A time warp. Like I'd been abducted by aliens in my late teens and returned to Earth in a pristine state. Maybe I could even go to one of those alien-abduction survivor groups and get a good burst of "oohs" and "aahs"—wide eyes, impressed girls.

Well, I think, at least I look older than I did when I first started! Six months into the hormones, as I was ambling down Church Street, I heard someone coming up fast behind me. A guy with a baseball cap on backward who looked as though he were intent on some mission. A bobbing grinning head on a stick, some odd teenage amble, hands shoved in back pockets, face shoved forward, he bent his face into mine and blurted out, "Hey, what junior high school you go to?" I stopped in my tracks, speechless. He looked closer at me. I was wearing a baseball jacket and had a flattop at the time. "You look like a nice boy who doesn't do drugs. . . ."

Who the hell was this guy? Older than junior high age himself, bobbing with a sinuous energy, tricksterlike. I thought this meeting might be a twisted message from the universe. Absurd, surreal, like so much of what my life had become since beginning transition. An unending series of paradoxes, perceptual shifts. A continuing deflation of expectations and unexpected exposures of feral knowledge.

Could it be, I wondered, that I *really* was in some way younger than before? In going into a second adolescence, had I reinvigorated my cells? I had so much energy. I was getting stronger physically and growing larger, too. If not in height, at least in bone thickness, neck size, the depth of my rib cage. My hands had even gotten a ridge of muscle I hadn't seen before. When I saw that, I banged on Will's door. "Will, I have a new muscle in my hand!"

"Wow," he said, *"I wonder where you got that from."*

As I stride down the street and consider this apparent pushing back of my biological clock, feelings of liberation and exuberance wash over me; I have found the fountain of youth!

CHAPTER 28:
IN THE GRIP
OF THE GODDESS

Once the eye begins to rove, it cannot be morally controlled.
—Camille Paglia, *Sexual Personae*

erhaps this skittish response to the girl in the booth was another sign of my freshness, my adolescent male perturbations and oddly skewed emotional textures. Raw and unpredictable. Usually, I'm drawn to femininity like a bee to honey. Curious, tentative, hooked in by the allure, the gauzelike dream of feminine charm. Intoxication of sex. That possibility. My nontranssexual friend Bob tells me that he's gone in these booths a few times and that the girls can be real nice, sultry, they get to know you if you're a regular. "Good for a quick jerk off," he says. I've begun to feel curious. Who knows, maybe a girl in a booth could be fun? *What would it be like as a guy on the other side of the strong glass?*

Aphrodite's dance of veils and mirrors, her tantalizing cries of pleasure. The temple prostitute, the escort, the street hooker, swollen vowels of sex silhouette sharply made-up faces on a damp yellow street after midnight. Satin colors and angular poses. Click of cheap high heels on pavement. Women in strip joints calling out for customers in North Beach. Promenade of gluttonous seduction, surging and calling out. Wheedling and cooing through red pouty lips, rouged cheeks, the enticement of wet panties. Switchblade arcade of bustiers and cantaloupe-round breasts, taut nipples displayed behind glass windows, serenade of sighs and gasps, women's soft throats and scented necks, their vulnerable agency of sex, enticement, the siren's call. I see. I hear.

I have suddenly become aware of a male vulnerability that had been hidden to me. Easy to be driven by this hunger, this excruciating sexual drive, there's a vulnerability in its propulsive urgency. *Easy to want to do anything, pay any amount, say anything you have to say, in order to get that sex.* To touch that woman, to hold her roughly against you, to part her thighs and lift then lower her down slowly on your cock. I could be taken in. I could go and blow all my money, like some of these guys I see, waiting in line to watch the women who dance naked in glass booths. A long line of guys. All kinds, young to old, some in baseball hats and baggy pants, some in sports coats and ties, good-looking guys, homely guys. All of them with a flame traveling through their cocks, from the root out to the end, a flame balanced perfectly on an arc of eyesight, the sheer pleasure of looking at a woman's naked body. That display of soft curves and elegant movements stoking the flaming of nerves and sensations. The way the flesh dreams.

Hugh Grant stopped for a quick blow job in his car from a street hooker. Charlie Sheen hired Heidi Fleiss's girls for thousands of dollars a pop. Nietzsche had sex with a prostitute, got syphilis, and it drove him mad. He lost his vision, his genius, from a fuck. Men do it all the time.

Anonymous sex, public sex in cars and bathrooms, phone sex, circle jerks. John Lennon used to do circle jerks as a teenager in Liverpool and call out "Winston Churchill" as the other guys were calling out "Brigitte Bardot," "Marilyn Monroe," or "Jayne Mansfield" when they came.

Bill Clinton couldn't resist Monica Lewinsky's thong panties.

I see entire female audiences on talk shows pursing their lips, shaking their heads at sheepish or smug male guests who are supposed "porn addicts" or "womanizers." Sometimes these men look awkward and contrite, other times they're unrepentant, arguing with defensive, angry voices. Almost always, they look confused by the reactions of the women in the audience, and later, the so-called expert, a therapist (usually a woman) who generally blames their appetite for sex, or their four or five rotating girlfriends, on a bad relationship with Mom, and a consequent seething, profound hostility toward the female gender. A blurb appears under these men's faces across the screen: JOHN—A WOMANIZER—REALLY HATES WOMEN, a pop psychology sound bite framing a criminal mug shot. "No," the accused protests, "I really *don't* hate women!" The mostly female audience sneers in disbelief and moral superiority.

Now that I am Max, I see that this rift, this fundamental chasm between men and women's perceptions and experience of sexuality, is one that may never be bridged. There certainly can be no hope for understanding as long as society pretends that men and women are really the same, that the culture of male sexuality is simply a conflation of misogyny and dysfunction. That the male libido is shaped and driven *primarily* by socialization, that it can be legislated or "psychobabbled" out of existence.

Jimmy Swaggart cries and begs forgiveness from Jesus for his trysts with prostitutes in motel rooms. Tears stream down his cheeks under the glare of television cameras. Jim Bakker had private orgies with both male and female members of the flock. Although they both tried to be "good boys," these guys failed on an operatic scale. The preaching and repentance continues, with unwavering and grim determination. Mellifluous temptations, guilt orgies that scour the small screen with tears and archly dramatic cries of shame.

But the carnage continues, unabated. Guys jerk off in their rooms and watch X-rated videos. Surf the Internet and find foot-fetish rooms, big-tit folders, bleached-blond beach-bunny bikini-party photo files, Victorian corset catalogs, high-heeled women posing next to Arabian horses. The "male gaze" is analyzed, deconstructed, and sneered at with academic excision, the drone of postmodern feminism, the joining of hands of the religious Right and the shrill invective of the antiporn feminists. Jesse Helms and Andrea Dworkin in bed together with the lights on. From the sex-scandal-slanted eyes of the U.S. Congress, to the church ladies and the antiporn feminist professors at the "Take Back the Night" marches—the rabid Republican right wing, the Catherine MacKinnons of the world—preach, cajole, and write torrid, censoring legislation. They mount intermittent assaults on sexy websites, and sweep *Playboy* and *Penthouse* off 7-Eleven display racks and behind the counters. They actually think that this will change something.

It's odd to understand, to see clearly where prostitution and pornography function as a service, a real profession filling a genuine need. It's that relentless sex drive. I can understand the need to just have it taken care of, to get off without having a "relationship" with the woman. It's a market that demands exploitation, the lubricious market of male libido.

Throng of hard-ons. Tomcats traveling over broken glass to find a female in heat. Gay men lingering in back alleys or train station restrooms for blow jobs. When he interviewed Camille Paglia, Tom Snyder said that women didn't understand what sex was to men. He said that it was food.

I go with lesbian friends to the Lusty Lady, and once we are all in one of the larger "group" booths, I notice that everyone else, all my friends, are laughing. I don't understand what is so funny. The naked dancers are posing on a small, raised platform in a brightly lit room. I feel tense. Something crucial has changed.

Later in the week I'm at the Roxie theater with my friend Bella. We're out for an evening of feminist-oriented short films—arty and ironic. A film of a woman with short, spiky, bleached-blond hair posing near some railroad tracks. She's putting on makeup: mascara on her eyelashes, and a slash of bright red across her lips. Crossing and uncrossing her sheer legs in bald, bright daylight near a group of gray industrial buildings. Bella is laughing hard, a derisive sneer, too wise to take this seriously. This woman's polished poses are too deliberate, as though she's practiced them for hours beforehand. The emotional distance required for parody is built into the film with its conflation of nightclub glamour and railroad tracks. A strategic pantomime of the highly self-conscious, ritualized language of seduction. Most of the women in the audience are laughing. In fact, the entire place is lit up with hoots of female laughter, knowing, hard-edged laughter. I shift in my seat, grip the armrests. I don't think it's funny. Not in my gut. I feel so alone, surrounded by laughing women. I'm turned on, in the grip of the goddess. I can't be derisive or superior. That luxury has evaporated.

As the men crash into the rock where the sirens sing, the sirens laugh and glance at each other, "Can you believe they went for it? Come on, girls, let's clean out their wallets and slip the corpses back into the sea." Watch them float out like empty plastic bags into the morass of water and swirling ocean life, deflated heroes stilled by the subtle nuance and erotic pathos of women's voices.

Men are so vulnerable to the ransacking seduction of feminine allure.

Oshun's (the Yoruban orisha of love, beauty, female sexuality, and wealth) shrill, intoxicated laughter as she dances on the graves of lust-struck men, with her smoky lips in a tantric pout and her happy sexual eyes gleaming.

I understand that for most of these women—these hookers, call girls, streetwalkers, strippers, massage parlor women, porn actresses, glass-booth dancers—this is survival in a male world of commerce, it's a job and not a pleasure. A desperate measure to survive. When I was twenty-three, I met a porn filmmaker in a McDonald's in Berkeley. I was desperate for money—young, sick of working clerk jobs that paid next to nothing and zapped all my energy for writing and creative work. Doing a flesh film, he promised, I could make a bundle of cash fast. I hoped that I would be allowed to do lesbian scenes, that I wouldn't have to fuck a guy. I'd be paid so much for so little of my time. The filmmaker was cagey, with an air of furtive espionage, like he was on a secret mission for some obscure Peeping Tom club. He looked me over narrowly, speaking in a cold, monotonous tone, "Ya got any marks on your body?" When I said no, he was quiet, scanning me with hard eyes. He wanted proof. It gave me the creeps. I gave up the idea. I wasn't *that* desperate.

Although I understand something of the lure of sex work for these women, now that I'm Max, I also am aware of another dimension. A biological fiat that propels this industry of controversy, lust, and considered outrage that fattens the wallets of Hugh Hefner and Bob Guccione on the one hand and propels the antiporn crusading careers of the late Andrea Dworkin, Catherine MacKinnon, and the Howdy Doody religious Right on the other. They've all made careers out of male sexuality. These players are at the top of the feeding frenzy, the apex of the pornography pyramid.

My friend Diviana sounds nearly Transylvanian with her thick Italian accent. Her voice is low and soft with sex melted into the edges. She's an expert stripper, actress, and performance artist; she does performances informed by her extensive and acutely intelligent involvement in the sex industry. She's stripped for a living for quite some time, in New York and San Francisco, and understands instinctively when I tell her about the sex-drive-elevating qualities of testosterone: "Yes, when I talk to these guys and let them think I might let them feel me up, that's all I need to do, tempt them with a squeeze, a peek at my breasts. They go crazy. You can get all the money you want from these guys, just get those hormones going. You get men by their hormones."

Testosterone drives this flesh circus, the elixir of sexual fantasy. Since I got on it, I've become more visual in my turn-ons. It's as if photos, previously only flat and one-dimensional, plastic, came alive.

On Market Street, advertising billboards and the flashy, frigid veneers of porn stores and strip joints have taken on another dimension. The faces and breasts of women pull me in. The night is lit with neon and sex. Men walk concealing erections. All around, the street crackles with a restlessness that feels electric.

The eye, my eyes, held and stoked by sexual imagery. I notice that I am aroused by even a benign television commercial featuring a sleek woman climbing into a sports car with its top down. I pay more attention to women on the street. I catch myself *watching,* like so many other guys. Since being on testosterone, it's almost as though I can *see* better in some way. Everything appears more three-dimensional: Lines are more sharply drawn, perspectives seem enhanced. Will notices this as well, and many other transsexual men report the same phenomenon.

It isn't only that testosterone makes men hornier in general, it also provides the key to the way in which male sexuality seems to work. Now, I'm not as interested in stories about sex. I get a more palpable sense of pleasure from looking. Anita wasn't so magnetized by a copy of *Juggs* magazine. My sexuality has become more driven by what I see. Looking, gazing, measuring, watching space and flesh intersect.

Women do tend to enjoy reading about sex more than looking at images. Not that they *never* enjoy those things, of course, but *Playgirl* is probably more widely looked at by gay men than by straight women. Words allow more of a *relationship* to develop between the reader and the experience described. Images are at once concrete, static, objectifying; they freeze and quantify our perceptions. Images easily become fetishes. Desire held and concentrated in the viewed object or image. A talisman.

I find myself looking at cheesy porn shots and thinking, "Who cares? Just put a bag over her head! She's got great tits!" It's happened to me.

It's eerie to be experiencing firsthand so many of these differences in perception between the sexes as I biologically change from one sex to another. And this is only the surface! Reds stand out; for the first few months on testosterone, I noticed I would often spot the color red from a distance. It appeared more vibrant, catching my eye before any other color.

My friend Kelly asks me, "Does this mean I should wear red if I want a guy to notice me?"

"Yes," I answer. The male eye is excited by red. Does this have anything to do with the dance of bull and bullfighter, choreographed and driven by red banners? And why scarlet is often associated with brazen female sexuality? Why are prostitutes and "easy women" portrayed wearing red dresses?

Will and I discuss these changes, comparing notes, reevaluating our perceptions and values; we're a gender think tank, an unfunded, underground research project driven by an obsessive sense of exploration and ceaseless investigation. The necessity of our lives. This is treasure, and we are plundering it. The information that transsexuals pass back and forth among ourselves is often not in the scientific journals or magazines. And we rarely talk honestly about it to nontranssexuals.

Once on testosterone, I begin to understand a whole arena of cultural cues and conventions that had previously been meaningless to me. There is a reason, a biologically encoded impetus, for many of our cultural preoccupations, rituals, and symbolism. As someone who had always felt and thought that so much of the "Western patriarchal capitalist hegemony" was mere caprice, the result of a conspiracy of exploitative bogeymen, I'm surprised. There's more sense and grounded *real* intelligence in the cultural signs around me than I've ever imagined. I'm beginning to understand sexual politics and its impact on religion, world history, literature, fashion, art history, and science from a point of expansion, an illuminated threshold.

CHAPTER 29:
URINE, SCENTS,
AND BATHROOMS

It's a good thing men and women have separate restrooms. A restroom is a temple of sexual codification, of unrefined, unself-conscious masculine and feminine motivations, obsessions, and expressions. Each sex's respective restroom has its own particular atmosphere, distinct from the other's except for the common human function of pissing and shitting. Here's where the truth comes out. Guys piss in an exuberant arc, miss the bowl, and scribble graffiti about hard-ons and wet pussy without fear of women's prurient detection and subsequent censorship. They can let themselves go. Women socialize without male leers or derision. The so-called male gaze is nullified within the mirrored confines of the "ladies' room." It's a memory, an echoing yet distant yelp. Inside the women's restroom is a sense of security, a safety that women crave and serenely enjoy.

There aren't as many mirrors in men's rooms. And the ones that are there are not as generous in size and are often smudged or cracked. In the women's restroom, the mirrors are central to the atmosphere and function of the area. They invite the luxury of looking, preening, the discourse of style and vanity. They're part of the general cultural encoding that discourages male vanity while encouraging a cult of feminine vanity. Before, in my female life, I was more likely to discuss a problem with a coworker in the restroom, complain about the boss, brush my hair, and gaze without hesitation into my reflection in the mirror. I seldom wore makeup after the age of eighteen, but I always paid a great deal of attention to my hair (and still do). Women powder their cheeks, check their lipstick, strike a pose in the mirror. Side and front. They don't seem to be in a rush. Guys, I've found out, seem harried in comparison.

I quickly realize it's not the norm to make a lot of eye contact in the men's room and that there's not a lot of conversation to be had in general. Every now and then I walk in and see some guy checking himself out in the mirror, looking proudly at his V-shaped torso, brushing back his hair, but it's an unusual sight. The atmosphere in the men's room is utilitarian, less social or loungelike. There's a nervous homophobia in the air, a nearly palpable tension that precludes more than a minimum amount of socializing.

Guys seem to relax only on the pot itself. That's where they really unwind—reading, jerking off, taking their sweet time, with their pants down below their knees. And men take *so* long in the stalls. Really now, dudes, it's true! *What the hell is going on in there?* I've often wondered. Is he dead from an overdose or a heart attack? Or, more likely, I've come to suspect, hasn't he come *yet?*

Striding into the men's room my first few weeks on testosterone, I am in for a rude awakening. As I open the door, a rush of urine smells hits me in the face like a sledgehammer. *I can't go in there!* I think, mildly panicking. With sheer force of will I hold my breath and step inside. Oh god, is it going to be this bad for the rest of my life? Will I be condemned to a lifetime of going inside men's bathrooms and smelling *this? How can they stand it?* And the place is a mess! Piss on the seat (why even bother to raise it, I guess, if it's only dudes coming in?) and wadded-up paper all over the floor. Doors ripped off the stalls. Cigarette butts. A crude drawing of a penis near the mirror, with tiny droplets coming out of the head. COME HERE SATURDAY NIGHT, GET HARD, GET SUCKED. TOM LOVES BIG DICKS UP HIS ASSHOLE. I LIKE TO SUCK OFF STRAIGHT MARRIED MEN, ESPECIALLY THOSE WITH BIG FEET AND TIGHT BUNS. CALL 445-0000. ASK FOR JUNIOR. And one of my favorites: EVEN FRIDA KAHLO GAVE BLOW JOBS. A drawing of a large-busted woman with tits pointing off like missiles into expanding space, a woman with breasts so large they drag on the ground. I examine these signatures of fetishistic lust, amused, repulsed, fascinated.

Sure is different from the women's room. Yeah, sometimes in the women's room there's stuff like ARNOLD IS A GREAT FUCK or KURT'S DICK IS HUGE, but more often it's a long political dialogue concerning battered women, lesbianism, or recovery twelve-step. Someone might scribble in a few lines about their multiple personality disorder or childhood sexual abuse. At least in San Francisco. And of course, almost everywhere there's the ubiquitous romance graffiti, like MARILYN LOVES PAUL or LANITA & SAM 4-EVER—TRUE LOVE, NEVER TO PART, 4-EVER MORE. Lots of big hearts with arrows drawn through them instead of penises or big pointy-breast drawings. I've never seen COME HERE FRIDAY NIGHT GET WET, GET LICKED in a women's restroom, not even in the most swinging dyke bar. Life will be different from here on out, I can tell.

Men's pee smells. Face it, guys, it's true. Many of you may not be aware of this odious reality, the specter of male urine. Now, lots of guys get embarrassed when I tell them this, especially if a woman is present.

Others are simply shocked. *"No,* you've got to be kidding! *No* way!" As though I've insulted a precious elixir. On the other hand, well, I guess it would be embarrassing, it always is embarrassing, to be told that one stinks. Especially if one is totally unaware of the fact. Wandering around leaving the seat up, not realizing you leave a spray like a tomcat. Guys have no idea that their piss actually harbors a strong, unmistakable odor! Like a horse in a stall. Or a wild animal secretion.

Now, here's why. It's the testosterone in our pee. After being on male hormones for a month or so, my pee also begins to give off that pungent odor. It also foams more. Now, here's the clincher. Testosterone dampens the olfactory sense, which is why guys are clueless about their stench. Men can't smell their own urine! In fact, as I learned in time, compared to women, men can't smell much of anything! This may be one of the great hidden female one-ups of all eternity—the nasty smell of men's pee. The embarrassing little thing women know about men that they don't know about themselves. Yet, most women are unaware they even have this privileged information about men's bodies. Women are unaware that they are able to smell something about men that men themselves can't! They just assume that guys can smell it, too. Perhaps this is just one of the many differences in perception that contribute to women's general notion of men as "clueless."

Luckily, I'm not to be condemned to an existence of holding my breath and nose each time I have to use a public men's room. (Or, I suppose, since my own urine has taken on that raunchy scent, holding my breath and pinching my nostrils shut in my own bathroom at home every day for the rest of my life.) One day, after being on testosterone a few months, I can't smell the wild stuff anymore. Zilch. I have nearly forgotten what it smells like now. Maybe a tendril-like waft curls into my brain's olfactory receptors from time to time, maybe not. I can't be sure. Now, I'm clueless like all the other guys, stinking up the world and not even aware of it.

My first experience pissing at a urinal is nerve-racking. A transsexual man discovered a way to pee standing up at the urinal without recourse to surgery, and I'm trying it out. It sounds simple enough. Take a coffee-can lid and shape it into a funnel, place it under the urethra and there you go, stand and pee. I've got a yellow one in my pocket. I clinch it in my sweaty palm, take a deep breath, and walk up to the urinal. Nervous and alert for onlookers. What if someone strolls in and sees that the object in my hands is not a penis but a small funnel? Oh well, maybe they'll think I'm just sticking it in something new and unusual for the fun of it. I won't be the first or last. Perhaps there's a lining of warm raw liver inside the plastic funnel. In any case, I'm sure to avoid detection since the urinal is off to the side, not easily visible to anyone who walks in. So I do it.

Peeing standing up isn't easy. I have to aim. A little to the right, no, maybe the left. I hit the sides of the bowl and splash. For the first time in my life, I can *see* my urine arcing in the air, a long warm stream. It seems to take longer than when I sat. The experience has been transformed into a task that requires concentration, some small degree of artfulness. I have to visualize, aim, control my bladder as I direct the urine to its target area. It isn't as relaxing, as passive, as simple. Peeing becomes more visual, more complex—possibly more fun. I can imagine having contests, developing my aim, creating a lexicon of urination based on an individual's ability to control and direct the contents of his bladder. It will be easier to vandalize public property. To leave a marking like a tomcat on a special, coveted site.

CHAPTER 30: AUTHORITY

My male voice appears to have more authority. People listen to me with greater attention. If I'm out with a woman friend for dinner, I get the attention of the waiter or bartender more easily than she does. They look to me for direction and act as though they expect me to be the one to pay. Authority—the ability to move and change situations in the world, the privilege of being listened to as though what I'm saying is true.

This feels odd at first, like being recognized for a talent that I don't actually possess; I am exactly the same person I was before transition. Or am I? Well, I know that regardless of the fact that my transition to a new sex is genuine, I certainly have no new expertise suddenly.

Lou said that this is what happened to him, too. People seemed to listen to him with greater attentiveness. He even got a sudden, unforeseen raise at his secretarial job after becoming male.

"Would you be interested in a management position?"

I gaze across the table at the headhunter. She's around my age—perky, efficient, with a crafty edge. There are toothpicks on her desk, a bowl of small green mints, a heart-shaped paperweight. Is she kidding me? I blink and ask, "What?"

"I'm asking if you think you might be interested in management positions."

"Management?" I repeat.

"Yes." She flashes her teeth at me.

I've never been asked if I was interested in *management* before. I can't imagine such a thing.

"Uh, what?" I lean forward to see if I've heard her right.

"Management."

I squint at her. What am I to say to that? "I'll think about it." I clear my throat, shift in my seat. What's going on here?

I'd pumped my résumé up a bit, an American tradition. And I'd been getting better jobs—technical writing and database programming—as a female right before starting transition. But this is crazy. Unprecedented. This headhunter doesn't know about my female past. At least not yet. I figure that she will eventually call for references with old employers. I've contacted those employers and asked them to use my new name and the appropriate masculine pronoun when referring to me, but I know even well-intentioned people make mistakes out of habit. This makes me nervous, but I will have to live with it. I worry about many potential problems, imagine all sorts of awkward or embarrassing situations. But in all my imaginings, I hadn't foreseen being offered interviews for management positions.

I wonder about the possibility that I'm being offered management positions because I'm a man. On the other hand, it could just be that my résumé is pumped and primed enough, that the experience I've had as a tech writer recently has cracked open some doors. Even so, the prospect of management with only the experience I've had seems a bit far-fetched.

Are people starting to listen to me with more seriousness because I feel more confident? A confidence that's partially a result of testosterone and its expansive qualities, and partially the result of my feeling more authentic and less conflicted with my gender. Of course, I don't always feel brimming with confidence and authority. I often feel vulnerable, as though I am setting out along a tentative, nearly invisible pathway. Without a doubt, regardless of whether I feel more confident or not, or what drives that confidence, the men and women around me react to my male voice with a greater attentiveness. They appear to take me more seriously. This reaction must be a deeply ingrained automatic response, since even feminist women appear to consider my words with greater seriousness.

This automatic authority must be a symptom of the wildly touted and infamous "male privilege." Since I've never experienced it before, I wear it like an oddly fitting set of clothes, not sure how to take advantage of it, if I want to, or even if I should or need to do anything differently at all.

CHAPTER 31:
SAINT PRIAPUS

The most perfect type of male beauty is Satan . . .
—Charles Baudelaire, *Intimate Journals*

ands reach up out of sallow light. Hands grab at flesh, any flesh, at me, at the guy next to me. On each side, at every angle, another pore, a flesh stain, a sweat mark in the dank heat. A dim yellow bulb lights the center of this small area shaped like a short hallway or crawl space. I've squished through a group of men to get to where I'm standing now. Scaling up and scaling down—faces shrink and grow in the humid yellow light. Anonymous faces scaled by soft, diffuse light, smaller or larger as they loom closer and then farther away. The men are very quiet in here, and we're all men. I'm stretching my neck around to see what's going on, but it's hard to tell. It's so crowded, but so quiet. That's one of the first things I notice in this club, the quiet. Silent men are jammed in, one on top of the other, all the way to the back of this indeterminate, odd space. I think, *How can I get to the end of this hallway? What's at the end?* Then, as I squeeze into the narrow space, I realize there is nowhere to go. This is a grope space, where men stand in a small area, all squeezed in together, and reach for and touch each other, feel each other up without even looking into the other guys' faces, just grabbing for parts. Reaching out and grabbing, yanking, twisting, holding, feeling whatever you can get ahold of—an arm, a leg, a cock, a pec, an ass, the inside of a muscular thigh. When I realize that this is actually a gropefest, that I am being groped, I panic and squeeze my way back out into the air of the larger room.

It's the Church of Saint Priapus, and the services are manifold. Two floors and no women allowed. Alexander, Jack, and I are here tonight. It was Jack's idea. We'd been walking around the South of Market going to gay clubs. First to The Stud, then out to the Watering Hole, past My Place, dark and cramped. Some nights we go to the Rock and Roll Queer Bar, a club night at a bar on Ninth and Howard. They actually play music we like: The Runaways, The Stooges, The Cramps, The Sisters of Mercy. I love going out with these guys. We have an abandoned yet easy fun, I dance with a wild energy, sweat my brains out on the dance floor, dance with either or both of them. There are rumors I'm gay, I don't care. I am proud to be seen with Jack and Alexander. To hang out with them and be a part of this scene.

So when Jack suggests we check out Saint Priapus, an all-male sex club, I'm game. I've never been to one of those before.

The place is large, roomy, airy even. There really is a guy here who calls himself a reverend. Jack, Alexander, and I walk into a large room that is as close to being completely dark as a room can be. "Nothing's going on in here," I blurt out.

"Shhh . . ." Alexander hushes me. "The services are happening all around us." I notice a tall blond getting a blow job in one corner of the room. His pants have been jerked down past his ass and a man is kneeling in front of him; small sounds of sliding, slipping—the movement of lips on skin. As my eyes adjust to the darkness, I see a guy in another corner at the other end of the room with his cock hanging out. It's huge, an enormous wanker, pouring out of his fly. "There's a big ol' cock," Alexander notes as we walk past and up the stairs to the next floor, which is more populated. Men walk past me, it's a continuous flow of traffic back and forth in both directions. I follow the flow to the room nearest the back. We stand in the middle and peer around. Many of the men are just looking, intent on an unseen shape in the dark, waiting for a fantasy to materialize in flesh. Others wear blank faces. It's difficult to read their expressions. There isn't a lot of noise in the room. Only the movement of men pacing back and forth, watching in the dark for a motion, a sign, scanning our faces as we walk by.

I watch as two men approach each other from opposite ends of the room, walking straight toward each other in a steady, unbroken line. They stand nearly motionless for a few moments, looking with a detached intensity into each other's eyes. They pull out their dicks and jerk off. The men don't touch; only their eyes meet, a slight smile bending their lips. A faint clicking sound. Cocks out, straight. Closed hands move up and down on the length of their erections as they watch each other's faces and dicks. Jerking off and watching the other man do the same, wordless in the filling silence, gazing eye to eye, silent from start to finish.

We're not here to participate. Although I guess something could happen. But we didn't come here with that in mind. I'm the "straight guy" in the group, although I have no qualms with experimenting, if the mood should suit me. But what would I do, anyway? In this large, public space the options are limited. And surely, in this age of AIDS, one has to think constantly about safety. I'm not into giving blow jobs; the idea turns me off completely. I don't want to be on the receiving end of anal sex, which isn't allowed anymore in public spaces anyway. If I had a proper cock, one I could wrap my fist around, I might do what I see these guys doing, the jerking-off-and-looking-at-the-other-guy-as-he-jerks-off routine. Yes, this act would be possible, almost like a circle jerk, which so many guys participate in as adolescents, whether straight or gay. But I'm not sure, even then: Could I keep it up, get hard at all, would I have to think of women, of tits in my face?

I usually do have to think of women, of a woman, more specifically, getting fucked by my ample and rigid erection, in order to come. Her legs spread, or possibly her sitting on my cock and facing me. Her coming as I screw her, slowly then faster, at different angles. All the different strokes I can use. I'm hopelessly straight. These thoughts float through my mind as I stand and watch, peering around the room. Possibilities, curiosity, a sort of mild titillation, then a realization that this is fine to watch, but I don't think I want to go any further than that. Even if I had the equipment.

I've always been the great experimenter. Some transsexual men do experience a change of sexual orientation once they have been living in their new sex. The crucial element is that others relate to us as men and not women, and that we are able to relate to our own bodies as male and not female. I'm not talking about gender roles here, but specifically about *body*—the tangible physical presence of maleness. Everyone relates to other people and to the world in general from the vantage point of their physical body. The body provides the basis for exploration of feelings and sensations, erotic and otherwise. It is the grounding element. Relating to a man as a man from a male body is very different from relating to a man as a woman from a female body. This basic idea is difficult for many people to grasp, simply because most people take their bodies—the physical sex of their bodies—for granted.

Sexual orientation and gender identity are two different and distinct areas, though there is, of course, a relationship between them, just as there is a relationship between gender identity and body. This relationship may vary from individual to individual. Even within an individual person that relationship, between body and identity, between object attraction and individual gender subjectivity, can be fluid or nearly indefinable.

Many transsexuals who later identify as gay may actually have been bisexual to begin with, but were unable to express their attraction to men until after their body had masculinized. The power dynamics of being the female half of a heterosexual relationship may have been too difficult to navigate in a manner consistent with their internal sense of themselves as male. This is what I have surmised, although I cannot speak for these men, as I am not one of them.

As a woman, my sexual orientation was ostensibly lesbian. As a man, it is heterosexual. If I am still queer, it is because I was transsexual, not because of my sexual orientation. When I go to queer events, however, I often feel like I am the only straight person there, since most of the people are gay or lesbian. This alienation feels new and puzzling. Am I still queer? In some ways, the hardest thing to give up is identifying as queer, at least in terms of sexual orientation. To give up that marginal state, that realm of real or imagined subversion—outlaw status.

Jack knows better. He has a healthy dose of cynical disdain for everyone. He looks around the room and says, with knowing sarcasm, "I hate fags." Jack was a wily street punk in his teens who hung out with various punk and death-rock bands in L.A. before nearly burning out. But he survived. Now he's twenty-five, pale with black hair and beautiful light eyes framed by long lashes. Faunlike. There's a slinkiness to Jack, an aura of danger and boyish vulnerability. "Fags" to Jack means guys with sweater vests and airs, affectations of taste, guys who are super neat and clean, who blow dust motes off coffee cups that have already been washed and put on the shelves. Or else gay men who affect butchness with handlebar mustaches and tight jeans. Of course, Jack is a fag himself, and his sneering is the insider's prerogative; he feels that much of "gay culture" is too trite and self-congratulatory for words. However, straight people are from "the suburbs" and that is much worse. "The suburbs" are more a state of mind than an actual place. The suburbs are not outlaw. They are bland, and normal, there is no edge or inspiration. Everyone is a kind of glorified worker bee—the Stepford wives and the white, clean sterility of strip malls.

The truth is that there are many transsexuals, transgenders, perverts, fags, dykes, and talented free spirits in the actual suburbs. And there's the fact that most fags, dykes, transsexuals, and transgenders are just normal nice people, good decent folks. Average. Susie Bright has said that if you could peer into everyone's head, that everyone would be a pervert. I wonder if she's not giving most people more credit than they deserve. Then again, what if it were true? What if this droll observation becomes reality and we have a future world of explosive sexual perversity! America loves outlaws.

Being an outlaw always seems like the better deal.

Being an outlaw is so all-American. It's the Old West with six-shooters, that individualistic rugged attitude. It's Bonnie and Clyde, gangsters, gangstas. Glorious, wild, and on the edge, solitary, bloodthirsty, mad with the territoriality of the outsider.

These days, outlaws get a lot of their hubris, their detonating pleasure, from their status as victims, oddly enough. Outlaw has become victim. This seems to be particularly big in feminist circles. Victim culture and outlaw culture entwine and meet in a New Age, self-help head space. Women introduce themselves as a laundry list of abuses and strange outcomes of said abuses: "I'm a multiple personality, attention deficit disordered incest survivor and date rape survivor, and am allergic to chocolate, furry animals, and lightbulbs." Ultimately, oddly enough, victim is a more traditionally "feminine" choice, the choice of swooning fragility, of someone who needs to be protected, buffeted from the harsh realities of the world, whose sensitivities are nearly abnormally acute. Words sting, foods bring on allergies, bright flashing lights disturb and start seizures, pornography rapes, rock music eviscerates with aggression, memories of sexual abuse are invoked by lusty lyrics and male strutting. The world is one hell of a place to live in.

Since "transgender" is the new thing, introductions have become even more colorful: "I'm a stone butch, hyperfemme drag queen, fag dyke boi, transdaddy with a tiny voice inside that screams, 'Curl that hair, put on that dress, and wear those heels now!'"

In this century, we have gone from extended family, to nuclear family, to individual, to family of one. The individual is fractured all over the place, inside and out, a multiplicity of identities. We teem with ourselves. Who needs kids when you've got *identity?* Andy Warhol said that in the future, everyone would be famous for fifteen minutes. Little did he know that in the future, which is now, *everyone will be everyone and everything for as long as they can stand it.*

I remember that all of this self-labeling started out humbly enough. It also had more of a traditionally radical, political emphasis. When I came out as a plain old lesbian in 1975, we all sat in a circle and introduced ourselves one by one at the meeting of the Lesbian Caucus of the Women's Liberation Front on campus. Even then, women didn't just state their names. They always had lengthy rejoinders, subtle anthems. But things were simpler. "Hi, I'm Sally and I am a socialist feminist, not a separatist." "Hi, I'm Naomi and I am a socialist feminist who is against imperialism in all its forms, and I am leaning toward lesbian separatism." "Hello, my name is Janet. I'm a Marxist-Leninist and a lesbian feminist." "Hi, I'm Nadine. I am a lesbian separatist and a member of the Isis Women's Community Orchestra in upstate New York. We are trying to demystify the process of music making and clarify our struggles with class and women's oppression." When it came to me—eighteen years old, green, just arrived on campus, looking at the first really out lesbians I had seen in my entire life—I was scared to death. I cleared my throat. I had only just heard of this strange thing called "lesbian separatism" the week before. What to say? An impish impulse in me thought, *What if I say I am a Republican and I like girls?* No, that wouldn't do, that much was clear. I figured that Marx was probably right about some things. I had read *The Communist Manifesto* in high school as well as

Marcuse's *Eros and Civilization*. Socialism sounded sane, tenable. Of course, I *must* be a lesbian feminist. I was for the liberation and equality of women and lesbians, wasn't I? I also wanted to meet women. I figured I'd better do some studying to catch up on what I believed, solidify my politics. I hadn't realized that being attracted to women, declaring one-self a lesbian, could be so complicated. I took a deep breath and said in a scared voice, "I'm Anita and I'm a, uh . . . socialist, lesbian feminist." Couldn't go wrong with that. I got polite nods and a couple of smiles.

Things have come a long way for today's young lesbians. They have so many more choices. Just think what it must be like to be eighteen now in that same circle . . . there's lots more reading to do.

A few of my friends hope that I will become a gay man. Properly and permanently "queer identified"—and not a predatory threat to society or to the female sex. I've had moments when I've hoped it would happen as well. The suburbs beckon with shined and scrubbed children, PTA meetings, and docile women with bad hairstyles. Certainly, that couldn't be my final destination. Yet, although it is far outside the bounds of convention, ironically, being a gay man appears to be the safer option. Not focusing on women as my desire and romantic fascination would soften my edges and diffuse the nature of my masculine threat.

I walk around that night at the Church of Saint Priapus watching the men and considering this option foggily. As female, I had been with men a handful of times here and there. The first time I slept with a guy I was sixteen. Johnny was my friend Helga's older brother. A Vietnam vet who lived at home with his mother, Jet, who used to practice knife throwing at their dad, a small, kind, withered-looking man whom she towered over with her jet black hair and enormous weight. She was a witch, Helga said, and swore me to secrecy.

Johnny used to play guitar and talk in a soft voice. We listened to Leonard Cohen and Pink Floyd. I wanted Helga, actually. I had a crush on her that was scalding, but I was only sixteen and didn't know how to begin to really reach out and get what I desired. We all took acid one night, and Helga and I danced together in the trailer out by their small, run-down house, pressing our bodies together hesitantly, tenderly. Helga ran her hand across my cheek. Then I went inside their house and fucked her brother. It was my first time on acid, too. I figured, *Well, why not?*

I wanted to find out what these things were like—the famed LSD, sex with guys. Johnny was as good a candidate as any. He was handsome and kind, older. Twenty-four. I knew what I was doing and I did it willingly. The sex was over in a couple of minutes. The acid was lousy, too, but I was thankful at the time that it wasn't too intense. I remember thinking, *So is that all?* No wobbly elephants coming out of the walls or melting windows, no elegiac strains of eternity whistling into the corners of the room. And the fucking, the taking of my hymen, didn't really hurt, though I was horrified, in a way. The blood running down my leg afterward and the sight of his bloody dick, small and wrinkled looking, like a weird kind of turkey neck. Not appealing at all.

I could at least say I'd done *it*. When I was a teenager, I decided that I had to try everything once. I wanted to experience as much as I could of human sexuality, of consciousness-expanding drugs, of life. But I could never really get into kissing boys. I tried. They were always too big, too grabby, their bodies too hard. Tongues huge, moving into my mouth way too fast, thick and muscular. Muscular tongues, who wants to be on the receiving end of *that*? They just didn't feel right. These early feelings of repulsion, of physical distaste and discomfort, never completely changed. Although physical contact with men finally got to the point where it was not completely unbearable, I would never ignite.

However, I have come to appreciate male bodies, especially since I have begun my quest to achieve one. I enjoy looking, scrutinizing, and comparing myself, or just gazing with no goal. There is no question that the human male is a magnificent animal. But I still don't enjoy the actual physical contact. I don't fantasize about it, although I have attempted to push that envelope just to see what would happen in my head. I always end up thinking about a woman screaming in agonizing pleasure as I pump her. Considering all this, I smile wanly in the dark of the sex club, realizing my friends' hopes are likely to be in vain.

In the Church of Saint Priapus, the atmosphere is tense and soaked with a male sexuality that is anything but delicate or mincing—none of those stereotypes people associate with faggotry and fairydom. These are men in a most extreme male realm. Men together without having to tone down their sexual impulses for the purpose of attracting and holding a woman's attention. There are no honeyed words, no promises of "relationships," no "I love you's" in order to cop a quick feel. These guys are objectifying each other. They're cruising with an abandonment that borders on cruelty—a lustful, cruel rooting out of desired body parts. *Cut his head off, just look at this dick.* There's a "glory hole" area where anonymous mouths feed on cocks thrust through holes cut out of the board dividing the two rooms. Because of AIDS, no anal penetration is allowed, and the glory hole area is brightly lit so no one can sneak in his asshole in the dark. Press your dick through the board and get sucked off by an anonymous mouth waiting to receive on the other side.

This scene brought home to me in stark terms the differences between male and female sexuality. Although there are lesbian sex clubs in San Francisco, there is no equivalent to the glory hole. Glenda tells me about her experiences at a lesbian sex club in the early nineties. The evening started out with a lengthy discussion about safe sex techniques, including latex condoms over sex toys. A few women who looked as though they already knew each other went off into private areas to get it on, generally in couples. The rest of the group sat attentively listening to the lecture. At some point, Glenda says, the woman giving the talk asked, "Is there anyone here who hasn't been fucked, who needs to get fucked?" Two or three hands shot up shyly. Glenda says there was a lot of blushing, squirming, and discomfort. The unfucked ones had to talk about why it was that they hadn't been fucked yet and what they were going to do about it. Lots of talk, very little action. Lots of emphasis on fairness, safety, and civility, even in a sex-club atmosphere that aspires to Dionysus in a female form.

In 1985, as female, I'd been to a women's sex party—an S&M sex party—and certainly there were some wild women there who did some mean rope tricks. Selene and I tied a woman up and sprayed whipped cream on her, we chained two girls together and paddled them. Later, I fisted one in a sling. It was the first time I'd met this woman, so this was certainly casual sex. No doubt, women do casual sex—both straight and gay. But Selene had prearranged our meeting, and the atmosphere in the place was not as intensely impersonal, as fired with the heat of lustful sex for sex's sake as the holy church of St. Cock. Which meets not only at the proper Church of Saint Priapus, but also at Ringold Alley, where men cruise after hours once the bars close, or at the Amtrak restroom where I wandered in one afternoon and discovered all the stall doors ripped off and men—some who looked like just average married guys in polyester with slight paunches not having any gay fashion sense or stylistic cues, and some street guys in greasy jogging clothes and hair nets—wandered in and out with huge erections, staring at each other hungrily at the urinals, going off together in the open stalls. I had never seen anything like it, anywhere. At the dyke sex party, I was properly introduced to the woman I tied up and fisted. I had a conversation with her afterward, she got my number. She wanted to continue and called me up. Something tells me that most of these Amtrak restroom guys and Ringold Alley men are not exchanging numbers or even names; they may not even get a clear look at the other guy's face. If you're a straight guy, you have to pay for anonymous sex, generally speaking. If you are gay, it is all over the place. Especially in a town like San Francisco, but probably in many places all over the world, there are bus station restrooms, truck stops, gymnasium showers.

William Burroughs said, "I think that the whole antisex orientation of our society is basically manipulated by female interests."

I remember my reaction when I first encountered that quote at age fifteen in *Homosexual: Oppression and Liberation,* Dennis Altman's seminal book on gay liberation. I was puzzled and mildly offended. Altman offered this quote, taken from an interview that Burroughs did with Daniel Odier, as an example of "the quite fantastic misogyny of William Burroughs." Now, as an adult, after having lived through the antiporn feminists' tirades, and after becoming a man and experiencing sexuality from a hormonally biological male perspective, my reaction to this Burroughs quote has changed. Recently, I came across it again and was startled to find myself thinking, *You could make a case for that.*

I'm not always sure just what is true and what is not anymore. I used to be sure, I used to believe that I knew.

I wouldn't say that I agree with Burroughs. It isn't so simple. I believe that the final answer (if there is one) as to why sexuality is so rife with superstitious prudery, censorship, and lurid, skin-peeling debate is more complex than an omniscient, omnivorous coterie of "female interests." However, I can understand now why Burroughs, who also believed that romantic love was another female plot to ensnare and ruin men, would make such a statement coming from a starkly male perspective, a gay male perspective where women's concerns and compunctions about sex are not even a consideration. Women do seem to be trying to spoil the party sometimes, with their rules, their feminist analyses, their ladylike delicate sensibilities, their torrid accusations of sexual harassment and abuse, their demands for male accountability to feelings and romance, and finally, that c-word, commitment.

Alexander told me about a Queer Nation meeting in San Francisco in the early nineties and the problems that sprang up there between the lesbians and the gay men. The men had put up pictures of naked men with erections on a bulletin board, as emblems of a male sexual potency they loved and desired. To lust and admire openly another man's hard-on was an act of hard-won freedom for them, and they reveled in its display. However, many of the lesbians did not see things that way, they were incensed. A vocal few were upset enough to make a very loud stink. They wanted the men to take the photos down: They were traumatic and oppressive, they were ugly and crude, they reminded the women of their sexual abuse as children. Alexander and many of the other gay men were surprised and offended. How dare these lesbians tell them what kind of photos they could or could not post? And, they felt, the photos of the men with erections were beautiful, emblematic of the glory of male virility.

The lesbians who were upset screamed long and loud. Meetings were held, feelings were processed, shouting matches ensued. Eventually, the pictures were taken down. The "victims" won out. The "ladies" were upset by the "dirty" pictures of naked men and so the men took them away. Now, these "ladies" are at a Queer Nation meeting, they are pierced and tattooed dykes with lots of attitude and bluster with short hair or shaved heads and combat boots who pride themselves on their sex-positive attitudes and riot grrrl rebelliousness. Not Victorians, not Tipper Gore, certainly not Focus on the Family Christian bake sale ladies. *Isn't it amazing, how when things change, how much they remain the same?*

These sharp, nearly irreconcilable differences between men and women are driven primarily by testosterone, the hormone that creates and informs sexual desire in both men and women. This is what my experience has taught me. I laugh at the absurdity of it all. Socialization follows and augments biology, not the other way around. In *The Sexual Brain,* Simon LeVay says, "In sex as in so many other fields of action, consciousness may serve as much to rationalize instinctive behavior as to provide its real motivation."

Jack, Alexander, and I walk around and sample each room. Looking, nodding, listening. Downstairs there is a congenial barbeque area, hot dogs are roasting on the grill, buns are available. Here the guys relax, get into conversations, introduce themselves outside the arena of lust that goes on elsewhere in the church. Jack and I grab some beers, watch the night stars from lawn chairs set out on the patio. Alexander is philosophical, observant as always. He sighs, "I guess we came to the right place. The rituals of this church have a strong foundation in historical phallic obsessions. Snatch the loincloth off Jesus on the cross, what do we have? A totem of Priapus. What *were* all those monks and priests praying to, anyway?"

CHAPTER 32:
VENUS OF DATA ENTRY

D ebbie's a flirt. She's blond and pretty in a Midwestern sort of way, and I have to admit she's sexy in spite of the fact that I can so easily imagine her strolling through a shopping mall.

We're both working for a temp agency and have been sent out on a swing shift data-entry job. My first job as a man that's lasted more than a few months. I decided not to take up the possible opportunities for management positions. I don't want that type of responsibility. I needed time to stretch out and adjust to my changes. Now I feel ready to go out and into the world.

There's a guy named Mark who's around my age, with a full beard and long dark hair. Mark's always kidding around with me. Although I've managed to change my sex, I haven't managed to alter my generally rotten work habits. I have always made a point of coming into jobs five to ten minutes late. The hormones haven't changed that. Mark makes a point of giving me a hard time about this: "Hey, Max, late again!" he bellows in a loud voice when I creep in, worried that I'll be caught and read the riot act.

When Debbie, slender yet buxom, flirts with me, making jokes and lingering at my work area, Mark remarks on our age difference. "Max, I bet you have a ton of gray hairs under that black dye!" Debbie is only twenty-two, a sweet young thing, wide-eyed, just arrived in California from Cincinnati. I am thirty-four, although I look closer to her age. Still in my time warp, though yes, I dye my hair black on and off, a habit I picked up from my punk days.

I feel hurt by his teasing, although I know that's all it is. Will is working at a job at Pacific Bell. He's also made a male friend there, Larry. Larry's a painter, a leftist kind of guy who talks about feminism and herbal medicine. Yet Will always ends up feeling that somehow Larry is putting him down. It's the kidding around, the little rowdy remarks routinely delivered with a twinkle and a guffaw, like the time Larry teased him about stuffing his face at an office party. "Look at you, man, you are like a wild animal with that cake! Hey, Will, control yourself this once, leave me a slice, okay?"

Women don't talk to each other like this. Will and I discuss this odd fact one night when we are going over our prickly sensations about being teased, which to us feels like we are being made fun of. This is an aspect of being male we didn't anticipate, one we aren't used to. Women, even dykes—in fact, especially dykes, with their consciousness-raising, their endless processing, their "don't say that word, say this other politically correct term," their walking on eggshells to not hurt anyone's sensibilities, to make everyone feel included, their downward mobility, lowest common denominator leveling of talent and intellectual precocity—don't poke at each other in this jocular way. This is a masculine sport, a slice of male culture Will and I had never experienced.

Certain aspects of maleness can only be understood through the process of living them out. For us, this is resocialization. In other words, finding out the hard way.

There's actually a lot of affection in all that kidding around. "I guess ya gotta learn to roll with the punches." That's what Charley tells me his dad always says. "If you're a guy, ya gotta let things just roll off your back." Charley makes whacked-out jokes that to many seem "inappropriate." He is not as serious as Will. Together we do Beavis and Butt-Head imitations, chortling under our breath together as we intone with wild grins, "Heh heh heh breasts . . ."

Transsexual men get a lot of male socialization secondhand in our female childhood through looking up to, identifying with, and imitating male behaviors that we see in the media, our family, or our communities. However, we don't have insider's knowledge of many of these masculine behaviors and attitudes, since we were not expected to emulate them. Also, there are male attitudes and expectations that transmen were not exposed to as children, since we were not brought up in the male role.

We do get exposed, whether we like it or not, to female socialization. I learned how to put on a garter belt, buy tampons, smile at people, avoid weird strangers in cars, appease, and make nice verbally. I also learned a great deal about communicating through my years of processing as a feminist, although I really did hate those long-winded meetings when we'd all sit in a circle and someone would inevitably hold the whole thing up with her emotional tweaking. Perhaps my maleness leaked through even then, because many times I had no idea what these women were making such a big deal about. *What were they talking about?* On the other hand, the verbal articulation of nuances and undercurrents of feeling, being able to analyze and talk freely about my emotions, thoughts, and life situations is a skill I learned growing up as a girl, while talking to girlfriends on the phone as we picked apart our increasingly complex emotional lives, giving each other support and condolence. Estrogen does give that enhanced emotional volatility, that intensity to many of the "gushy" emotions. Possibly this is one reason why women are better able to perceive and verbalize emotions and complex interwoven entanglements of feeling. It's where women live.

There's no doubt Will and I talk on the phone more than the vast majority of guys. I'm sure there are other "phone queens" out there, but we are aware that we've picked this up from our days living as women. Well, it's not bad for us, and provides a cheap and clean form of entertainment. More guys should try it.

Which brings me to another interesting phenomenon. Many transsexual men report that testosterone has actually made them less verbally articulate. These men note that they find it harder to find the "right word." They're more prone to adding in "uhhh" and "yeah" into their conversations—filler words, longer spaces between words, more verbal groping and grasping for an accurate or even adequate term. I admit it does seem more difficult now to say exactly what I mean out loud. My speech doesn't seem as fluent, there are more stops and starts.

I joke with Will that if we had our conversations taped over time, perhaps we would be able to witness ourselves becoming less and less articulate, with more silent spaces and more grunting until finally, after a few years, we would be reduced to, "Hey, dude, what's up?" "Nothing much, man . . . uh . . . just sitting around, doing okay, uh . . . thinking about getting a job. Uh . . . you want to . . . uh . . . go out, or . . . uh?"

"Uh, maybe later, I want to just sit and watch somethin' here. It's called, uh, you know that thing? That soft-porn channel? Yeah . . . I couldn't believe it, gawd . . ."

This hypothetical downgrading of our conversational skills has brought us a lot of laughs, but I haven't noticed it getting quite so extreme. (Although Will and I have actually discussed the soft porn on late-night television through a series of unintelligible grunts and half-formed sentences.) In any case, I'm more aware that words are sometimes more difficult to access, that there are more of those "grop-ing for words" spaces in my speech patterns.

Also, I have noticed that when I'm emotional, it is even more diffi-cult to put my feelings into words. This is where women have a distinct advantage. I find it very hard now to explain or articulate my feelings when I'm actually in the throes of feeling them.

Thankfully, this hasn't carried over to my writing. Writing and speak-ing are distinct, controlled by two separate areas of the brain. Gram-mar is stored in the left hemisphere, and metaphor, rhyme, and song are found in the right. Also, one's handedness has a great deal to do with how the brain is structured insofar as language and spatial skills are con-cerned. The corpus callosum of lefties, whether male or female, has been found to be larger in size. This might enable at least some lefties to have better communication between the two halves of the brain, greasing our verbal ingenuity and skill. I can only pray. . . .

Of course, many men are extremely articulate and verbally adept. Possi-bly testosterone amps the aggression of male lawyers, or at least shortens and speeds their reaction times. In spite of my fumbling for words, I do interrupt conversations more often since I've been on testosterone. I feel more energized and it is difficult to contain myself. I notice that I react more quickly to stimuli, including noises or sudden occurrences. My re-flexes are on alert.

Certainly, these changes are relative to the individual. However, I think it's significant that many transmen do report less verbal agility, a straining at articulating out loud, particularly when emotional, once they are taking testosterone.

Debbie's flirtatious, alluring. The only problem is, she claims to be a les-bian. I talk to her about dyke culture—the Michigan Womyn's Music

Festival and rumored ancient matriarchal cultures such as the Amazons and Crete. I'm careful not to reveal why I know so much more about these topics than she does. Debbie's only just come out a year and a half ago, as long as I've been transitioning to living as male. There's a lot she doesn't know about the dyke world, however I don't think that I should necessarily be the one to fill her in.

Why, if she is a lesbian, is she flirting with me? Am I only imagining it? Does she suspect I am transsexual? Would that make a difference to her? Do I want it to? Is she picking up on some kind of female cue?

Juan, a young gay man Debbie pals around with, also works with us. He appears to be interested as well. I catch him staring at me from across the room. He's a drag queen, and I imagine he isn't bad, with his rotund body and swishy mannerisms. He brags in a loud voice that he won the Miss Drag Panama contest. "I have to shave my ass and legs and put on a wig, but girl, I am hot!"

I ask Debbie if she ever shaves her ass. She's aghast: *"Of course not!"*

Juan and Debbie talk about going out dancing at a gay bar and inviting the whole office to come along. I definitely have the hots for her. Debbie is sexy in a breathy Marilyn Monroe-ish way. One day, as I type in numbers and watch the clock, bored and restless, she stops her own data entry and saunters slowly to my desk, singing in a sultry tone the song, "I'm Gonna Wash That Man Right Outa My Hair." She gazes at me with a long simmering.

One night, we venture out to the gay nightclub, along with nearly everyone from the office. It turns out to be a dyke club called Quest, held twice a month in a large, warehouselike club near the Western Addition. Debbie and I stand around chatting amicably; I am wondering what will occur. Without warning, she wanders off and goes to the bar, buys a drink, and promptly picks up a tall blond woman. I stand around wondering how this entire scenario could have just happened. As female, I'd been attracted to straight women, and now, the first woman I have a flirtation with as a man is a lesbian! This predicament strains inside my brain all night as I watch Debbie dancing. What would she say if I told her about my past? Would it make a difference? Outside the club, as rain is beginning to sprinkle, I test this impulse. "Debbie, I was once a lesbian."

"What's this, Max, a past life?" she asks, looking amused.

It's impossible. I can't tell her now. I breathe and pause, "Well, sorta. . . ."

She's smiling at me like I'm some kind of nut.

"Ah, nothing. I didn't mean anything by it. I'm just joking." I look down at the sidewalk, then across the street through the wet air, feigning a sheepishness I don't feel. I know what Debbie thinks. Here I am, a man trying to get into her pants by telling her I was a lesbian in a past life. In a really weird way, it's true; I *am* hoping this will make her more open to me.

After taking it back, I walk with Debbie back into the club. We decide to leave, and her date is coming with us. We all pile in Juan's car to go home. Debbie's pickup is a loud Southern woman with an Arkansas accent. She keeps talking about Debbie as though she isn't there. "That little thing, she can dance!" "That little thing, she is one sexy little woman, I tell you!" "Did you see what she's wearin'? She was squirmin' around on that dance floor . . . yee-hah!"

Debbie seems amused. Apparently, this loud commentary doesn't turn her off. I sit in the back seat, wondering at the strange twists my life has taken.

Eventually, I tell Debbie that I'm transsexual. Once she's over her initial disbelief, she ends up telling me that yes, she is attracted to me, she has been flirting with me, and yes, she is occasionally still attracted to guys. "Gee, I couldn't tell," she exclaims. But when all is said and done, I am a man now and so she can't follow through with her attraction. "I'm a lesbian," she declares. For the first time in my life, I will be rejected for being a man. It appears that, after a couple of years, I have definitively arrived.

It's a bittersweet milestone for me.

Eventually, this night at the club will feel like an odd misadventure. My interest in Debbie will fade and this rinky-dink night job will end. I know this will happen no matter what, and I nod as the lights of the city flash by the car window. But right now, in the back seat of Juan's car, the woman from Arkansas is still whooping up a storm about Debbie's sexy hooters, her wiggly behind, and tight dress! She yelps and grins. The window is a panorama of blurred lights, someone is smoking in the front seat. I watch Debbie listen with a coy face. I know that I couldn't talk like that even if I wanted to. I would be seen as one hell of a male chauvinist pig.

CHAPTER 33:
MAN WITH BREASTS

If I was Madonna, I'd, like, fondle my boobs constantly.
—Beavis (of *Beavis and Butt-Head*)

After two years on male hormones, I'm way past any comparison to Madonna, but I do discover nipple sensation. I've never had erotic nipple sensation in my entire life. I've never known what women were feeling when I touched their breasts or nipples, only that I loved to do it and they certainly seemed to appreciate the gesture.

When Will and I saw the movie *Switch,* we both felt a real identification with the main character, a man who one day wakes up transformed into a woman. There he is, suddenly a dizzy bleached blonde, teetering on high heels, shocked to look down and realize that he doesn't have a penis anymore, feeling like a weird klutz in women's clothes. We both laugh at the way he, now she, comes barging through the door with her hand stuck down her blouse, squeezing her breasts like they're wild rubber toys. She races to the phone and calls up her best male buddy, frantic with the discovery of her very own busty pinup girl yelling into the receiver, "Hey, I'm stacked!"

Yeah, that's the feeling.

A friend from high school, Rick, tells me that I used to complain in high school and college that my breasts were too big, that I wished they were smaller. "Afterward" he tells me, "you would get embarrassed by this complaining and say that you didn't really mean it."

In retrospect, they actually weren't that big. Only a 34B or 36B. Medium size. But to me, they seemed huge. It took years before I got an accurate sense of their size.

By the time I got to university, I was already developing that lesbian feminist coating of wishful thinking concerning my feelings about my body and supposed "womanhood." I was an emanation of the goddess. I looked at the round, curvy figures in lesbian art and tried to identify.

This image rang hollow for me; it didn't arouse my passions. Yet I've always had the fantasy of women raking their fingers across my bare, hard chest. Sexy soft fingertips touching my taut body, a male body, dusky with sweat.

I realize now how when I wore a man's undershirt, a so-called wife-beater, I always unconsciously thought of myself as having a sort of male chest. Tama would sit looking at me in my man's undershirt at breakfast, her eyes shining. I felt she saw virility. Now I realize that she must have been looking at my breasts. Well, maybe I had virile breasts.

Much like a woman with an eating disorder who is skinny and thinks she is fat when she looks in the mirror, the actual reality of my female body was not always evident to me. My mental image of myself was often more male than I was in reality. Situations would inevitably occur that would make it extremely difficult for me to not be aware, acutely, that I actually had breasts and not a flat chest. Situations I often worked to avoid.

Long before I became Max, I decided to give up the grim task of allowing women to touch my breasts when we had sex. I'd tried my best to appreciate this inevitable moment. I'd close my eyes and attempt to feel pleasure, breathe deep—but feel nothing. Having someone touch my breasts felt intrusive, unnatural. I'd grit my teeth and feel tense. Faintly embarrassed. Having my breasts fondled was like having an exam at a doctor's office. Nothing. *No* feeling at all. My bed partners may as well have been squeezing my wrists. Those breasts didn't really seem like parts of *my* body.

My breasts had simply been attached, and over the years I'd adjusted. I was aware of them from time to time, and if I could be objective about it, and not think of them as *mine* in the most acute sense, I realized that these breasts, my breasts—were attractive. . . . In a bikini, they didn't look half-bad. It wasn't that I hated my body, I just had a difficult time relating to it completely as—mine.

I knew by the age of twenty-five that most women (apparently) enjoy having their breasts touched. They experienced their breasts as integral to their self, they had sensation, they connected.

And I enjoyed that connection. I loved touching breasts. No doubt about it. Still do. I'm a tit man. Love to fondle, squeeze, suck, and kiss a woman's breasts and nipples. Bring her to orgasm that way if possible. I always have, it's a natural impulse, the impulse to get to "second base," reach up inside her tight soft sweater and squeeze.

It's a lazy and long afternoon, and I finally have time to catch up on some long-delayed reading. Flipping through a porn magazine, my eye is caught by a singular, pulsating image. A guy is sucking on a woman's tits as he fucks her. She's facing him, he is deep inside her. He looks completely blissed-out.

I can identify with this guy. I hunker down on my futon. Imagine a woman sitting on my cock, swinging her tits in my face. I have a strange impulse. What will happen if I squeeze my own nipple? Forbidden territory. Do I dare to touch my own breasts? Yet today the idea of touching them has an intriguing hook. I am alone. No one can see. *Who will know?* I ask myself.

So I do it. I touch my own chest, sweep my fingers up to my nipple . . . I feel erotic sensation!

How ironic, to finally experience pleasurable sensation in a female part of my body, now that I am on testosterone and becoming a man! *Is this normal?* Worried, I call up Will and ask if he knows anything about this. He does. In fact, when I spoke to other transsexual men, I found that many do. This is high irony. Apparently, many transmen had never experienced feeling in their nipples before taking testosterone, and now, with the hormones, they do. Some report elaborate and twisty fantasies surfacing once they're on testosterone, before getting their top surgery. Fucking the daylights out of some woman, squeezing on her tits, while squeezing your own nipples and fantasizing they're hers! The objectification of one's own female body parts. One guy said this was like having your own harem, right in your room, in your bed even, always available!

Does this sound pretty out there? Don't worry, I thought so, too. I also found that the best way for me to enjoy this newfound sensation was to imagine that my breasts were someone else's. A real hot girl with great tits.

When Will and I recounted these odd idylls we laughed. This was truly bizarre. To have that kind of distance from your own body—to be able to turn it into someone else's. Surely I shouldn't tell a soul. Who would understand? And it was embarrassing. I mean, these were my breasts, I guess. Somehow the idea that I actually had breasts was still removed from who I felt I was, even though I now felt sensation.

I talked to other transmen about this sudden and unheralded gaining of sensation in areas of the body we'd never identified with. Some guys never had any erotic sensation in their vaginas until starting male hormones. This transformation is the ultimate irony. They were not quite sure what to make of it, but some took advantage of this newfound source of pleasure and sensation. One guy justified exercising his right to explore this previously unspeakable female netherworld by declaring, "If nontranssexual guys had vaginas, they would probably be sticking things up there all the time!" He's probably not completely off base. After all, men who are willing to experiment with anal penetration, whether gay or straight, experience pleasurable erotic feelings because of the prostate gland. And pleasurable erotic feelings are an important dietary requirement for most men. Transsexual men don't have prostates, but we do have G-spots, which are analogous.

Many transmen have experiences like these, where areas of our bodies that had previously been in sleep mode suddenly wake up. We talk about why this is. Is it that, now, being men in the world, with our bodies virilized, we are more comfortable with our physical selves and can accept the "female" parts more easily? Whatever the reason, transmen don't think of these parts as entirely female even when we do start using them for pleasure. We *are* men with vaginas. A new concept, one whose time has come.

Possibly, another word is needed for this quixotic state of affairs, maybe "manginas." Or, if that's too gimmicky, there are other terms out there. Some call it "the tranny hole" or the more generic "front hole."

Although it is a feat of imagination, many transmen think of their vaginas as part of their cocks. My friend Sam laughs when he tells me that he fantasizes that his vagina is part of his penis that has been shoved up inside him, maybe by space aliens at birth. Sam also fantasizes, like many transmen who use their vaginas occasionally for sexual sensation, that his vagina is part of his balls or the root of his penis, which glides up inside nontranssexual men and anchors their cocks in their bodies. When his uterus contracts in orgasm, he translates the sensations as those of his ejaculate shooting out.

Was it just because we were so damn horny that we didn't care one way or the other anymore? On the other hand, some transsexual men don't experience these surprising erotic awakenings, or at least don't mention them. Everyone is different and there are no rules.

Breasts are a phenomenon.

Will declares one day how he realizes that women like him better if he doesn't stare at their breasts while he talks to them. As a dyke, Will had gone through a long, relentless phase in which he preached that breasts were not for sex, but only for giving milk to babies. He felt that the patriarchy was the sole reason that breasts had been eroticized and fetishized. Will realized that this notion was a little off the mark before he made his change, but he had not been a big tit watcher nevertheless. After taking testosterone, this relative indifference evaporated and he is only now beginning to adjust to the fantastic and eloquent infusion of sexual magnetism into the breasts of the women he sees each and every day! Now, even if it can be argued that this is an intrusive and evil patriarchal influence, he no longer cares.

My mother used to brag about how she would get bras made with underwire support from traveling bra salespeople. I'm not sure if these traveling bra salespeople came right out to the houses on the reserve, traveling along the gravel roads in the remote night to the Indians' houses out by the deer and the bobcats to sell their underwire bras to the young Native women, or whether they came out to the Catholic boarding schools and got the French nuns to allow them to hawk their underwire bras there. For whatever reason, the fact that she'd worn underwire bras made Mom proud and she threatened to get the same for me on principle. Bras that were sturdy, wire-bound, manufactured to give support that would last a lifetime. No sagging, no gyrating, no unsupported tender flesh, no fascinating movements.

When I was an adolescent, it had been tough for my mom to get me to wear a bra at all. Bras should be burned, I thought.

Bras, breasts, bra burning, Wonderbras, cleavage, sagging tits, tits with luminescent curves, bras with underwire cups . . . My own breasts, if I could bear to contemplate them at all, had become flatter than pancakes from the hormones. Inert. A lot of transmen I know who haven't gotten top surgery yet have breasts covered with hair. Hair on the chest. My chest was smooth, I liked that. But the breasts had to go. They definitely put a dent in my male image, even if normally no one could see them because of the binding. But where to come up with the money?

I imagine saving, saving, and saving. But I have to face it. Saving is not my forte. I am reckless with money. I don't even work steadily most of the time. I write poetry, do idiosyncratic, intense performances. What money is there in that?

I could be like Rimbaud. Go off and be a businessman, get practical, abdicate the muse. Working in San Francisco's Financial District is almost like working in the Abyssinian desert—dry, parched, an expanse of unbroken claustrophobic tedium. And I'm not always writing anyway. I write in fits and spurts. Also I have retreated from performing since beginning my transition. I can't go up on stage at this point. I am still being strategic, conserving mental and emotional energy.

Even so, saving thousands of dollars is no easy task. And I need money. I have to have money for the surgery . . . and first, most crucially, the top surgery. Whack those tits off! I sometimes feel that I can't take the binding anymore, or the absurd pain and unsightliness of knowing what is beneath it, of being a man with a pair of stringy knockers.

I wear layers. I am lucky since I don't have huge breasts. I only have to wear a couple of pieces of clothing to disguise the bulging contour. A T-shirt and a heavier shirt over it. I can get away with only a T-shirt, since the binder makes me so flat, but then I am paranoid about my binding showing. Even so, strapping my tits in has become easier over the last couple of years as my breasts become progressively more deflated from lack of estrogen and lose their punch. I snap the binder closed in front with an indrawn breath and march out to meet each day. Rarely does anyone see me without this piece of elastic on, and never does anyone see my breasts. The binder is becoming a part of me. This experience proves to me that a person can get used to anything.

The tight corsets and powdered wigs people used to wear in earlier centuries . . . the bustles, the wooden dentures. I have a hard time breathing, but eventually endure even vigorous exercise with my binder on. I run up to five miles or dance wildly in an ecstatic sweat. Damn thing keeps falling down, worse than my old bra straps, which I would feebly yank back up, only to have them fall again. The binder is worse than a bra—a sweaty expanse of elastic and cotton that loses its snap over time and I have to buy another. I go back in to Eva's Corset Emporium, where Eva gives me a snide sideways look and silently grabs a box from her shelf, sneering, "You still got that back trouble?"

I take off the binder and peer into the mirror, trying to imagine what I will look like when I am finally free of these breasts. . . . Hard to look, hard to see the two shapes hanging there, they get in the way of the nascent male form shaping underneath and around them. Do I have pecs yet? I stand up straight and focus on the shape and contour of my chest muscles. My pecs are in there somewhere. I pose front and side. Make a muscle, stand up as straight as I can. I can flare my lats. That's new. I never had lats like these as female, and I hardly ever work out these days. If I do work out, my lats stand out even stronger—male markings. In some ways, the musculature on the human male is analogous to the bright markings of birds or the manes of male lions, the developed and flamboyant physical features of males in nature.

In the old days, Plains Indian men would parade on their ponies around the camp. Many had paint on their faces and bear grease—like pomade—in their hair. They were showing off, exhibiting their beauty to the women, who would then pick from among them. Once mirrors were introduced into the tribes, it was not unusual to see a young man gazing into the mirror to check his appearance. Vanity and masculinity were not considered to be in conflict. Men were often expected to be vain, careful and proud of their appearance.

I am beginning to understand male beauty. I pick out the male bodies I want to emulate and begin to figure out which ones I *actually am able to* emulate. Genetics are genetics, and there's more to musculature than exercise and diet, although some of our physique is under our control. I gaze at the male form and at my own prescient shape. I am emerging.

The breasts constrain me. Hobble me, take my posture down a notch with the binding's pull. I push out my belly and waist as the binder cinches me tight. I am imprisoned. There's no way out I can see, although it must be there. There must be a way, and I wait for the answer to come. Waiting, scheming, trying to have faith.

Taking off these breasts will be like unfastening a couple of deflated balloons. I want that contour, tight and masculine. I fantasize about finally being able to work out in a gym without worrying about the binding. Being able to see my pecs, instead of having them disappear under my flesh. Being seen as a man, feeling manly in my body without these barriers. I can't wait. I can't wait, but I have to.

CHAPTER 34: NORMAL GUY

At home at my place on Folsom Street, I have a room fit for a writer—cramped with boxes, stuffed with books, an electric typewriter on a blue-and-silver typewriter table in the middle of the room. There's a sink in the corner, papers scattered and piled, and a large window looking out over the street. Folsom Street is lively and home to trendy straight nightclubs and lots of gay leather and S&M bars. At BrainWash, a Laundromat café just a stroll down the street from my room, I begin most mornings with a latte. Read the paper. The day expands as I watch and analyze people walking in and out of the place, ordering their meals, stepping out into the street.

I'm writing again. After a series of poems, I work on a series of prose pieces. The poems don't appear to be affected by my transition in any way, though it appears that the testosterone is making my prose more blatantly sexual, aggressive, reflective of the way my mind has come to work. I write a couple of erotic stories in a flash, swept up in this new energy.

No wonder Burroughs wrote the way he did! All those boys, naked, getting fucked, coming on every other page. It all makes sense now—the long masturbatory fantasies of Genet, *Our Lady of the Flowers,* and the Marquis de Sade with his florid, violent, sexual imagination flowering with blood and sperm, moans and sex, in every position with every possible type of person in each and every book. Henry Miller with his endless cunt and the land of fuck.

That amoral driving quality, obsessive, hard-edged, cold, and nearly abstract in its salacious fury, feels more male than female overall. Although there are women who write with insatiable sexual appetite and aplomb: Erica Jong, Pat Califia, who since has become a transman, and the late Kathy Acker, with her long postmodern pornographic rants. Certainly, sexual writing isn't a strictly male realm. Looking back, I'd always had a sexual, dark quality to all my writing, pulled taut beneath the surface of the images and sounds. A visceral, gut-pulling amorality that always bothered the do-gooders of the world, the fainthearted. Even so, there's a definite shift. On testosterone, the sex has taken over, driving the work more than ever before. The same way sex drives my mind.

I take more breaks from writing.

Jerking off and coming back to the task at hand. My sexual imagination on fire.

For work, I've settled in at Time-Life Books, where I have a job selling videos and CDs over the phone. Selling on the phone, something I've done on and off for years. Didn't want to go back to it; I thought I'd finally left the slick talking and endless manic dialing. But work is slow. It's 1992 and we're in a recession.

On the night shift there are long-haired heavy metal musicians, ex-used-car salesmen, former housewives, and Tom, a guy from Salt Lake

City who just got to San Francisco and is looking around for a better job. Meanwhile, he's here, well scrubbed, with a sleepy expression, in a plaid shirt and Dockers. Although I wouldn't ask him for fashion advice, I would ask him to lend me five bucks. Tom is a friendly, jocular guy, approachable and unpretentious.

Taylor is a musician with long, dark hair and large, expressive eyes, lots of earrings on each ear and tight, ball-choking jeans. He used to work as a manager at the O'Farrell Theater and tells me how he would just stand there and play with the strippers' breasts while he looked straight into their eyes, without betraying any emotion or arousal. "That really gets them going, man. Playing with these girls' tits, staring right into their eyes . . ."

"Sounds like a great job, man," I say. And it does.

Taylor tells me these tit-fondling stories after work at night. On the narrow island, waiting for a bus, he breaks into his stripper stories, eyes glowing.

A part of me is thinking, *I like hearing this tale and I probably shouldn't. Here I am laughing at what many would consider a sexist story.* But no female ears are present, and I understand instinctively that this is "guy talk." If I were still a woman, this wouldn't happen. Taylor wouldn't be talking to me like this. He'd probably be putting the make on me.

The context for my thoughts and feelings has changed. Values and feelings collide. Memories are framed in my new experience of manhood. I remember what it was like on the other end of this male lust. Even so, I decided a while back that I didn't want to be the kind of man who was apologetic about being male. It's mawkish, smacking of manipulation and a self-conscious insincerity. The last thing I want is to become a "sensitive man," speaking loudly for all to hear about how in touch with my "female energy" I am. Or the transmale version of that, proclaiming how I am so different from all those other "sexist and patriarchal genetic men," since I was brought up female and not socialized as male. I have always found these types of proclamations to be an oddly irritating form of sanctimonious ass-kissing, or a surreptitious male braggadocio.

Still, I feel uneasy. I am not sure how to ethically evaluate my reaction yet, since it is mixed in with many feelings. Being so completely one of the guys is a new experience. Part of me is still surprised that Taylor is talking to me about sex and women. I am passing regularly and with no effort; in fact, even when I tell someone and the incriminating conversation is overheard, the eavesdropper doesn't know what to make of it. The idea that I am a transsexual, that I was born female, is the furthest idea from anyone's mind. I still find this hard to entirely believe.

Yet, it appears to be so. Juan, at my old night data-entry job, was convinced that I was a genetic gay man, even after he realized that I had a crush on Debbie. After I came out to Debbie as a transman, she regularly asked me questions about the hormones. I noticed that Juan occasionally seemed to be listening in from his cubicle, catching bits and pieces of our conversations. Apparently, Juan concocted an elaborate story to account for overhearing us use the word *hormones*. He began to spread a rumor around the office that I had been a hustler on Polk Street in my late teens and that I'd taken female hormones and dressed in drag. At some point, I apparently decided to go straight and give it all up, and here I was today, lusting after Debbie. He was convinced that deep in my heart I was really a queen. Someday, I would go back to my former gay ways, he predicted. He refused to believe anything else about me, no matter what Debbie said.

I'm staking out my territory, trying on different roles and attitudes. What kind of man do I seem to be to other people? Obviously, it's hard to know for sure.

Tonight, my supervisor, Fidela Adams, named by hippie parents for Fidel Castro, paces and struts. Fidela is a short, plump woman with red hair teased at the sides. She's in her early twenties but looks older, not because she's prematurely aged but because she is so perky, so saleswoman-like, so careerist. It's hard to believe that her parents were hippies. She's a real talker, able to go a mile a minute when she's giving us pep talks. I've been in a number of phone rooms over the years and it's always like this. There's someone front and center getting everyone tanked up with adrenaline and hype: "Money, there is money to be made, ladies and gentleman. Dial dial dial. Don't take *no* for an answer. That word does not exist. Let these people say yes to you. Give them a reason to say yes to you. They *want* to say yes." Fidela ends her speech in a paroxysm of screams, her face exploding in a series of wacky expressions, P. T. Barnum meets est.

It's crazy work, exhausting, stressful. A hurtling contest of will, grit, manipulative skill. I'm good at it, but never one of the biggest players. Dogged, aggressive, but not always consistent. My sales soar, then go down. I have a hard time sustaining the mood. Still, I'm one of the better salespeople, and I stay on long past the time when most of the others who started with me have been fired or left. I have recently embarked on one of many attempts to save the money needed for my top surgery. I'm working two phone jobs and counting up the dollars.

Fidela is joking around with the guys in the first couple of rows, exchanging repartee with Taylor and Tom. We all have our phones glued to our ears. Dialing in between smiles. Suddenly Fidela declares in a fit of inspiration, "Max is the most normal guy in here."

Taylor looks sideways at me, "Yeah, Max, we know that's true." I know he's saying I'm a square or a dweeb, normal as in *the norm,* dull. Tom, whom *I* perceive as Mr. Normal, nods and agrees.

"Yes, Max is the most normal guy in here." Fidela's gaze is fixed on me. She isn't putting me down, simply stating what she believes as fact.

I'm taken by surprise. I squirm. I've never prided myself on normalcy; it has always felt too close to conformity, although actually they are distinct. This idea about me is ironic. *If only they knew,* I think. I want to shout out in pride, *No, I am* not *normal. I am the weirdest guy in this place!* I want to twist a devilish grin and say it loud, *I'm weird, I'm a freak, I'm an outlaw, and I'm proud!*

Taylor is looking snide and smug. "Yeah, Max, face it, you *are* Mr. Normal."

Confusion. . . . Maybe it's good that they see me as so normal. I guess I am *making* it now . . . I'm a "real" guy, indistinct from any other guy, ordinary in my masculinity. It's been a year since Juan thought I was an ex–drag queen and hustler. I am now three years into the change. Have I changed so much? The idea that people would perceive me in this way is so new that I find it difficult to believe.

Alarms go off in my head. No, I don't want to be "normal"! Not that kind of normal, the bland normal. True, I do have a certain stability in my demeanor, but what is Fidela seeing?

"You don't know, Taylor," I say, feeling defensive.

"Oh, yes I do, Max, you are the most normal guy here," he replies.

"Sure . . ." I want be above it all, to let it roll off my back, but I am unconvincing. Then the irony hits me in waves. I begin to laugh.

Fidela stares at me; she blinks. A doubt clouds her features. *Of course, he does have that weird laugh; who knows what that weird laugh really means?*

My laugh has been determined to be "weird" since adolescence, it's the laugh of a demonic robot or a prerecorded laugh track, fake or faintly malevolent. When I transitioned, it simply went down a couple of octaves.

I laugh again, a knowing, vibrating ha ha ha hah. Fidela is gazing at me, puzzling over this mystery, knitting the elements in her brain.

I walk home that night and can't stop thinking about her remark. I'm slightly stunned. Normal . . . I couldn't be *normal.* I mean, I don't want to be seen as crazy, as sick or twisted or anything, but . . . normal? I am devastated. Should I get a piercing on my face, shave my hair off again and bleach it, get some visible tattoos? What am I doing wrong? Is it something about my manner? *Why?* All the way walking to Folsom Street I think about this new concept. At home I'll gaze into the mirror with a question mark. Normal. The most normal guy in the place. Me.

CHAPTER 35:
COCK IN MY POCKET

**I just wanna fuck
this ain't no romance**
—Iggy Pop, "Cock in My Pocket"

Sex is like a feast now—an absolute smorgasbord. I am in a porn store in the Tenderloin; I'm here almost by accident, on a whim while walking by. Suddenly, I feel an insatiable rush. I grab through the magazines. There's all kinds of stuff: women over forty, fat women, girls who like to fuck big cocks, women in bondage, motorcycle sluts, white women with black men, black women with white men, Asian women with black and with white men, black and white women with Asian men, women with breasts so huge that they can barely walk, women with tiny breasts, women dressed like little girls, snarling dominatrices tying men up and stabbing their balls with stiletto heels, women being paddled over the knees of men or women, women being fucked in every conceivable and inconceivable position in almost any environment you could wish for—beaches, barracks, classrooms, cafeterias, crosswalks—and in the background of the store, on television monitors, women moaning in orgasm. And the other men here, all of us, are wolves, a pack of wolves, hungry, panting in excitement.

With a jolt I see myself here in this store with all these men, one of them. No one can pick me out as being different in any way. *Here I am, once a lesbian feminist, now a hungry wolflike man in a porn store, browsing girlie magazines.*

I go up to the counter and get five dollars' worth of tokens for the video arcade, impatient. *Make that change fast, man, I've got to get off, now.* Up the stairs, into a booth—which one? In and out of doors in a hurry, some of the booths smell bad, acrid from semen. Finally, I get into one that seems clean and search for the knobs in the dark. Lock the door shut. There, in the flickering light of the small screen I undo my pants and reach for my clit, which is big from testosterone now—a small penis. Hold it between thumb and forefinger, stroke up and down, like a cock, up and down fast. Flip through the channels with frenetic intensity.

There is a texture to my sexual fantasies that is different now. I was always more of a "top"—more dominant in my fantasies, aggressive, the pursuer not the pursued—as female. Yet now, on testosterone and fueled by the contrast of male and female bodies, that context of edges and vulnerability, my fantasies are more aggressive than ever.

Standing next to Laura, a coworker, at break time, I slide into an expanding sexual dream. Lately, we've been flirting, and suddenly she's standing at a nearly intimate distance. So close, in high heels and a black dress, tight and revealing of large, perfumed breasts. I can smell her fragrance, a sweet scent, flower petals crushed under the tongue of a bull. I watch her breasts move under the taut stretch of black, her nipples outlined and erect, her tits globes, wet melons. I imagine tasting them. In heels, she's teetering off balance, just a little. If she falls, I could catch her. Standing there, face-to-face with her in that outfit, I simmer in the intensity of this new male sex drive, the aggression of it. I have to hold myself back to keep from touching her. A sheer effort of will, I grit my teeth. I want to fuck her so bad, grab her and throw her down on the floor and fuck her so hard she aches for days. This impulse almost overpowers my better sense. It's so strong, a rush of white lust from groin to gut to flaming solar plexus, a hard stretch of flame. The eyes of the bull inflamed and entranced by the red cloth. I have to stop and take stock. This feeling is different in intensity from anything I'd known before in its pleading for release.

No wonder guys lose it sometimes, I think. *How can they not?* In the beginning, I think this a lot. *My god, if this is how men feel, how come they don't rape more often? Rape and plunder. Take.*

It is wrong to rape. I knew that before; I know that still. Any man who acts out these fantasies or impulses, no matter how strong, is doing a wrong act, an abominable act, and should be punished. Even so, I understand now the force of will it can take to keep from running wild with these feelings, the temptation.

Rape is an act of violent sex. Power and sex are entwined, joined in ancient communion within the brain, in the hypothalamus, seat of the id. Many people feel more powerful when they feel sexual; many people are turned on by other people's power or lack of power, aroused by their strength and perceived ability to vanquish and control, or their vulnerability, their fragility. This is as ancient as hunter and hunted, prey and predator, the abduction of Persephone by Hades and the tender romance of Beauty and the Beast.

I've talked to many transsexual guys who wonder out loud, "If we had normal penises, would we rape?" With that piece of meat dangling between our legs, so easy, so ready. Will tells me that he got turned on one night when he realized that a woman he was walking behind was afraid of him. This was a new feeling, scary and strange. He didn't know what to make of it.

This jacked-up sex drive freaked out another transman I know so much that he stayed inside for his first few months on testosterone, afraid to go out, unsure of what he might do. In time, the jagged edges of these sexual feelings become less intense. We grow into our new sex drive and learn how to deal with it. Even so, some transmen say in dark tones, half-scared, drunk on libido, and hallucinating sexual abandon, *I might do it, I could rape a woman. Maybe I couldn't control myself.*

I would not rape a woman. And I bet these guys wouldn't, either. But the stuff we take—that virile hormone testosterone—grabs you by the edges of your scalp and holds you tight. You begin to wonder. And if *we* wonder, knowing what it's like on the other side of the threat, knowing how afraid and vulnerable a woman can feel, what must it be like for nontranssexual men?

Around this time I went with my friend Aleister to the Exotic Erotic New Year's Ball, a colorful San Francisco cavalcade of costumes, bands, and naked people. There are hardly any naked babes to be seen, mostly just out-of-shape pasty-skinned middle-aged men with leers smeared on their faces. I'm disappointed. Aleister and I wander around with beers in our hands, watching the celebration and the yuppie band playing soggy rock music.

At the end of the evening, a woman begins to masturbate with criminal glee. She looks as though she's in a trance. She has on a red corset. She's yanked off her silk panties for the occasion, leaving them crumpled beside her. She pulls her breasts out and over her bustier and stares into the distance as she fingers herself. The light is dim and shines all over her body with a sticky yellow glow. Men begin to gather around her, a crowd that grows from every angle, an approach of sentinels with transfixed faces. Male animals driven by the sight of a female lifting her ass into the air, making anguished lustful cries. A pack of men, muscular and strong-breathed, breathing down on this lone woman touching her pussy with light, dancing fingers. She keeps on, circling her clit with an expert touch, finely honed, as though she's massaging a jewel. I walk in closer; the crowd tightens around her, a noose of bodies. I realize all at once, *I am a man drawn by hypnotic power to this woman, to watch her.* The men are tense with sexual feeling. I am one of them, turned on like being branded by hell's irons. I feel the surge of it, a force close to unstoppable.

We breathe down on her in that clamp of bodies, all the men now sweating, frantic with excitement. She begins to give one man a blow job, her lips sliding up and down along the length of his pole. Everyone watches, tight, not moving, transfixed. "Let her breathe! Back up and let her breathe!" one guy's yelling from within the crowd. I keep watching myself and watching the crowd and watching her, feeling only a dim ability to control this strong urge. "Let her breathe!" The guys are not moving. What will happen? Then some begin to back up, just a step. The crowd's chomping at the bit, close to pandemonium, reeling at the edge of mob violence. Tail hook, panty raids, gang rape—men often commit acts in groups that they wouldn't alone. It must be what those situations feel like, in the beginning, when they are contained, before all hell breaks loose. A vein of violence pulses beneath the surface. I can barely move back. I'm enthralled, held by fascinated lust and the thick movement of the group. I force myself to move back a few steps with a mechanical effort, *because it is right, because I have to*—sheer moral force.

It's breathtaking to watch this happening, to be in it and of it. A man in a crowd on the edge of . . . what? What could we and might we do if we could get away with it? What are we almost about to do to that woman?

I walk with Aleister to the band area, shake off the arousal I feel. We stand for a while and watch the band, then walk home in blazing rain. My umbrella snaps in the storm, and I watch as it tangles up in the gutter, a maze of steel spokes and torn black cloth.

CHAPTER 36: JULIET

Juliet's from Australia, with shoulder-length dyed black hair and an impish expression. She wears baby-girl clothes, or tights and long silky men's shirts, tuxedo jackets. Tiny dresses that hike up even higher when she saunters down the center of the room. Juliet has a mischievous glint in her eye. When I point her out to my friend Charley, who has just started at the job on a tip from me, he proclaims, "That girl's got a body on her."

She does have a great ass, heart shaped, and small breasts that beg for attention on her slender body.

Juliet gives off a hint of high-wire erotic mania, flirting with the guys in the office, flitting around the room with an uncontainable energy. You never know what she'll be up to. She sits in the corner and makes kitten sounds, or goes out on the roof where no one's allowed and walks around, peering in at the other phone interviewers with a goofy grin on her face, a glint in her eyes. She's a musician and plays keyboard, guitar, and drums. She has a droll wit, a cutting observant tongue—she's a renegade pixie, a quixotic nymph with charisma and seductive charm.

Everyone's convinced at some point or another that Juliet is coming on to them. Even the women. She'll sit too close, lean over too long, or find the new guy at work, stroll up to him and linger, grab his wrist and gently raise his watch up to her face: "What time is it?" Juliet brings an overnight bag of clothes to work and picks a pink lace nightie out and holds it up to the guy who's sitting next to her, saying in a sweet, low voice, "See?"

It's an office joke that she works the male supervisors, getting them hot and bothered, manipulating them into letting her take long breaks or sit with her feet up on their desks, or run around without shoes. With the women she isn't so lucky, and there's often a mutual distrust and antagonism. They are immune to her wacky charms.

Apparently, she never actually does anything sexual with these men, she just carefully places the idea of sex in the air.

There are rumors that she leaves her panties scattered around the room—on desks or on various chairs. The guys half expect to find a pair in the sink of the men's room.

I don't find out that Juliet has a reputation for such nymphomaniac provocation until it's too late.

I hear her voice before I see her face. She hears my laugh before she hears me speak.

"Your laugh!" she screams.

I'm standing near her cubicle, joking around, laughing, waiting for directions from my supervisor, Bart. Juliet's back is to me; she swivels and looks in wonder. Immediately I understand; Juliet is adorable, absolutely cute. I know that she's the femme fatale of the office. And she's a foreigner.

Instinctively, I want to tease her. "Where are *you* from? The South?"

"The South?" she's indignant. "I'm from Australia!"

"Australia? Well, you *are* from down south then, in a way. What's your name?"

"Juliet. And you?"

"Max."

"Max." She repeats my name with a look of inner satisfaction, as though she is being spoon-fed on the sly by the goddess of love.

I make a split-second decision to have Juliet as my own. In some respects, I recognize her as my type immediately. She's slightly crazed, frayed around the edges, with a look of daft poverty, a waif. Also feminine and slender, energetic. I've always been attracted to waifs. To eccentric, talented women, strong with an effusive vulnerability.

I've begun a new job doing market research on the phone. We're starting a survey on baby diapers, calling up new mothers from a screened list and asking them what kind of disposable diapers they use. I don't know how much longer I can take this kind of work. Now that the recession is in full blast, no place I call wants a technical writer, especially one without very specific technical experience. I toss around for direction. Do temp jobs, do the Time-Life gig till I can't stand it any longer. I'm floating and, soon, desperate. I talk a lot with Will on the phone. Should I go back to school? And, if so, for what? Computer graphics? Broadcasting? I've been told I have a "broadcast-quality voice." My male voice is developing into a deep baritone. Still getting deeper, though the process is slower now and more subtle as time goes on.

A small group of surveyors goes upstairs for the training on the baby-diaper survey. We work the late-afternoon to night shift, and there are many unconventional and artistic people on the job. Here I meet my new colleagues: Anna, a young woman with large, liquid eyes and stringy hair who plays organ in a spooky goth rock band; Joel, another musician in a punk band called the Cruising Boners, he talks a lot about getting "woodies" when he sees his female roommate coming out of the shower in the morning; Isis, who wears pink sweaters and does a lot of chanting; and Leonard, an African American guy who was a basketball player at UCLA before he dropped out from partying too much and ended up here in his thirties playing chess in the park and reading Camus, smoking on breaks outside with a wistful, elegant aura.

Juliet leans over and taps me on the shoulder from behind. We sit next to each other almost constantly, and in time she begins to get in trouble for talking to me too much. A trouble magnet, she pouts.

"Do you sleep alone?" she asks.

"Uh, yeah . . ." I say, puzzled.

"I hate to sleep all alone," she purrs.

I sharpen my pencil and turn around to see Juliet watching me. She inquires in an innocent voice, "Are you sticking your big piece in the hole?"

Bart appears to be infatuated with her. He asks her out to lunch often. I hear he asks her out to dinner, too. Lingering over her desk. Bart knew me from my female past, had worked with me years before at Decisions and Opinions Market Research in 1986. When I walked in the first day he was startled. A flicker behind his eyelids, a quick glimmer of stunned recognition. But, for some reason, possibly because it's awkward, Bart acted as though he was meeting me for the first time. I'm glad. I find out later, from a friend, that he does remember, just as I suspected. I've become accustomed to the various expressions on people's faces when they recognize me.

Bart appears alarmed when he sees me and Juliet spending so much time together. He probably wants to warn her, and seems jealous when we talk and laugh together. Today Bart is watching me as I come into the office. "Hi, Max."

"Hi, Bart. How ya doing?"

I haven't taken off my mirror shades or leather jacket yet. His eyes widen as I march up to Juliet's desk and linger while she looks at me with a sweet gaze . . . "Oh, look at him, look at that leather jacket and those shades . . ." She sings a Heart song, "Magic Man," to me.

Bart looks like he is about to explode into a dozen cut-up confused little ribbons. *How could this be?*

I make a point of sitting next to Juliet.

Juliet and I hang out more and more on our dinner breaks. She gives me her bag to carry on my shoulder. We whisk away laughing into the break room, clandestine like two escaping convicts. She cautions, "Shhh . . ."

I'm making moaning sounds in the break room for all to hear— "Ahh, agh, yeah, ah, oooooh"—sexual sounds, grunts and tiny roars, as though I'm ravishing her slender body.

Juliet giggles, "Shhh, don't make any sounds of enjoyment!"

I'm increasingly attracted to her, but I don't take it too seriously. Although it's an immediate attraction, it isn't an entirely enthralling one. I can sense that Juliet might be a bit immature or unstable, although she is also loads of fun.

She would have to be told, of course.

Should I go for it? Will it be worth the risk of rejection if Juliet freaks out? She could let everyone in the office know about my past. Which might make work uncomfortable, although since Bart and a couple of other people know, I sometimes wonder if Juliet hasn't already found out. I try to ascertain this; I don't think so . . . but I'm not completely sure. After all, once one person knows, the news travels fast.

I have not yet had sex with a woman in my newly masculinized body. I'm aware that this is new territory.

In the beginning of my transition, I decided that I didn't want to have a relationship right away. I needed to be on my own. The process was too all consuming to add in the unpredictable ingredient of a romantic relationship.

I have never gone this long without having sex with a woman. Although I miss the intimacy and excitement, there are emotional changes I hadn't expected that have enabled me to cruise through this period. I don't feel a flickering, haunting loneliness as much as I used to. I remember feeling more nostalgic as female, more acutely vulnerable. More inclined to a thin chill, a melancholy feeling. Now, this atmospheric loneliness seldom surfaces, although I'm actually more solitary than ever before.

One could surmise I no longer feel the chill of melancholy loneliness since I've rectified my gender issues. Although living as a man has brought on an overall well-being and happiness, a kind of overall "rightness" with the world, this particular emotional change feels more fundamental to body chemistry. Another important change I didn't notice immediately, but which has crystallized with time, is the realization that I'm more emotionally self-sufficient on testosterone, more independent.

Perhaps the time has come to test the waters. Should I try and get something going with Juliet? I turn the idea over in my mind, watching the ceiling as I lie on my futon after work.

She got fired. Bart kept warning her, "Stop talking to Max." She'd pout, then just keep on talking to me, poking at me, sending notes across the column of cubicles. We were thick as thieves. Then Bart called her into his office one day, and that was the end. I came in and found out from someone else. Called her up right away and, joking, pretended to cry into the phone. Juliet laughed with that mischief-making ferocity that endeared me to her, and we talked. She was upset about being fired but she sounded resigned. She wanted to go to the movies.

CHAPTER 37:
TWILIGHT ZONE

I arrive at the movie slicked up. My hair just right, spiked with a bit of scrunch in it, black leather motorcycle jacket slouched on my shoulders. On a mission. I'll make my move in the night air. End my long celibacy, begin my next phase of initiation into maleness—a heterosexual relationship.

Juliet is not a lesbian and has never been one. Actually, most of the women I'd dated when I was Anita hadn't been dykes, either. Since age twenty-six, I'd had a long pattern of finding women who primarily identified as heterosexual. I'd pick them up at clubs, sometimes right out from underneath the noses of guys who were swarming on them. Many heterosexual transsexual men have this pattern; even before transition we respond primarily to straight or bisexual women. I think this is because we wish to be responded to as men, even if we aren't completely aware of it at the time. Quite possibly, these women I dated before I started taking testosterone were responding to my masculine energy, even though it was enclosed in a female body.

Juliet looks bashful when I see her, peeking through the front doors of the movie theater. I can't tell if she has the same intentions I do.

After the film we walk around to her small car and sit together in the dark. She pops a tape she's made of herself for voice-over auditions into the cassette player. Her thin voice is musical with a slightly strained, warbling American accent that she's had to put on for the mattress commercial she's doing: "Come, come to the wonderful world of comfort, rest, enchanting dreams. You'll wake refreshed."

"Wow, that's great. You do sound American there. How do you do it?"

"It's hard." She does it, pronouncing her hard *r* like an American broadcast news anchorwoman, looking strained in the streetlamp's yellow light.

Watching her in the car, I feel her pure reckless appeal.

I reach for her across the stick shift. She shrinks back, *"No!"*

"Oh, okay." I'm deflated.

"I just want to be friends," Juliet declares.

I'm surprised, not completely distraught, but let down. How can this be? She'd seemed flirtatious. I wonder out loud, "Really? Well, that's okay. But you did seem to be flirting . . ." I thought back to all the times I'd carried Juliet's bag slung over my shoulder, marching protectively into the night after work to her bus stop, thinking this must be part of the male role with women—protector in the night. I'd thought she'd given me that bag to carry for some reason. As though she were getting me to claim her, or possibly she was claiming me.

"Well, I do want to be just friends," she repeats.

I sit in the still of the car for a moment. If we are going to be just friends I figure I may as well just tell her and get it over with. Juliet will be a fun person to hang with, in any case, and I'm always honest to a fault with friends. We can't be close until she knows about my past. "Well, that's too bad, but I have something to tell you anyway. You have to know if we're going to be friends."

"What is it?" she asks.

"Well, it's hard to say. . . ." Suddenly, it seems so huge, how could I tell anyone something like this? Like jumping from a parapet.

"What is it, tell me!" she repeats, impatient.

"Well . . . I don't know how to say it. But . . ." I grasp at the words.

"Tell me!" Juliet is beginning to look frantic.

"Don't worry, it's nothing bad. I . . . uh, I . . ." I stop and begin again. "I'm a transsexual, Juliet. I'm in the process of having a sex change. I mean, I am a guy now, but I wasn't always."

"What? What are you saying?"

"I'm a transsexual man, Juliet. I haven't had surgery, but I'm taking hormones. That's why my voice is so deep. I've already changed a lot." I pause. Her face is lit with alarm.

"What are you saying?!"

"I'm a transsexual, Juliet." How can I make it more clear? "I used to be a woman, Juliet, and now I am a man, I—"

"What *are* you?" She gazes at me across the tight space in the car, from her place behind the steering wheel, to the glove compartment, peeling green vinyl, in front of me. I shift in my seat, uneasy.

"I'm a guy. But I wasn't always. I'm on male hormones. Testosterone. That's why I look the way I do. I've become a man, I wasn't always."

"*No!* No no no no no no!" Juliet begins to scream and smash her head onto the steering wheel. Her hair swings back and forth in the air. "No no no no no no no no no no no!"

I don't know what to say. I've never experienced a reaction like this. Perhaps I shouldn't have told her after all.

She stops dead still and peers at me across the stark interior. "What are you saying?!"

I will have to be as graphic as I can. She isn't completely grasping what I've said. *"Well,* I was a girl once, Juliet—*like you."*

"No no no no no no! Aaaaah . . . no no no!" Juliet keeps smashing her head on the steering wheel, up and down, up and down, swinging her head, her neck-long hair sweeping through the air, up and down. Silence. She becomes quiet, looking in front of her. Calm with a suddenness.

"You're scaring me." Her voice is thin, that Australian accent sketched inside every word. "I feel like I'm in the twilight zone." She takes a deep breath and peers at me again. "Are you kidding?"

"No, Juliet. It's true. It's been nearly three years now."

"Three years." Juliet contemplates this pronouncement. It's meaningful to her.

"Do you want to see a picture of what I looked like before?"

"Yes! Let me see a picture!"

I have one handy for cases like these. Eventually, in another year, I'll lock it away in a photo album. But tonight I have it in my wallet. An old California driver's license with a hole punched through it, no longer valid, relevant only because it's a clear photo of Anita, looking glum. I was tired, after waiting in the long line at the DMV, the interminable bureaucratic photo opportunity. I'm sulking but there's no doubt it's my female likeness.

Juliet peers at this photo for a long time in the small light. Holding it close to her face, she says, "Let's go somewhere and talk. I was going to take you home, but now . . ."

We go to Zim's. She has to know everything about this unforeseen revelation. I am ready and willing to talk. Juliet listens and drinks decaf. She grows increasingly tired-looking, but wants to hear as much as she can possibly take in. Coming back from the bathroom, she sees me from a distance and breaks into laughter! A giggling fit.

Later, Juliet tells me that she told her male roommate about me. "Have you ever heard of a man who used to be a girl?"

"Huh?"

"Well, I met this guy at work and he used to be a girl."

Her roommate, Rod, grunted from where he was sacked out on an overstuffed chair watching television.

"How do you think he felt about it?" I ask.

"Oh, I could tell he didn't like it. I think it freaked him out, the idea of *a man who used to be a girl.*"

CHAPTER 38:
WEIRD, WEIRD WORLD

Juliet shows me pictures from her past: a photo of her holding a kitten she saved and nursed, photos of her, looking pouty in tights and green hair, with her all-girl rock band. I show her photos of myself as Anita. Fascinated by the mechanics of the change, the titillating and amazing process, I'm always eager to share my enthusiasm and wonder. Many transsexual people are reluctant to show their "before" photos, and I understand why. Many of us prefer to keep the image of ourselves as our birth sex very abstract, a mirage. Perhaps being so open hasn't always been a wise move on my part, but I've always had a candid nature. It's not so much that I trust other people, although I often do, but that I trust and know myself, and feel a need to share my transformation, my real life struggle, with whomever I get close to.

Juliet looks at my old photos with a captivated intensity. I snap on a tape of my old voice.

She sits on my futon and watches me while I move around the room, putting photo albums away, straightening things. The voice of Anita blares from the stereo speakers. For a split second, I don't recognize it. Is that woman speaking with a resonant, lilting, nearly seductive tone really me? *I sounded kinda sexy,* I think to myself. Then, I take in the fact that other people might have thought the very same thing, and feel suddenly embarrassed. Here I'd always thought I had a very masculine voice. *What was I thinking?* I shudder to myself. At least now my voice sounds the way I'd always felt or imagined that it should.

Certainly, my previous speaking voice contained male intonations, even male speech patterns, and was fairly deep, contralto in its deepest notes. Even so, I'm amazed at how much I actually sounded like a woman.

This sharp and irreversible change feels poignant. Like listening to someone who's died or moved away forever to another country. This voice will never exist again. A thin thread connects my two voices, male and female, and I can hear it if I concentrate, but they are distinct. Poignancy hangs in the air, the reality of this profound and permanent ending.

Juliet senses my feelings. She asks me, "Are you sorry you did it?"

"No, of course not, but it is an incredible change. It's like hearing a ghost."

She wants to know whether or not I am happy now. I say yes, although this question has always struck me as inadequate. I am happier, but *relieved* is actually closer. My first feeling when I began my transition was enormous relief. A burden had been lifted off my shoulders. Some invisible battle had evaporated. When Kristine Ambrosia, the performance artist, saw me, she said, "So, the battle is over now, isn't it?"

My counselor, Joanne, told me that the battle never ends, it just changes. "It will go on for the rest of your life," she said. The texture, the stakes, the outcome, the feelings all shift. The fate of a transsexual—the battle continues, but the ambience and context change.

Transsexuals have an opportunity to probe deeply into the intrinsic nature of identity—its slipperiness, its preconditions and expressions—as well as the ways in which we determine or know who we are and who we want to become.

My identity is still undergoing growing pains. I increasingly feel like some straight guy stranded around gay people. I don't go to lesbian bars anymore, unless it's with an old friend, and that's becoming increasingly rare. If I do go, even my friends treat me differently than before, talking around me and over me. I stand around feeling isolated and bored, like some guy with a bunch of dykes, which is exactly what I am in those situations. In gay bars with Alexander and Jack, I often find myself watching the few straight-looking women in the place. It's possible that I'm clinging to queerdom to protect myself; it's an outpost on the path toward finding myself in the larger world. After all, in some respects, the lesbian world never did feel comfortable to me, although I did cherish the outlaw aspect of being a dyke and tried to ignore the goody-two-shoes part.

Juliet watches me, apart from this world of conflict and memory. Juliet is no feminist. She uses the word *girl*, never *woman*. She's never heard of the phrases "womon-identified womon" or "womon-loving womon." She doesn't know a butch from a femme or a top from a bottom. She has no idea what the Michigan Womyn's Music Festival is. She's an innocent, in some respects. A free spirit. Like most women her age, twenty-eight, she's been influenced by feminism, but it doesn't inform her entire vision.

"You come from a weird, weird world," Juliet says to me. Her accent outlines this sincere declaration with distinction and exotic aplomb.

As the tape of my old voice winds down, Juliet stretches out across my futon. For awhile, I talk to her from a small distance at the foot. I get closer and she doesn't move. I climb on top of her and press against her for a long time, barely moving. We breathe together quietly, holding each other in a full-body embrace. I'm not sure what to do next, how much further it can go. After all, she did say she just wanted to be friends. I begin to kiss her ear, softly, with a tentative, tiny tenderness. Taking time, not wanting to startle or upset her. I kiss her neck and then her ear again, nuzzle and hold her. I feel her loosen beneath me. A quiet heat begins to run along her skin. Juliet begins to moan softly, squeezing me tight.

"I don't have a penis," I warn her of the obvious. I've already told Juliet that I haven't had my bottom surgery. Getting up and beginning to pull off my pants, I glance at her watching me calmly, unblinking. Juliet nods. She gazes at my naked lower body without any expression—no surprise, judgment, or any discernible emotion. I yank off the black tights she's wearing, pull her panties off gently. Open her legs with my leg between, not too wide, just wide enough to enter at the edges of her wetness with my fingers. She's hot and liquid. Fucking her with my hand, in and out slowly with small motions, then faster and thrusting on top of her. We are free and awkward at the same time. It's familiar to me, yet tenderly new.

Afterward, Juliet sits up and begins to cry softly. I put my arm around her and hold her close. Ask if she's okay, and she says yes, she always cries after the first time with someone new.

We talk for a while longer, linger on each other's expressions, and then she leaves. I sit on the bed and contemplate this first experience of making love with a woman as a man.

Moving against Juliet I felt a pronounced and new sensation of difference between our bodies, a contrast between male and female that I had never experienced before physically. For one thing, I was physically much stronger now in terms of brute strength. I had felt almost as though I had to be careful with her, be gentle to keep from hurting her.

The next morning she calls and declares, "I'm pregnant."

That next night she comes over and we make love again. Beforehand, I put on Diamanda Galás and we lie together listening. I hold Juliet in my arms quietly and ask her to listen. I really want her to hear Diamanda shrieking like a fire-drenched demon with a thousand tongues—beseeching, invoking, cursing, mourning, howling: "I am the Holy Fool . . . /I am the Antichrist."

"How romantic," Juliet quips.

CHAPTER 39:
SEX WARS

Juliet throws herself on the bed and begins to kick and scream. She curls herself into a tight ball and begins to weep with a convincing agony. "How can you say that?" she wails, eyes tight, fists held tight and close to her body, tears streaming down her cheeks.

I watch Juliet writhing on the bed. "What?" I ask. She's a twisting form on the bedspread. *Am I missing something important here?* "What are you so upset about, Juliet? You can tell me, really. I mean, what's wrong? Please, I mean, don't cry. What's wrong?"

She wails, turns her back to me, clenching her fists, literally gnashing her teeth.

"What?" I cry out. I'm beginning to feel desperate. Is she for real? "Why are you so upset? My god, Juliet, I'm sorry, what is it?"

Juliet quits crying long enough to look at me, her long dark hair tangled over red eyes. "Oh," she stifles small sobs, gasping, "How can you say that . . . that 'Madonna is hot'?" She screams again, agonized. Hot tears run down her cheeks. This is only our third date.

"Juliet," I say. "I'm sorry. She's just a singer. I mean, I don't know her. Lots of people think that about her. It's nothing . . . really."

Juliet and I had been discussing music and she told me she liked Madonna's music. I said that I prefer harder-edged music, although Madonna certainly composed or sang hummable, danceable, stick-in-your-head tunes. "I love her dancing. Madonna is hot!" This last opinion is what got Juliet upset! I blink back disbelief.

"Oh, you're all the same. All you men, *you are sexist.* How can you say that about someone you don't even know? You are objectifying women!"

I am—perplexed. Is she serious? Does she really think I'm sexist? Part of the objectifying hordes of male humanity because I told her that I think Madonna is hot?

I think for a moment, creasing my forehead into a puzzled scrunch. I try to give Juliet the benefit of the doubt for a moment. *What if it were true?* Am I objectifying women? Is it now wrong to say that Madonna is, well, you know, really cute? How does this appear to Juliet, a man calling Madonna "hot"? I frame the scene in my mind. I am now a man calling Madonna hot. Does that make this statement different from before? I mean, I would have said the same thing if I was still Anita.

I check to make sure Juliet is really saying this. Maybe we're just not communicating. Worst of all, I realize, still feeling trapped in a tightly squeezed puzzled box, Juliet called me "sexist"! How weird. No one has *ever* called me *that* before. Me, the former radical feminist, featured in the historic *This Bridge Called My Back;* me, the former lesbian more feminist than any straight woman in a corner of my mind, ever so slightly superior, saved. I have to see if this is for real. "Juliet, what do you mean? Why do you think I'm sexist? Lots of people think Madonna's attractive."

"But you don't even know her! You are objectifying women. So sexist!" Juliet wails, inconsolable, writhing on the bed. She balls up into a tight wad with her back turned to me.

I'm beginning to understand that this wildly strewn epithet, clumsy and blunt as it feels, is yet another indication that I've arrived. Even though Juliet knows of my female past, she's deeply convinced that I am actually a man.

I approach Juliet delicately, carefully observing her self-protective, rigid posture—like a pill bug. Should I try and touch her? My hand stretches out to comfort her, tentative fingers touch her shoulder. Juliet is moaning and rocking. Softly crying. My intrepid hand attempts a soothing gesture. I stroke her hair. I settle a firm grip on her shoulder, apologizing and speaking in a constricted, sweetened voice.

Desperate, I make a contrite speech. I tell her I remember how it felt to be objectified as female. "You know, Juliet, I remember walking down the street, the guys hooting and hollering on Mission Street, or construction workers . . . the endless catcalling. I remember how horrible that was." I tell her, "Madonna means nothing to me."

Juliet doesn't strike me as being too concerned about sexism. Is she really outraged at the thought of me objectifying a woman I've never met? A public persona making her living and actualizing her dream by being worshipped, analyzed, lusted after, denounced—objectified? Or is she simply, as I suspect, *jealous?*

CHAPTER 40:
"IT'S A GREAT GIMMICK"

In the first few years, when I compare myself to many of the men at the straight clubs I frequent, I feel green and vulnerable. I wonder if this feeling will change in time; it is hard to believe I will ever approximate their hardness, their rough and agile virility. There's a bravado just underneath their skin. It's confidence, ultimately. They've been at this a lot longer than I have.

Juliet is aware that I'm different, although she remains immune to the complexities of my vulnerability. Her worries revolve around disclosure. She is afraid that people will think she is a lesbian if she tells them that she is seeing me. She acknowledges that this might be unlikely, since I don't look at all like a woman, and she doesn't experience me as a woman. Even so, Juliet is convinced that her parents would never speak to her again if she told them. She is also afraid to tell her roommate or friends. She's isolating our relationship from the rest of her world, drawing the curtains on us. I tell myself that she just needs time, but I don't know. She's my first woman as Max, and it presents different challenges than my previous relationships.

Altogether, in spite of her fears of being labeled a lesbian, my male identity feels confirmed. Juliet experiences me as a man, some kind of odd guy from a parallel but not altogether foreign universe. She tells me, "You look like a guy, you smell like a guy, you seem like a guy," and her weeping and gnashing of teeth concerning my appraisal of Madonna appears to indicate a genuine and heartfelt perception of my intrinsic male self. She compares me to past boyfriends without any self-consciousness, speaking about us as though we are essentially the same. Still, I'm insecure about her perception of me.

Even so, I feel free with Juliet, lucid. She seems imbued with some kind of joyful life force.

I go wild on her body, it's been so long—biting her nipples, nibbling at her small breasts, giving her as much pleasure as she and I can stand. Because of the testosterone, I'm stronger and more aggressive than ever. It drives me crazy with lust to feel so masculine, so male in comparison to her. The conflict I always had going on in my head has abated. My fantasies feel natural now, since my body fits in more closely with what I feel is my actual self. When I penetrate her with my fingers or a toy shaped like a realistic cock that I wear in a pair of tight-fitting underwear, I feel nearly complete in my manhood, more tangible to myself as male.

It's comforting that my anomalous situation doesn't appear to deter Juliet's enthusiasm in bed. I fuck her slowly from behind or have her sit on top, which she is only too glad to do. Sex feels tentative and wild at the same time. I'm relieved to find that it isn't difficult. I'm able to pull it off. My confidence increases. She says, "You're exciting, I've only told two people that."

I not only come from a "weird, weird world," as Juliet claims with a kooky and serious tone in her voice, shaking her head, wide-eyed, but I introduce her to many wide-ranging and eclectic sexual activities. Spanking, role-playing, rough sex, talking dirty. I tease and push at Juliet's fantasies, provoke with a series of well-timed tactics to pull threads of heat from her.

I take her a little further each time, spanking her lightly. One day, I take off my belt and give her a couple of good, strong whacks on the bottom. She lies still on her stomach, then wiggles a bit on each stroke of the leather strap, clutching at the sheets. The next night she asks me to hit her.

Not everything I do or say is understood and appreciated as sex play.

We're driving out to the ocean and Juliet asks me why I call her a "slut" sometimes when we make love. Her voice is innocent and clear, a ringing slender chime. I glance at her in the car, her hair flying in the breeze from an open window. She's been bouncing to a Judas Priest tape and grinning that slightly mad grin every time we stop at a red light. Stomping on the brake, I recoil as the car ahead of us looms dangerously close, springing up then bouncing back as we slow down. Looking both ways into the intersection, Juliet makes a mock heavy metal scream, high pitched, snapping back her head, open mouthed, up to the sky: *"Aaaaaah!"*

"You want to know why I . . ." I grope for words.

"Yes, why do you say that? I'm just wondering, you know? My old boyfriend used to say that once in a while when we were having sex, too. Why do guys say that?" Juliet glances at my perplexed eyes.

I'm not sure how to explain. My mind races to the lesbian S&M and anti-porn sex wars, the Susie Bright *Penthouse Forum* columns I've read, the Dr. Ruth I've overheard on TV. Suddenly I feel tongue-tied. *Why do I say that?* "Uh, well, it's supposed to be sexy," I finally manage. "Like, you know, pointing out how you are really hot and wild."

Juliet is doing mock drum solos now whenever we stop at a sign or light. Her hair is a banner in the car wind, a rock-and-roll shape. She doesn't seem to notice my discomfort or my smiling at her antics. I continue, "I mean, I'm not saying that to insult you. I want you to know that." I lick my lips, realizing that I look too earnest and grim to get across the sexiness of this expression.

She glances at me from the steering wheel. "Yeah . . ." A look of concentration is on her face, she's trying to understand. "I see." Juliet is nodding. Serious. The road is expanding in front of us now, on our way to the ocean.

And here I thought she liked it. This informal remark, tossed out in passion, meant to ensnare and arouse, had been merely puzzling. How much else of what I'm doing or who I am is going right by Juliet?

At the beach together, we sit watching the seals on the rocks. She brings food and watches me eat with watchful, protective eyes.

Juliet's moods wash over her with titillating grace. Almost every time we see each other she pouts or bursts into a round of tears. Without question, she is talented (at music) and quirky, and she's certainly fun to be with, but I begin to wonder what is behind her moodiness and sudden outbursts.

As though to answer my unspoken questions, Juliet declares once, after a long day spent walking around town, while we're sitting in a café to rest, "I'm crazy. I'm so crazy, I'm schizophrenic."

I peer into Juliet's face, her gleaming eyes and intrepid smile. She is coasting on some kind of revelatory mood. This outburst about insanity is her way of being candid, of announcing the truth to me, a clarion call to my better judgment. She smiles later and adds with a note of satisfaction in her voice, "I'm a bitch."

"Oh, yeah?" I say, eyebrows raised.

"Yes," Juliet grins.

I brush the hair from her eyes and study the elemental emotions sliding behind them. Is Juliet putting me on with this "crazy" business? "I don't think you're crazy, Juliet."

"I am," Juliet insists.

"Why do you say that? I know what schizophrenics are like . . . I had a friend once who was. I mean, do you hear voices?"

"No."

I ask Juliet a series of questions designed to pull the truth about her sanity out of her, to make it apparent to her. No, she has never seen things; no, she has no special mission and no one is watching her from the TV or plugging into her brain from the radio; but yes, she really is crazy.

I laugh at her. She smirks at my disbelief as though she is holding a secret weapon.

This revelation or declaration is filed away by me for future reference, although I really don't know what to make of it at the time.

I never take my T-shirt off, or my binder. I tell Juliet I've got breasts, they're there, squished and sweaty, held in by the faithful elastic band. I'm amazed by how much I can do with this thing on. Dance, jog, and now, have sex—vigorous sex. For all I know, it could be that the breasts are purely theoretical for her. On the other hand, I cannot know all that Juliet is feeling or thinking about this and I don't want to probe too deeply into an area that could lead to potential trouble, leaking pain and doubt into an otherwise positive situation.

It is when she sits down and plays piano at another party, for her friend Carla, wearing a green tuxedo jacket that is worn and glittery, hunching over slightly at the keyboard, that I begin to fall for her. We are at a Memorial Day weekend barbeque at Carla's place, a big house overlooking the city. Juliet and I stand on the balcony and survey the city outside, the landscape of San Francisco stretched out with its painted Victorians and promenades of palms, skyscrapers in the Financial District distant in weekend solitude. "This is great," I declare.

"Yes, but I've seen better," Juliet replies. I shift in closer to put my arm around her shoulders and she moves away with a start; she doesn't want Carla to see us together.

Carla had driven us here and we'd held hands, stealthily, with a slick sneakiness, like guilty teenagers with a chaperone. Every time Carla would turn around in the car to glance at Juliet, she'd drop my hand like it was on fire.

After the barbeque I take her home, and we make love on my bed and she leaves, as she always does, never staying the night. I hear a woman screaming outside a bit later and feel worried. I relate this experience to her the next time I see her. "I was worried it was you."

"And, you didn't do anything!" she pouts. "You just thought, *Oh, she's dead already!*" I smile at Juliet. At that moment, lying side by side on my small bed, everything feels perfect.

I ask Juliet what changed her mind. Why did she decide to start sleeping with me after initially saying no? Apparently, the fact that I was a transsexual hadn't deterred her; in fact, I suspect that this intrepid fact about me had actually made me more attractive, or at least intriguing.

"It's a great gimmick," Juliet declares.

Juliet decides to quit seeing me. I never completely understand why, and she never gives me an answer that feels true. Or, possibly, the reason she does give is too depressing for me to believe. Although she is fickle, I might be the one in denial. Without question, dating a transsexual was not something that she had planned on. Even so, Juliet had warned me once that she sometimes suddenly leaves boyfriends—or men she dates or is sleeping with—for obscure reasons. There was one guy whose eyebrows were too light: "He didn't look good in the dark." Another who had muscles in his arms that were exciting during lovemaking but far too large upon further reflection. She hardly spoke to him again, although they were roommates.

We go to the St. Francis Theatre for the last round of cheap movies and sit on the frozen escalator as the people leave. It is close to midnight. Just last week I had declared my growing feelings for her, and Juliet had echoed my growing ardor. I wasn't completely sure what all of it meant. I wasn't even sure where my feelings would evolve, whether this was simply infatuation or something ultimately more enduring. Everything was still so new for us, undefined. Perhaps the time had come for Juliet to decide one way or the other what she wanted. I also knew that my being a transsexual man was a likely factor in this sudden change.

"Is it because I'm transsexual?"

She paused. "Maybe . . . I just don't know what to tell my friends. And my parents would never speak to me again."

We make love one more time, on the narrow bed in my room with the yellow lights on and green and gold drapery, a musty smell in the air. She hadn't wanted to, but I seduced her easily, pulling her toward me on the bed. I can hear her heart beating fast under skin flushed with a rash of sexual feeling. I play with her small breasts and tug at them with my lips, teasing with a concentration into abandonment. I fuck her one last time, but I can feel her fading away from me. Juliet's attention isn't with me. She seems distracted and distant, dreamy in fits.

Afterward, we switch on the television and stare absently at the screen. A show about Ted Bundy comes on, Juliet is stretched out beside me. "Maybe you're like him," she declares.

"What? Come on, Juliet."

"Maybe you are! You are charming and attractive. Maybe you are like him."

I watch her eyes with amused disbelief. "Come on, Juliet, I'm not like Ted Bundy. That is crazy."

CHAPTER 41: PREDATOR

A woman walks ahead of me on a dimly lit street. Her heels click on the sidewalk. She's alone. It's around midnight, and there aren't a lot of people out. Cars now and then, metal shapes in the dark floating down a dark ribbon of road, ghostly, without voice or identity. Streetlamps create an intermittent rhythm of light. I'm fast and coming up behind her, not thinking of who she is or where she is going, but about my life, about getting home. The woman turns and sees me behind her, a flitting glance—she glimpses a man in a leather jacket, black pants, dark boots. She crosses quickly to the other side of the street.

This startles me. I remember crossing the street when I was alone at night and an unknown man was walking behind me. The feelings—

strands of fear lighting up my chest, heart beginning to pound a slightly faster pace, the beginning of a tightness in my throat. An alarm that was slight yet ominous, hypervigilant, on alert for rapists or murderers. I can't say that I blame her. And although I understand why she must do this intelligent and small act of self-defense, it does make me sad to realize that this anonymous woman is afraid of *me*. A still feeling settles in my heart, a tiny and tender pain. I'm perceived as male now, and therefore, possibly a predator—a rapist, serial killer, or strong-armed thief.

On a visit to New York City, I walk a measured pace behind a young man who's around my height. I'm in a dangerous part of town visiting a friend. I figure if I can keep someone in my sight, their presence will act as a compass, a kind of protection for me. But the young man is increasingly nervous. At an intersection where we both stand waiting for the light he glances at me several times. Later, as he walks ahead of me by several yards, he turns again to look back at me. Suddenly, he breaks into a run and takes off down the street, glancing nervously back over his shoulder. I'm shocked. It's hard to believe that this guy would be scared of *me,* and then I realize that here, in this part of Manhattan, in my black leather jacket and dark boots, I might look intimidating.

Juliet and I find ourselves working at the same place again, another market research firm, about six months after our breakup. It is not uncommon for people doing market research jobs to work at a small circuit of market research companies, following the projects as they begin and end, a kind of migrant office work. A person will often work with the same people, at a different company, on a new project. I had written a letter to her, and called a few times, hoping to see her and at least become friends. She never answered, so I reluctantly gave up. When I see her at the company on my first day I am stunned to find that she won't talk to me or acknowledge my presence. Later, I find out that she thinks I'm stalking her and that I found out where she worked and got myself a job there just so I could be close to her. Although I do still find her attractive and have not entirely gotten over our short episode of dating, I most certainly am not stalking her. When I find out she thinks this, I try and tell her that I had no idea she was working there. She is stepping out into the hallway as I approach to tell her I mean her no harm and begins to run, screaming, down the long hallway and into the elevator. People dash out of their offices to see what's wrong. At this point, I realize that many things I do as a man with women can be seen as sinister. Things that I might have easily done as a female are now seen in an entirely different light.

Over time, I recognize that people see me as more powerful than I feel and more menacing than I am.

It occurs to me that I must be careful when talking to children. After all, men are often seen as child molesters or kidnappers.

CHAPTER 42:
STRIPPER

At Diviana's birthday party I give her one whack, a resounding whack that is one out of thirty for her, a tender and decisive parting of the Red Sea. She's bent over, her ass round and inviting. I am the only guy in a long line of women, so when my turn comes, I whack her ass once with a firm, honest stroke. "Ouch, that hurts!" she screams. No one else has made her scream like that. Her sharp shriek surprises me and again I'm reminded that I don't know my own strength anymore.

A friend of Diviana's who works as a stripper is lounging on a sofa in the main room. She's got a long, thin white dress on. Her breasts are in a push-up bra, decoys. I watch her from across the room, feeling alone in a roomful of dykes. Everyone's relaxed with an effusive happiness, popcorn is passed around, and the women couples on the couch sit close together, squeezing each other's hands. Diviana introduces me to her stripper friend, Cynthia. "This is my friend Max, he's an FTM. I knew him before, when he was a dyke." Cynthia's eyes sparkle—surprise. Suddenly friendlier, she begins to speak with a more trusting tone, smiling at me more often, making eye contact in a way that indicates that she perceives me as a friendly kindred spirit instead of a *man*. Part of me is relieved, I enjoy being accepted and liked, after all. Yet another part of me feels uncomfortable; in order to be accepted by lesbians, I have to give up some portion of what I have worked so hard to achieve—my male identity.

Generally, I don't care to be introduced as a transsexual man or as an FTM, but simply as Max, a man like any other. However, with old lesbian friends, I understand how they sometimes feel more comfortable when their dyke friends know that I too was once a sister on the island of Sappho.

I watch lesbian sex videos, get bored, walk around and talk with the guests. Cynthia is catching my eye from where she's sitting on the couch. I lean against the doorway, feeling hungry and new. Later, we go home in a cab together, an odd accident that is planned by both of us surreptitiously.

"I am a lesbian!" Cynthia announces, as we walk through her door and down the long hallway leading up to her bedroom. I'm aware right away that I would never have gotten this far with her if she hadn't known about my past. I tell her that I haven't had any surgery yet, but I bind, which is why my chest is flat, my breasts undetectable.

We go into her room and I grope her, feeling her curves and fleshy round bottom. The sensations of a woman's body pressing against me feel almost new, delicious. Her breasts are large, I unhook her bra, impatient.

I've noticed something different about my sexuality since becoming Max. I'd suspected this with Juliet, but tonight confirms my emerging suspicion. I'm more aggressive. Once I get going I go at it harder, faster, with a flare of hot lust; I remind myself of the teenage boys I kissed in junior high and high school. I remember how they were so nearly out of control, reaching, squeezing, and grabbing, panting with a widening excitement that pushed at me. Now, here I am on the other side. There is a familiarity to my own sexual responses, like a memory from a distance. I've always been aggressive in bed, but this heat, this aggressive and intense flare of lust, is new. It is harder to stop once I get going.

"Slow down, slow down." Cynthia backs up on the bed with a sudden, breathless motion. Abruptly, she pushes me back gently. "I'm not used to being with men, this is new for me."

A triumphant feeling goes off inside me. I know that she's taken me home thinking that since I am an FTM, that I must somehow, deep down, *really* be a woman. A real butch number. . . . It's becoming clear to her—this is not the case. I am, for all intents and purposes, a man. As this fact becomes clear, Cynthia isn't as sure.

Once someone knows of my past, there's always that tendency to try to put me back into my former biological sex. Cynthia's heated announcement is another indication that in spite of that tenacious and disturbing tendency, my maleness feels real. I've scored an experiential coup.

Cynthia and I stay up half the night, talking and listening to Bob Dylan. Although we kiss intermittently and lie together talking about our sex fantasies and experiences, we don't do much more serious messing around. Before I leave the next morning, she says, "Don't tell anyone about us being together, I don't want anyone to think I'm straight."

I think back to Juliet as I walk out into the street and her admonition to me: "Don't tell anyone we are together, I don't want anyone to think I am a lesbian."

CHAPTER 43: COMMITMENT

With Jane, I realize that I can have perfectly decent, hot sex with a woman and not be in love; in fact, not even really have romantic feelings. It's different than before as female. Somehow, the line is more emphatically drawn. I can have sex and be more detached.

Jane is a biker and a student. She has long, torch-blond hair, brilliant in its white sweetness. Jane is tough at the edges—smart, skinny, and blunt. Every time we go out for a drink together she gets mobbed by guys. Usually, this mobbing occurs when Jane is up at the bar ordering a pint. I realize there will always be lots of hungry sharks out there who are only too glad to take my girlfriend off my hands. This is a different experience than when I was a dyke; for the most part, other dykes are not as aggressive about approaching a woman who might be alone at the bar for a few moments ordering a drink, even if they find her attractive. Guys appear to not waste time.

I meet her at work. This seems ill-advised, but now that I am a straight man there appear to be so many more opportunities on the job. When I was a dyke, I did not meet women at work so readily. Risky business, but I go for it.

I liked the snakeskin outfit Jane was wearing the first night we met. She responded to me immediately and we walked to the bus together talking about Aztec religious rituals. She had strong opinions and once nearly got in a brawl with a woman at the office over whether or not the window should be shut. I figured she might be too stubborn for me, too scrappy.

There is the usual problem of how to tell her I am a "bionic" man, once I've decided that I want to pursue her. This is the life sentence I must endure—how to tell and who and when.

Deception, honesty, trickery. I don't feel it's fair to make moves, to kiss or do anything without telling first. Even so, I'm torn inside. And of course I have to tell her I haven't had any surgery yet.

I end up kissing Jane before I tell her, feeling pangs of guilt about not revealing my trans identity first. We're in her room and she's reading to me from a book about the Toltecs. I pounce. We kiss for a few minutes. She melts against me. I freak out and excuse myself, running out into the rain.

Later, I give my disclosure such a buildup, telling her that I want to talk to her alone, telling her that it is kind of "intense and important," warning her that she should sit down first, that Jane is terrified. She blurts out, "Don't tell me! Don't tell me!" Finally, after agonizing, I spit it out.

Jane's reaction is unexpected. "Oh, is that all? I thought you were going to tell me that you'd been in prison and were some kind of rapist or something." She seems nearly disappointed.

"No, I'm just a transsexual," I quip, relieved and puzzled.

It never seems to make any difference to her.

In a very short time, I can see clearly that although I certainly enjoy her, this is not "love" and never will be. Even so, the sex is good. Eventually, my lack of strong, romantic feelings strains the relationship to breaking.

Jane becomes aware that I'm not "in love" with her. She complains to her roommate, who tells her that I must be using her for sex. I wonder if she's right. Maybe I am.

Am I becoming the man who can't commit? Or is that beside the point? Eventually, I begin to feel Jane's bitterness pulling at me, and I end the relationship. She agrees with vicious green eyes over breakfast that we are going nowhere.

A friend of mine who works in the sex industry tells me that her clients complain about how they feel "misunderstood" by women. "I'd rather pay for it than go through the misunderstanding," these men remark. The misunderstanding revolves around the fact that many men don't always need a committed, intense, and emotionally intimate relationship with a woman to enjoy sex with her. When confronted with this reality, their partners chide them that they just aren't in touch with their feelings, or that they're afraid of their feelings and of commitment. Actually, the "romantic feelings" just aren't always that important, and, if truth be told, for a man to have a sexual relationship, they don't even have to exist.

CHAPTER 44: TERRITORY

There's a strange thing men do while walking down the street. It has to do with territory. *Do I move or will he move?* Some guys take this more seriously than others. Take Joe, a guy I work with. Joe's a wiry dude with a Mohawk. He looks rapid, with quick, tight movements to his shoulders and hands, holes in his army boots. Nervous, nonstop, a gutter gladiator. He's bright, with a strong, cynical streak. Joe loves to tell long stories about his past exploits as a bike messenger, a job he held for a long time before he turned it in after busting up his kneecap on a winding downhill slope where he mowed right into a crowd of pedestrians. "Secretaries and suits," he called them. They stood in his path—a malingering cluster of deranged animal life—and

Joe plowed right into them. Joe moved on in his career path and ended up doing what many on the cigarette-butt, caffeine, denim, and black-leather-jacket circuit do for money—telephone surveys. He and I hang out during work, lingering over breaks with greasy donuts and sour coffee from across the street.

By this point, after four years, I'm used to hanging with guys at work, feeling akin to them as well as distinct from their more ingrained ways of perceiving the world. I'm observing. After being sequestered by a lesbian feminist political outlook for so many years, a narrow frame of reference that nearly shut down my most free-ranging instincts, I don't want to judge. I want to learn, to ferret out the occluded, subliminal aspects of male life. All the conversations I've never had, all the male-bonding rituals I didn't have the opportunity to experience.

After work one day, I learn more about the male obsession with territory. Joe and I stride down the street, long steps in black boots. He's chain-smoking a thin cigarette with nervous fingers. A large, wide man in a dark blue suit waddles by. Joe jerks his head and looks, hypervigilant, "That guy in that suit . . ."

"Yeah," I look around, over at the wide man passing us, wobbling as his thighs rub together under his polyester suit pants.

"I almost nailed him. See, he's asking for it. He's looking for it, man." Joe cranes his neck to watch the fat man move past us and down the street. He kills his cigarette, pinching the end between his thumb and index finger, flicking it toward a flower vendor. "That guy was trying to get me to move first. I do not move, man. I do not move. You know, I slammed square, dead on into the mayor of San Francisco a couple of weeks ago, man. I slammed right into him. Boom!" He made tight fighter's gestures with closed fists. "Man, he was shook. Look, I tell you, he was walking right toward me and man, I don't move for nobody. Nobody, not even the mayor of fucking San Francisco. Nobody, man, only old people, women, and children."

Joe does have a trace of gallantry in him. A soft touch with the ladies.

He keeps a picture of his girl up near his desk and calls her several times a day. He makes a beeline to talk, in a soft, soothing voice, to a new female staff member wearing a tight, low-cut top, a short black skirt over slinky legs. He's protective of her, getting her oriented to the job, sharpening her pencils, offering to bring her coffee from across the street on his breaks.

"Nobody, I move for no-fucking-body! Only old people, women, and children, old people, women, and children!" He's shaking with wiry energy, smoking with old anger as he repeats that he doesn't move for nobody. I don't know quite what to say. Joe's stance seems tightly choreographed, an improvisational ballet of rage, territoriality, conniving macho spirituality.

Strange to me. I've always been spacey, I guess. After seeing me for the first time as Max, my friend Chrystos told me that I appeared grounded, to have a rooted sense of who and where I was. She said that I'd always seemed as though I were somewhere else, on some distant planet. I never seemed to be completely present when I was Anita. Now, as Max, I've landed. "You're finally here, present," she told me. This unexpected observation felt revelatory to me. Becoming a man, I've gradually become embodied. I've begun to inhabit my life.

Is there something grounding about testosterone? If there is, can that grounding quality lead to a strident preoccupation with territory, a hyperawareness of personal space versus other people's space? This preoccupation with *ground* . . . the literal ground upon which one walks, where it begins and ends, who else is on it or attempting to take it away, claim it, besmirch it. This is warfare. What wars are fought for: land, resources, honor, women. Joe's honor and sense of self are thoroughly connected to his sense of personal space, his ground. There is a possessiveness inherent in this attitude, it's a jealous state of mind. Prone to rage, to violent outbursts. To parading like a rooster with flaring curses.

I know that there is more to my landing on earth as Max than testosterone's chemical propensity to hypervigilance. I landed on earth because

I've finally arrived. As a man, I've begun to connect more wholeheartedly with my environment. It's age, also, getting into my thirties, the way age can weigh you down with a tempered realism.

Even so, the dramatic effects of testosterone pull me into my body with scintillating awareness. That energy, that *tension* in the cells that curls the hair on legs, coarsens it with a wiry quality, causing veins to stand out under skin, an all-over bristling of hair, then nerves. Hair texture is one of the first characteristics that changes when a person begins to take sex hormones. One transsexual woman reported to me that when she began estrogen treatment, one of the first changes she noticed was that her beard (which hadn't yet been removed through electrolysis) became soft and silky to the touch, as did the rest of her body hair. And, as transsexual women's body hair relaxes, they do, too. Another transsexual woman remarked to me how much more relaxed she feels on estrogen: "It's a tranquilizer." She found this alteration in mood unexpected.

I remember that soporific quality. Dreamy, nearly beatific in contrast to the charged, energized feeling I experience now. There are modalities or shades of perception and feeling more apparent to men than to women, and vice versa. Just as there are colors that certain animals or insects can perceive that humans can't. Because we have never experienced these colors, which are outside of the range of our human senses, we live our entire lives as though they don't exist. When I begin to grow my hair long, I'm surprised that it's acquired a wave. After rain, it almost curls. My whole life I've had completely straight hair—always lank, and a bit fine. My head hair is turning out to be wavier, coarser, stronger in texture. That tension, translated to head hair, body hair, to an overall alertness. Hypervigilance on the streets. Hair standing on end. Tension. Energy. An acrobatic distention of tendons, blood vessels, and muscles. Testosterone chisels at fat, sculpting my female adipose layer bit by bit, changing my frame slowly to leaner, harder proportions. Tension, clenching fists, and watching to see who crosses what line, looks in which direction, and how.

CHAPTER 45:
INITIATION

The universe must've been warming up to my maleness, catapulting me into the arena of combat, barbed wire initiation rites.

I watch and listen to Joe's rant, bemused. I know that this territorial attitude, although extreme in his case, is not unique. Listening to Joe I wonder, *How should I relate to this?* As a man I've already experienced guys getting bent completely out of shape because they think I've looked too long or too closely at a woman they're with. Male privilege: the privilege to be threatened or beaten because you cross an invisible, inviolate line.

When I'm walking with Joe down the street I wonder, *What if I were that man walking toward him, hands in pockets, lost in thought with a harmless expression, unaware . . . ?* Should I buy into this behavior, do the territory dance? Stare him down, force him to move, bust his balls? Do I have a choice? I know that Joe is out on an edge, not by any means typical of the average guy on the street. He's a fugitive from an abusive family—had a father who beat him and drank. His rage is an incandescent outburst fueled by his past. But there are plenty of guys out there like Joe, looking for trouble, stoking a muted hostility.

Now that I'm a man, I find that an invisible coating of protection, a soothing, sweet barrier, has fallen from around me. I hadn't even been aware of its presence. Women ask me, sometimes with a resentful tone, "So are you more safe on the streets now?" It's not that simple. It's true, I no longer worry about sexual harassment on the streets, about intrusive ogling, or rape. That's a huge relief. I don't make light of it. However, there's another side to violence that women aren't exposed to. The competitive angst and edge of man-on-man violence. The pecking order, the daily drills of masculine testiness. I no longer have any slack cut for me; men threaten me with their fists if I give them the finger or tell them to fuck off and die; I have to watch where I am in relation to their boundaries with greater care. Bumping into the wrong guy at the wrong time can be a prelude to a confrontation. It's a drag. One I wasn't prepared for. Everything in my feminist background informed me that I would be safer as a man, more secure walking the streets, being in crowds, going about my life out in the world. So when I actually begin to experience more violence being out in the world, I'm startled. I've been mugged, punched in the face, and threatened on more than a few occasions. I've had to learn a new code of conduct, to decipher a fresh set of signals. I'm not complaining, but I can't say this is my favorite part of being a man.

The first time I wimped out. Tried to do the "smart" thing, de-escalate to avoid confrontation. Actually, this wasn't the first time I'd encountered threats of violence, but this episode was a private milestone—the first time I almost got into an all-out fight.

So here's how it happened.

David and I are walking in the Tenderloin, one of the testiest parts of San Francisco. We're involved in some run-on conversation—his girl-friend, my living situation. I've just been kicked out of my room on Folsom Street since the landlord has decided to convert it from an arty and reasonably priced rooming house into a tourist hotel. I'm feeling depressed, energy low and lagging, slump shouldered.

I've known David for nearly twelve years, but we've been on the outs for more than five years, and he had no idea I was doing the change. One day, we walked past each other on the street; I stopped and did a double take. There he was, thin, rangy, just like before with his glasses and large, expressive eyes, the same mouth working in a tense rhythm. Looking smart and hungry.

"Hi, David," I said, conscious of the startling change in my voice and appearance. I wasn't sure he would recognize me. David gazed into my face for a long fifteen seconds with a quizzical expression, and finally he asked, "Anita?"

Now we're hanging out again, comparing notes on writing projects. He seems to have adjusted remarkably well to me being a man. Without hesitation, David calls me "Max" now, and "he." You never can tell who will be able to adjust.

So, we're walking in the Tenderloin when two young guys on a motorcycle follow David and me up onto the sidewalk with their bike roaring. Seconds earlier, they had been turning the corner—driving fast—and one of them spit a wad of gum out into the intersection. It hit me right on the cheek. I winced and pulled the small wad from my cheek. Shook my head, *Damn jerks.* David yelled out, "Asshole!" without missing a beat.

Their faces are smooth and youthful, they appear to be older teenag-ers. Like me, they wear black leather motorcycle jackets. David says they may have thought that I was their age—a peer, and a competitor. I look younger than I am because of the hormones.

"What did you call me? What did you call me?" The motorcycle is on the sidewalk behind us. The driver is the blond one; he's doing most of the yelling. "I don't care if you got a knife, man, don't call me 'asshole'!"

The pattern that I've observed concerning this territorial testiness and violence is this: There is an incident in which an insult occurs, real or perceived. The guys think for awhile about whether or not this insult has actually occurred. When they decide that it has, they come back and take vengeance.

David had called out "asshole" at the quickly disappearing motorcycle; then the action went flat for awhile. Nothing. We'd nearly forgotten the dynamic duo when we heard the bike coming up from behind and onto the sidewalk.

The wise-ass kid is looking straight into my face. This is all strange, yet familiar in a faint and removed sort of way, like movies I've seen about young thugs on motorcycles in leather jackets. I search through those movie memories on fast-forward to see if I can recall a strategy that will work in this situation. David is alarmed. Although he is a large man in height and frame, he's bookish and junkie thin. By slow degrees, David begins to back away. I glance nervously at him; close to the wall, his eyes look eclipsed behind his glasses, his forehead sweaty. I keep talking at the blond, watching his dark-haired friend, who's a bit taller and stockier—energetic—out of the corner of my eye.

"Pussy bitch!" the blond stringy-haired kid shouts at me over and over.

Why is he saying that? I think in a flash of confusion. *Does he know I'm a transsexual? Can they tell?* I worry for a split second. I shift, uneasy. Then this insult begins to make sense. I know that I'm being seen as one of the guys; this is how they insult each other. It is a curse and a pout at the same time, marking out ground, a challenge—*I dare you to prove me wrong.* A dare to prove my "manhood"—that fragile quality that can never be proven often enough and is often proven in contrast to woman-hood or at women's expense.

Some phrase I say satisfies their bloodlust, and both guys walk away. This is not the end, however. Later, we hear a familiar sound. The motorcycle on the sidewalk and the same blond guy shouting! He slides off his bike and marches toward us. David and I don't have a chance to turn around before he comes up from behind—fast. As I turn he hits me square, right on the forehead. I crouch down and put my hands over my head, ready for a rain of blows. But at that moment I realize a sweet and unexpected surprise: It doesn't hurt! I thought his fists would hurt, but they don't. Before I know what to do, David pulls the guy off me. The kid hits him and David falls down on the sidewalk, his glasses break. I am up and walking toward the kid. From his position on his back, David sticks his foot in the guy's crotch and forces him to do the slow backward walk. Later, he tells me that this is a technique I should remember—the ball-crushing technique. The kid backs up, sweaty looking, his nerve seeping out of him. His friend has lost interest. As I close in on him, he runs away, yelling, "Two against one, that's not fair, man!"

Later, I ask David about the guy calling me "pussy bitch." He confirms what I suspect: "All these smart-ass punks call each other that. That's their insult of choice." On one hand, it is all hilarious, surreal, a drunken, slanted reality. If only those wild-eyed jerks knew what those words had made me feel!

David calls me a wimp and I guess I deserve it. But this is all new to me. I tell him how amazed I am that the blows from the stringy-haired kid didn't hurt. In my mind, at that moment, as I watched him swing his fist into my face, I flashed back into my former female body. For a split second, I was a woman about to be punched in the face by an angry man; after all, the female body had been my point of reference for violent experiences up till that moment in my life. As a woman, although I would've tried to deny it for my pride's sake, I knew deep down that the average guy could likely beat the shit out of me if he really wanted to. In any serious contest of strength, I'd always been humbled, sometimes awed, by men's superior upper-body strength. With that in my memory, I'd expected a series of smashing blows that might be so powerful as to crush me, or at least bruise and batter me. When I'd straightened up and looked around, I'd realized that I definitely could have fought back. Although I got a small bump on my forehead, the young man's fists didn't make much impact. My new testosterone-primed body had capabilities of strength and endurance that exceeded anything I had ever known before.

Strangely, as a woman it had seemed easier to defend myself. I felt more confident. At a demonstration when I was nineteen, I punched a guy on the other side of the picket line in the jaw, nearly knocking him to the ground. All the women at the Women's Liberation Coalition on campus were astonished. They recounted this unheralded feat over and over again. At age twenty-five, when I was with Roxanne, I'd nearly smashed a guy in the jaw; later he turned out to be a friend of ours.

Roxanne loved to wear short, sleek skirts, lacy anklets, and high heels. Everywhere we went men whistled and hooted. In a crowded club one night, I'd just about had enough of the relentless catcalling. *One more,* I thought, *just one more time.* Sure enough, a long, wild hoot came up from the side of my head as Roxanne and I inched our way through the tight crowd. I lifted my fist to strike, pivoted, and there was Phil, a friend of ours we were scheduled to meet. I stopped mid-strike, shocked.

It's not that I never experienced fear and trepidation out on the streets as female. As I got into my twenties, I learned to walk tough—with my black leather jacket, my army boots, greasy dyed black hair spiked, chains dangling, black weight lifter's gloves on. I'd flip the finger to guys who bugged me or shout out "Fuck you, asshole!" I passed leering men on the street—striding big steps, loose at the shoulder, lurching with the force of a juggernaut. Even so, for all my posturing and blind force of will, the lurking of male predators wasn't vanquished.

Once, walking after midnight, I got followed by a strange van. As it slowed I perceived a silhouette, a man leaning forward in the driver's seat, observing me. Alone on the still streets I moved quickly, plucking a bottle out from under a parked car just in case I had to defend myself. I know that fear. The fear women learn and endure their whole lives. The warnings from my mother about strangers, the GIs on base whom I walked past as a child on my way to buy comics and candy at the PX. Haunting stories about girls or women being strangled, raped, stalked, killed, stuffed into plastic bags, cut into pieces, burned alive. Richard Speck, the Boston Strangler, Ted Bundy . . . All those girls and unsuspecting women lured or taken by force to their deaths.

When I was nineteen, I had taken a summer job as a maid in a hotel in downtown Denver. I waited on the street in the morning for a bus to work. A man in a red truck pulled up to the side of the street and asked if I wanted a ride. I hesitated. He seemed alright, I thought, and was friendly, but why such a need to be helpful? I got in, not sure it was the right move. We rode for a while through the center of downtown. The morning was crisp, a blue sky, strong summer scents. He made small talk, innocuous: Where did I work, what was my name? Suddenly, with a quick movement, he lunged at my leg with one hand, keeping the other on the wheel. I kept talking but shifted on the plastic seat, away from his thick fingers. His hair was black and greasy, he looked around forty-five, thick around the middle. Nothing in his tone of voice indicated he was doing anything strange; he kept talking to me, cordial, small patter, just driving along low-key, harmless. Again he lunged at my thigh. I moved up against the car door, scared. Was this really happening? I knew it had been a huge mistake to get in the car with him. When he stopped at a light, I unlocked the door, flung it open, and jumped out into the intersection, into the maze of waiting cars, and ran.

I would never again be as naive as I was that summer morning at nineteen. You learn. Still, I walked the streets late and all over town.

Careful but never allowing caution to completely cramp my style, my wanderlust, my adventurous vigor. I fooled myself in order to survive. Convinced myself that I could beat the shit out of any guy that tried anything on me.

Without a doubt, men enjoy a certain expansive freedom on the streets. Even so, this relative relief from particular threats of violence—from rape or sexual harassment—isn't completely what it's cracked up to be.

I knew this intense male combativeness and territoriality would take some getting used to. I have always abhorred violence. It seems small-minded, primitive, and unimaginative. All this testy male behavior seemed slightly ridiculous—a gang of pubescent apes beating on their chests, peeling bananas, and smashing them into each other's faces for a show of force.

John is one of my first roommates once I decide to begin living with people again, after I've gotten through the initial phase of transition. In the early years, I wanted to live alone, since I didn't want to deal with people's reactions to my transition in my own living room. Originally from Brooklyn, John has huge muscles anchoring a short, wide frame. He's a competitive weight lifter, and, once he starts doing drugs again, a holdup artist; I didn't know anything about John's sideline of breaking and entering houses or mugging people in Golden Gate Park until long after we'd lived together on Julian Street.

When I tell him that I am transsexual, John's response is one of the most memorable. A display of guts, brawn, and jocular mendacity. With a bottle of cold beer in hand, John gives me the lowdown on total guy-ness one Sunday afternoon. I stand with him looking out over the porch into the blue sky, three stories up. He advises me, "If you're a guy, you just gotta figure that at some point in your life, you're gonna be sent to the hospital after getting the shit beat outta you or you're gonna at least get your ass beat a few times. I mean, that's all part of it. It's no big deal.

I mean, so you get a few ribs broke, huh? It's no big deal. You can get 'em fixed. It's just part of being a guy."

Gulping at my beer, I gaze at him and stretch my lips into an expression of calm acceptance, nodding through a strained face at his reasonable, practical advice. John scratches his bare chest, grins, and shrugs his massive shoulders. "It ain't no big deal, man, believe me. It's just ribs. So they get broke! Ya fix 'em. Ya go to the hospital. That's what a hospital is for. You know, when I was living back in Brooklyn, there was a bar the guys went to on Saturday nights, all the guys in the neighborhood, it was called The Sand Lot. The Sand Lot. Now, you know what happened at The Sand Lot?" I shake my head. "Well, I'll tell ya. Guys beat the shit out of each other. That's what we did. Every weekend. For fun. You'd go in there, grab a beer, someone'd start a fight, there'd be punches flying, one guy'd be smashing a bottle over another guy's head, another guy'd be strangling some other guy. Man, that's what we did! On the weekends. It was, 'Hey, man, let's go to The Sand Lot!' and you knew, you knew, what would happen there. It was great!" I listen, nodding at what seem to be appropriate moments. John laughs loudly, pitching his head back on his massive neck, he gulps a stream of cold beer.

I am starting to get the picture about guys and fighting—the strange, dissolute shock treatment. All vaguely familiar, something I'd practiced when I was a kid, mostly with male friends, or alone in Oklahoma City in my back yard, playing cowboys and Indians, or secret agent with a sleek 007 spy rifle. Search and destroy, pursue, strategize, deploy secret weapons and forces, capture! The diversion of chaotic energies, of aggression or wanderlust, into an ordered, skillful reenactment of suspense, competition, risk. Coming close to the abyss, right at the edge, looking down into the widening hole, the gaping intersection of death and peril, falling in, then somehow finding a passage, a secret power, a formerly cloaked force, crawling back out, surviving, winning, beating all the odds.

I loved the friendly competition of wrestling and would challenge my male playmates to wrestle, sweaty in a ball of dust on the playground.

I could beat just about all the guys in first, second, and third grades, except for the fat boys, and then it was a draw. Fat Steve punched me in the stomach near the jungle gym and the world shook. I wrestled big Bill down to a stalemate, both of us exhausted, me in my required dress with scabby knees, always ready for more.

But I grew up, and my body changed. Tall and lanky, sometimes the tallest kid in my elementary school class, I grew into adolescence and then, to my resigned consternation, womanhood. As adolescence blossomed I felt weaker and smaller, softer, a lassitude crept on me. I spent more time daydreaming, reading, listening to music, singing, and less time being active. Although I was an ace long-distance runner, and established a school record in junior high with my first three-mile run, I was no longer as fired with ambitious fervor for athletic achievement. I took tae kwon do on and off for six years and enjoyed the rigorous workout, sparred occasionally with guys in class, and did push-ups on my knuckles. Although a rugged athleticism persisted, I would never again be one of the guys out on the playground as I almost was in elementary school. With adolescence, the underlying female blueprint for my body asserted itself. While the boys I had played with suddenly became larger, more muscular, I felt as though my body almost shrank in size. I experienced an encroaching fragility, a gradual lessening of sheer physical courage. Leaking out of me as childhood died with its dreams of manly heroism and spectacular superhero feats.

John talks to me about boxing as we watch it on cable TV. He describes the weight classifications—strawweight, flyweight through welterweight and up to heavyweight. I am a welterweight at 145 pounds, and he, although shorter than me, is a middleweight at 160 pounds, with his pumped-up weight lifter's physique. John, for all his tough talk and grueling eyeball-to-eyeball bar-fight, robbery, and prison experience, is also a sweetly handsome man with finely drawn, pretty features. He had once been a Chippendales dancer and was constantly being hustled by gay men for jobs as a bare-chested waiter. He confesses, "I tried boxing, man, it's a great workout. Tough. But, I'll tell ya, I don't want to mess up my face. Those guys, they really get their faces messed up. Smashed-up eyes, screwed-up noses, weird foreheads with bumps out to here, forget it." I agree. With a face like his, which could earn him money, and had, why risk it? Even the toughest-talking guys have their vain moments, their secret fears, their weak-kneed fantasies.

Just how common was this man-on-man violence? Were all these gassed-up stories chest-beating, talk like a short shot of piss to stake a claim on the Russian roulette of manhood? Was it all lies? Or just some of it?

At one market research company where I worked, two guys had been hospitalized after having the tar beat out of them; one for stepping on a guy's sneaker, the other for simply walking around on an early Sunday afternoon on Haight Street. These were young, straight white males. Once I started talking to men about this, I found that many had stories of sudden, violent encounters with other men, no matter who they were or where they were from. Threats, fistfights, shouting matches, sudden outbursts that would escalate into broken bones or blackened eyes.

While we were roommates, John had gotten revenge on a young guy who'd ripped him off at knifepoint by lying in wait the next evening. He beat the teenager mercilessly, with compacted, battering force. Pummeling him, steaming with wild rage and vengeance. He almost tore the guy's ear off. John made the guy bring him to where he lived, and while the young mugger looked on, crying and whimpering, John took his television and toaster, which was nearly all that the kid had in the empty apartment he lived in with his mother. When he came back to the house, John was so tanked up with adrenaline his eyes were popping and flaming, buzzing, he talked nonstop, in an obsessive rant, about ambushing the guy and beating his head into the concrete, ripping at his ear, making him scream and beg for mercy. He wanted to go back and do it some more.

The quintessential male experience is frontline combat. Women have fought in wars, it's true, and in the animal world, a female animal with her offspring is the most deadly. In the human realm, women whose lives and families are immediately threatened will also fight fiercely, and guerrilla warfare is an arena where women excel in many disparate areas of the globe. Even so, the totality of the picture is decidedly masculine. For the greater part of human history, to be male is to have to kill. Kill prey for food, or kill other men to defend or expand one's territory. Kill to enshrine some abstract principle; kill for a religion; kill for a way of life. Men's bodies are aptly designed for the rigors of combat. Sleek and compact, with less body fat than women's bodies. Men are more muscular, with thicker, harder skin, more massive bones, larger frames. The hormonal stuff that builds and fuels male muscle mass, that regulates body-fat distribution and bone density, that shoots men's height up—honing male endurance and energy—also makes men more prone to wildly charged outbursts of rage, to stretching the limits of physical daring and capability, to a hypervigilant, nearly paranoid territoriality, to the combative resolution of conflict, to war.

CHAPTER 46:
TESTOSTERONE, ENERGY, AND AGGRESSION

igher testosterone levels do seem to make for higher aggression levels. When I told Monika Treut, the director of *Max,* that I felt as though I had more energy on testosterone, she asked, perceptively, whether or not I also felt more aggressive: "When I think of someone having more energy, I also think of someone being more aggressive." I actually wasn't sure how to answer this question; it is difficult to view and judge oneself from the outside. However, I know that I've had experiences which indicate that my level of aggression has risen.

Aggression in males is fanned into an array of distinctive expressions: flamboyance, impatience, irritability, a calm and watchful paranoia, heroic physical courage, and the intoxication of daredevilry, a burning intensity energized, a heightened urge to control and dominate. I've noticed that I do take up more airspace in conversations now, especially with women, and have to hold myself back, watch that I'm not soaking up all the airtime without realizing it, on a roll, spinning out, a slight euphoria. Expansive, full to bursting, sitting on top of the world. Marilyn Monroe once said that men were too talkative, and I think I understand why now. Even though there may be more groping for the exact words, the urge to gab is undiminished as the energy level is high. Talking, often to impress, is also another way of staking out territory. Talking like a slow strut through a stage door.

Looking back at old journal entries from the time I began testosterone, I see a pattern emerge.

Journal entry, August 1989:

Told off Tama today. I'm not sure how it happened. She called and we started arguing about some fine point in the conversation, she started to attack me, I'd tried real hard to be reasonable, help her to see my side, to understand that I wasn't against her, my usual diplomacy. Her words were curt, nasty, ringing, and sharp. I felt she was unfair. I attempted to take responsibility. She circled back, bitterly patronizing, accusing me of being morally and emotionally defective. She sounded paranoid. I reassured her. And calmly hung up the phone. Then, it happened. Before I knew what I was doing I had the phone in my hand and called her back. I was speaking to her emphatically, telling her in no uncertain terms that she had no right to talk to me in that tone of voice. I was shaking, livid with rage. She backed down. Stunned. The feelings I had were amazing. A brutal ascension of anger, unbidden, unexpected, and rising out of my depths, taking over. I wasn't going to take shit from her, and I let her know. I'm finding again and again that my boundaries are stronger somehow than before. Flares of hot anger shooting up from my feet through my solar plexus into my chest, flaming and swelling, shooting out into my head. I act; a primal, elemental impulse. Taking control through the loss of control.

Has the testosterone made me more aggressive? It has definitely lowered my threshold for anger and impatience, and frustration. When I called Tama back, it felt as though the call were an unbidden event happening *to* me. As though I was the random site on which an intimately confounded amalgam of emotion, tension, and expression was being created and set off. The site of an explosion. If I am more aggressive, am I also more insensitive, egocentric? More prone to acting out, to the flaying alive of my psyche with raw anger?

Journal entry, January 1990:

I see now how guys get into explosive fights. Over parking spaces or cutting each other off on the road. For most of my life, I've been easygoing, usually patient, except when I lose or I'm trying to find something. These days, since testosterone, although I am generally even tempered, I do notice an impatience gnawing at my gut much sooner, my threshold for frustration is lower. I draw boundaries faster, don't put up with as much shit from people. Could it be that because of their hormonal makeup, men tend to have stronger boundaries than women do? To not take as much shit or abuse?

I've watched transsexual men have marked personality changes once they've begun hormone treatment. One of the most predictable is an increased intolerance for bad behavior from others. Al had an extremely domineering and bitchy girlfriend. She was always at him about something—his clothes, his job, his taste in books or music. She would go on harangues that seemed to last forever, relentless, an acid tongue. I predicted that as soon as Al got on testosterone, things would change. I kept this information to myself and waited. Sure enough, after being on testosterone three months, he called me up in shock: "Max, I just told Sunshine off. I can't believe it. I told her all these things I would never have thought to say to her. I mean, it was terrible, I said really nasty things, but they just came out of me!"

"What did she do?" I asked.

"She's in shock. Totally shocked. I really told her off. I can't imagine ever saying those things to her before."

"Yeah," I smiled, "what would you have done before?"

"Oh," he laughed softly, "I guess I would have cried. She used to make me cry for hours and hours. It's good, I guess, but it is strange. It's like there's this anger coming over me so much sooner, instead of just the pain. Do you think this is normal?"

I laughed. "Don't worry, Al. It happened to me, too. Remember Tama? She was a lot like Sunshine, always going on long harangues where she would put me down, do these elaborate character assassinations. It would get me so upset, I would cry for hours, too, and feel devastated the entire day. Then, after I took the testosterone for a few months, I ended up telling her off one day. Out of the blue. I was in shock. I told her off and she shut up. She didn't say a word. And when I got off the phone, I only cried for a few seconds. That's it, a few seconds! It was unbelievable."

I told Al not to worry. His behavior was a direct result of the testosterone, that flash of hot anger rising up so fast. Initially, those feelings seem nearly foreign, you're reacting in such a dramatically different way from how you did previously. At least for us, the testosterone appears to have the beneficial effect of helping to put up barriers between ourselves and the negative, intrusive behavior of others.

I imagine this might sound like part of a brilliant advertising campaign for testosterone.

Two guys talking:

"Yeah, I finally told the bitch off."

"Yeah, me, too."

"Strange, huh?"

"Yeah, Al, what came over us?"

"Must be this great testosterone stuff."

"Yeah, must be, Al. No more of this crying for hours. *It gave us balls. Genuine balls.*"

CHAPTER 47:
FURTHER INITIATIONS

Mina's voice is in my ear, alluring, sweetly melodic, a scintillating narcotic. I've been out here on the street, talking to her on this pay phone for more than an hour. This is the section of Market Street where tourism and skid row collide. Tourists in shorts and windbreakers wait in line for the cable car alongside a loose crowd: men with most of their teeth missing, limber teenagers in knit caps and baggy pants, middle-aged women in red stretch pants with puffy faces out shopping, bleached blondes in cheap plastic high heels, long-haired wiry motorcycle riders wearing black leather and engineer's boots, homeless people asking for spare change, street preachers scowling and screaming at everyone to repent now, before it's too late. The street blurs dissonant, sharply outlined in a prome-nade of personae.

I've been on this line a long time. Twisting my weight from one foot to the other, standing up facing this metal box stuck on a pole. This pay phone feels too exposed. It's not an old-fashioned phone booth enclosed in glass; it's a phone box on a concrete pole set out in the open arena of the street—vulnerable. I've been standing so long my lower back feels like the metal pole—hard, rigid with tension. I clutch the black receiver tight in my fist, eyes darting, unfocused. Street noise. Random people stop, watch, and wait for me to get off the line. But this call is long-distance, and I want to talk with Mina for as long as I can. I have moved once again, but don't yet have my phone installed. Mina is traveling to New York on business, going to exhibit a small collection of her pho-tographs. This pay phone is the only connection I'll have until she gets back from New York and I see her in person again.

Mina has done a great deal of visual art—mostly photography—and worked shooting music videos and fashion. A delicate woman with hazel green eyes and jet black hair, she possesses a tensile, ener-getic grace. She's lived in Europe, is fluent in both French and Italian, her photography has been featured in magazines and exhibited both here and abroad. She tells me that in Europe men and women *like* each other. There is an unabashed erotic energy between the sexes. "They enjoy each other over there!" she laughs. Her voice is like a drum of honey, soothing, I feel transported.

The first time I heard her voice, it was on my answering machine. She spoke so quickly I could barely make out her first name. I played the message over a few times and still couldn't quite make it out. It was her voice that struck me—a sweetly articulate sexuality tugged inside her voice. I had to smile, *Sounds like a babe.* I felt like a satyr making the floor with bright, black hooves.

A friend of mine had given her my phone number; he said that she was looking for models for photos she was shooting. When we spoke

I sensed an enormously perceptive and rapt intelligence—a passionate mind. I felt an immediate rapport.

Mina told me that she had black hair and was small boned, though not short. I climbed into the front seat of her blue car and smiled at her. She was even more beautiful than I'd imagined, with her gorgeous, luscious mouth and pretty hazel eyes. Mina's skin was finely textured and stretched to perfection over high cheekbones. She looked petite at the steering wheel.

She drove slowly away from the curb, glancing at me sideways. "It's freaky, you know, to actually see someone when you have only been speaking to them on the phone." We had already had a few long conversations, finding ourselves immersed in conversations without meaning to. I must have looked slightly entranced. It was awkward for a moment as we adjusted to each other's physical presence. There was a femininity about her that was enchanting—she was like a doe.

All at once, sitting in her car, I could feel the length of my legs. I became conscious of their weight and strength, they felt cramped in the front seat. I was wearing my black leather jacket and tight black pants. My hair was long then, and I had a bit of a goatee creeping in. My masculinity hung over me with a playful power. It felt so good to really meet her, to be looking at Mina at last.

Our first stop was at the Laundromat—I was embarrassed. I imagined that she must have known that I was planning to seduce her as she helped me to fold the guilty bed sheets. I got a better look at her then—she was nimble and very youthful looking. Although she was in her thirties, she seemed younger; her legs slim. From certain angles, she looked nearly teenaged.

We became lovers. Making love for hours like angels. Angels drunk on sweat, dreams, and pleasure. Sex was easy with Mina; she responded like a beautiful, nubile animal with alert and fine-tuned senses. We went to the ocean and held each other, watching the water slip into the sand. She told me that she was afraid of passion, that she didn't want to burn up.

And so we begin to see each other, although she travels a great deal, making the time we have together precious.

I see him out of the corner of my eye. No significance. A guy about my height. White, probably around my age, although he looks older. Waiting, without complaint. A hint of tension, frayed agitation at the edges. The man glances toward me, shifts with an increasing scintilla of nerves, head cocked, hands jammed in pockets, a small tan briefcase stowed next to him on the sidewalk. I figure he'll get the picture that I'm going to be on the line a while. The waiting man vanishes like a fading cartoon thought balloon from my peripheral vision; I begin to forget he was ever there.

A woman with a tree branch tied to the top of her head saunters by, singing "Somewhere over the Rainbow" in a high-pitched voice. She walks back and forth several times in front of me, then crosses the wide street, breaking into a staccato laugh at the military-like procession of cars passing, obedient to signals and signs, straining toward precise destinations and hourly rewards. She looks amused by this busy scrawl of pedestrians and motorized consumers. Leans to look in the windows of the parked cars, a long row of resting machines, potentialities of speed and efficiency, frustrated dreams of long vacations. She steadies herself on their roofs and watches their interiors for a sign. An errant symbol. A clue to their inhabitants' habits or fears: gum wrappers, cigarette butts crammed into tiny ashtrays, a pink plastic Virgin Mary stranded on the dashboard near sticky candy residue, a half-emptied bottle of rum on the vinyl car seat, a Club locking the steering wheel with a tight grip. The street woman absently touches the tree branch tied to the top of her head as if she's remembering another time. Possibly, a time when she drove a car just like this one. A tenderness washes over her eyes, followed by a roving glee. I watch her and smile, listening to Mina tell me about the New York subway crowds, the seminars she's attending, the ambience and noise of the streets and clubs after dark. She tells me that she loves me over and over, I say the same to her. We could go on like this forever, and we do. I'm in a trance. Colors seem a little brighter, I have a heightened sense of place. Mina stretches my senses out as we talk, time warps and wraps around each word.

Then it happens. A hand steals the pay-phone receiver out of my hand—grabs it and slams it down. A propulsive burst of wind and force. *What? Where?* I turn and look at the man gliding away from me, feeling shock, disbelief. Gape at him, open jawed for a moment, spliced seconds. Anger. *This son of a bitch just grabbed the phone from my hand and slammed it down!* By the time I fully realize what he's done, he's off walking fast away from me up the street, his back to me, wearing a wrinkled beige jacket. He looks sedately nine-to-five, that same tan briefcase I'd briefly registered moments earlier, a businessman's haircut. Not a street person, not a young tough, just some impatient briefcase carrier. I swear at his retreating form, make the decision. *I'm going to follow this one, I'll go for it. I've had it.*

To be passive weakens the system in tentative degrees, softening and rotting the vital instincts. Survival—a primal and primary concern. How can a person survive allowing these violent incidents to continue without putting up any resistance? Got to learn how to fight back, at least make a gesture, at least learn to fake it. Thought escalates, a burning relayed from brain to chest, a scalding transposition of emotions. Sensations of fear and anger take over. I begin to walk with predatory intention, *follow the guy. Track him down.*

I've figured out by now, after four and a half years as Max, that this guy wouldn't have grabbed the phone from my hand if he didn't think he could take me on. I am close to his size, not built like a beef door. He figured I wasn't insane, or packing an automatic or a handgun. I didn't look like I was on antipsychotic medication. Maybe *he* was on Prozac. Who knows? He took a chance. Pushed himself toward a collision, a twist of fate.

I did the same. Looked him over in that split moment after he'd slammed the phone down. I assessed his build, his sanity, his capacity for cruelty or sudden inexplicable acts of petty violence. Was he a thief, an imbecile, a drunk jock, a bank manager? Was he waiting to call his drug dealer?

That could be the case. You never know. Even yuppies have drug dealers.

Concrete buildings, parking lots blur past us, I'm coming up behind him. I let out a wild roar, up from my guts, a bellow, using my new male voice to its deepest, most savage advantage. When I had a woman's voice it seemed easier to yell loud or scream. I could project my voice easily over a greater distance. Now it takes a larger effort, a more strained working of the muscles to throw my voice out into space, as though I now have to throw a heavier object.

It's all rushing in my head now, intentions, feelings, fantasies. I walk fast, propelling a long stride. Behind him a half block, in the middle of the city, people's faces roll past me.

Once he realizes I'm behind him, the man in the beige jacket appears to crumble inside. Crumble, crumple, and sag. He turns and glances at me over his shoulder, starts to run, slowly, lightly, a low-energy gallop. Stealing little glances, a quickening panic animates his movements. I'm behind him three-quarters of a city block, determined, glowering. My heart's racing. I keep yelling at his form diminishing ahead of me. A frantic quality stretches the air between our bodies, I can't believe that this is happening but it is, and *I am starting to enjoy myself a little.*

He keeps glancing back. Short looks, panicked. I play the part, with feeling. *"I'm gonna get you, motherfucker, asshole, fucker, I'm going to get you! What did you do? I'm gonna get you!"*

Is this against the law? Will I get arrested? Who cares!

He did it. He began this game, and now he has to face the consequences. The panic. The blood rushing, senses opening with adrenaline.

I pass a black guy on the street who gives me a concerned look. "What if that guy has a gun?" he says to me as I surge past him, glowering at the beige-coated man, yelling from time to time just to keep him moving.

Somehow, in my insides, I know that he doesn't and say so to this man as I hurtle past him loosely striding, swinging my shoulders in a long, ambling gait. I sniffed the wind before I began this and I *know*. Like a tightly wound animal, a wily predator.

Anger comes, fire shooting up in short stabs. There's an intoxication to this pursuit. Different from the way it felt being female, it's hotter. *A rush* as the hypothalamus surges, "Fight, flight, or fuck," the streetwise throne of id. That portion of the brain to which testosterone is annealed in ancient enthrallment.

The whole thing is comical as well. A balloon getting pumped up larger and larger, swollen with its own hot air, until it bursts, a rain of red rubber ribbons—a lunatic clown suit.

The truth is, I don't really want to catch up with this guy. I just want him to feel fear, to regret the second he reached out and snatched that receiver out of my hand. Around the corner, I look through the open entrance of a gate. We're by the art museum, an expansive area. He's walking fast, close to the white buildings, body pitched forward, the wind ruffling his coat. In this instant, he seems so ordinary, just some lightly frazzled man in a hurry. That's it. I'm done. I watch him lope away, stand still, feeling taut, squeezed full of adrenaline. Heart pounding, I stand and wait for a still, observant moment.

CHAPTER 48:
COLD DARK SHADES

I imagine and hope that Mina will laud my courage, my manly pursuit of the telephone interloper. I know that this is silly; even so, a part of me wants her voice to light up on the other end of the line when I call her back, glowing with sweet admiration, a nimbus of feminine sighs.

Am I buying into a retarded male trip? Probably.

Memories wheel back through my head of all the times I've been threatened by guys, punched, glared at. All since becoming physically male and living as a man. There was Jim, a houseguest of one of my roommates who threatened to beat the shit out of me because I accidentally ate his tomato. At the time, I was staying in an old flat on Church Street with a bunch of Deadheads and a bicycle messenger, Scooter. They had no idea that I had ever been anything other than a man. At first, everyone was friendly, and I enjoyed the camaraderie. The bike messenger was a fun guy, mostly into beer and bikes, and I reminisced with him about the days in the mid-eighties when I, too, had been a bike messenger. I taught him how to smoke cigars; he told a mutual friend that I was showing him some of the finer points of masculinity.

In time, the Deadheads' brand of peace and love appears to be twisted with a stilted and cliché-ridden political paranoia. They have a boorish habit of sitting around stoned on pot talking about "the pigs" in loud voices. Talking in circles, repeating the same phrases with compulsive vengeance, "the pigs, man, the pigs, fuck the pigs. Groovy." I end up feeling like I'm living with the Manson Family. And although Jim claims to advocate free housing and the overthrow of corporate capitalism, when he realizes that I've accidentally eaten his tomato, he flies into a rage, stares me down, and threatens to beat the shit out of me. I know by now to stand my ground. To not show fear, to be ready and willing for anything. We face each other down over the tomato, neither flinching, until one of my other roommates intervenes.

Later, there was the odd angry man who wanted to fight me because I accidentally spilled coffee on him as I was walking down Market Street. I'd had it. Each confrontation had pushed me further.

When it came to the briefcase carrier, I decided to fight back and beat one of these jerks at his own game. These guys will eat you alive otherwise.

I call Mina back. For some reason, she isn't worried.

"Sorry about what happened, but this guy, this guy with a briefcase, grabbed the phone out of my hand and slammed it down, hung it up. Right out of my hand!" Mina doesn't say anything. I continue, "I guess he was waiting for the phone a while. I didn't realize that he had been waiting, I mean, he never said anything. I was just standing here, talking to you, and the next thing I know, *bang!* He snatches the phone and slams it down! Can you believe it?" I'm breathless, explaining the abruptness of it all, still cranked up on adrenaline, spinning slightly.

"That's terrible," Mina replies.

"Well, I got so mad at this jerk I followed him six blocks or so. I actually chased him, yelling *'Fuck you asshole!'* I just wanted to scare this guy, I didn't really want to hurt him, I mean. It just really pissed me off. I didn't want him to get away with it completely."

Mina is quiet for a moment. I wait expectantly for her response. Finally, she speaks softly and firmly. "You are a very primitive man. Is that what you are going to be, Max, a primitive man?"

I don't know how to reply.

She continues in dark, somber tones, "This is very primitive behavior, so macho."

"But," I interject, "I had to do something! These guys just think that they can do this to you anytime if you don't do something!"

There is a void on the other end of the phone. Mina isn't responding. "Mina, don't you see? I'm not sure what to do, but maybe at some point I have to fight back, or at least show myself that I can. I can't just be totally passive and watch while this stuff happens. I've got to do something!"

Mina is silent. We are continents apart, emotionally and physically. Mina's world is far more civilized, quieter, less brash and violent. There are different rules and expectations. Now that I'm a man, I have a new problem, one I don't quite know how to resolve. One I hadn't anticipated. How can I communicate the vagaries and pressures of a male life to someone who can only imagine them? From her perspective, as I know from experience, this male posturing and fighting looks ridiculous and boorish. It parades at absurd angles and puffs itself up, bloated and beady eyed, foolish and full of chest-pounding vanity. On top of it all, Mina is a feminist. I don't yet realize that this will become a problem between us. The universe is about to play the most profound joke upon me. I, the former lesbian feminist, am beginning to argue with my beloved feminist girlfriend about feminism, sexism, male privilege, and behavior. Mina's silence and disapproval are impenetrable.

I start to worry that I'm doing something to attract this kind of testy behavior from other men. Do I look too much like a tough guy? Or a wimp? Some geeked-out weirdo, a fuzzy-brained intellectual, a guy with no clue as to his surroundings? Do I appear to be looking for a fight?

Bob looks me over. He is a coworker at Atlas Research, a market research firm where I work on and off. He has no knowledge of my female past. I trust his opinion. Bob has been in fights here and there, has a vivid temper, a fiery streak. Even so, he is far from being a mindless lout. Bob is a musician, a computer science major and a fitness enthusiast who's always drinking bottled water and talking about running and his morning regime of two hundred push-ups. We share a male camaraderie. Once, when I first began working at Atlas, he asked whether or not I was married and had a family of kids to support. It occurred to me that at the age of thirty-five, I could very well have said yes. A wife and children—the role of provider. Bob was relieved when I replied that I didn't. After all, supporting a family on the hourly rate we were earning would be hard to imagine.

"What am I doing wrong?" I ask Bob on a blue and clear afternoon while we are walking home from work. In the middle of Market Street near Civic Center, I'd just bumped into a crazy guy who bellowed that he would "go at it" with me after I accidentally spilled some coffee on him. Hot liquid swished out when he collided with the cardboard cup I was delicately carrying, absently watching people and stores, holding the steaming liquid out to the side and away from my body like a sour poison. Startled, I'd said, "Sorry." He'd grunted, but came back later, yelling at me that he was ready to "go at it"! I realized regretfully that I am definitely too spacey and should watch where I am going, especially when carrying a volatile liquid. Being too spacey as a guy in broad daylight could have explosive consequences! If I had bumped into that guy as Anita, he most likely would just have spit out, "Bitch, watch where you're going!" and that would have been the end of it. Or maybe he would have tried to ask me out.

Bob examines my appearance, searching for a clue. This episode has also made him nervous. Even Bob is not fearless. His eyes scour my leather jacket, a look of concentration tightens his features. "When you wear a black leather motorcycle jacket like that, man, you gotta be careful. If you do that, it looks tough, like you're ready for something. You present a challenge to these guys." Bob keeps looking at me for what feels like a long time, top to bottom, and finally concludes, "And those shades. Max, if you wear dark shades that hide your eyes, that's it, man, they're gonna go after you! People don't like mirror shades. Take them off. They look cold. People can't see your eyes. Those things are cold, man, they are cold!"

Compliantly, I take the shades off and balance them in my hand. I gaze at Bob in the fresh breeze, suddenly feeling very young—hazel green eyes vacant and at that moment—incredulous. I'd suspected that my look was at least part of the problem—my black leather jacket and dark motorcycle cop shades. I looked too tough, a challenge. It is almost a compliment.

What is intriguing about Bob's observations is that these are the same accessories and styles that had actually warded off trouble in the past. When I was a woman, I'd found that wearing a black leather jacket, spiked black hair, dark reflector shades, army boots, chains, and lots of metal seemed to keep away men on the streets. Looking like Tank Girl, I was able to walk around without being whistled and catcalled at the entire length of the street. Prepunk, when I had long, light brown hair, wore blue jeans, and was braless in T-shirts, Mission Street had been a relentless runway of "Hey, baby's" and hissing snake sounds. Once I became more androgynous, punked out, spiky haired, angular, and alien looking, that stopped. To my delight, many men appeared to be afraid of me. I wore a long, heavy chain over the shoulder of my black leather jacket and clanked around wherever I walked. A dead silence took the place of catcalls, along with eerie, fearful stares. Although people would scream "Devo!" or "Whip it good!" or sometimes even spit or lean out of opened car windows and pretend to vomit as I passed, at least the wolf whistling and ogling had stopped. This was before punk became any kind of familiar fashionable item in America—Queer Nation, MTV, or otherwise. It still had plenty of shock value—it was bizarre, anarchic, possibly dangerous. Teenagers would get hysterical when they glimpsed me. Once when I was strolling in suburban Walnut Creek (on an odd temp job), a carload of teenage girls swept past me, screaming in unison, a wild, joyful, hysterical shrieking. I wasn't sure if they were excited, scared, or having orgasms.

Although these reactions did make me feel as though I were venturing out into a war zone every day, in time, I got used to all this mayhem following me wherever I went and even learned to enjoy it. My slouching posture improved from feeling on display, I began to carry myself upright, with a long-legged stride blasting down the street. All this was an intriguing testament to the power of appearances, the ability of costuming to ward off danger and display power.

In any case, as a hard-assed punk rock chick I'd aroused fear and awe. As a cool-looking rocker dude in a black leather jacket, dark shades, and long hair, I was getting nothing but trouble—challenges, weird male angst. The look was similar, but the response it got was vastly different.

As a male, looking like a hard-ass can attract genuine hard-asses to you. Will had warned me about this in the beginning, he had stopped wearing his black leather motorcycle jacket for this very reason. It was a fine balance. I also discovered that wearing my hair short and wearing a black leather jacket often got me tagged as gay (at least in San Francisco or New York City). This struck me as odd, since long hair was once considered to be a feminine attribute on men, and therefore used to be associated in many people's minds with homosexuality. In fact, the short hair on gay men in the seventies was initially an attempt to look "butch." Apparently, times have changed. As a woman, long hair is definitely feminine, but growing my hair long as a man takes on new dimensions and tags me as macho. If I were to visit a gay bar with Alexander, many of the men would give me closed or puzzled looks, like I don't belong. Jack's roommates ask with some resentment, "So, are you going to become a macho heavy metal guy now?" My clothes, gestures, tone of voice, and hairstyle mean entirely different things than they did when I was female.

I am learning. The hard way. Each encounter with these unpredictable male forces motivates me to sharpen my wits. To question myself, my presentation, to interrogate my body, state of mind, my newly appointed manhood. I have never been hazed by any fraternity, but I sure am getting the treatment—initiation rites.

But what to do with this information? I don't want to buy into the cultural effluvium of masculinity, or, as they say in academic circles, perform the embodiment of heteronormative and hegemonic phallocratic institutional supremacist bodies. Still, when it comes to whether or not I am going to get my ass kicked, I really don't want to be a martyr for the cause of sensitive nice guys. On the other hand, I certainly don't want to attract all the frustrated dudes out there who are looking for a cockfight.

And then there is Mina's reaction. I can't convince her that I did the right thing by following and yelling at the telephone snatcher. Of course, there's a chance that I didn't. The truth is, I am experimenting. When she reacted with disapproval, with such dark, somber tones of judgment, I felt a little ashamed. Sheepish, like I'd been caught posturing, pretending to be something that is not worth being.

But what am I to do when confronted with this violence? I feel squeezed by inadequate choices—man or mouse, wimp or Sylvester Stallone clone—bleak cartoons.

In time, I will adjust and learn to stand up to man-on-man violence consistently, without encouraging it. This process of resocialization as male takes years and a great deal of thought. The complex process of resocialization is another aspect of the change that can only be lived through and not completely anticipated—an unscripted rite of passage.

CHAPTER 49:
THE END OF TEARS

Journal Entry: September 1989

I can't cry! I haven't really cried in four whole months. Outside, a damp gray mists the air. I'm feeling a tight sadness compacted in my chest. I've felt contained by its compression all afternoon. Slowly, I begin to realize that anytime I felt this way as female, I would have cried easily, released this pent-up sadness and frustration through tears. Now I can't. I find it impossible to weep.

I ponder this, understanding immediately and instinctively that this change is chemically driven, another startling and unexpected aspect of my hormonal transformation. I look around at the

walls of my apartment and out the glass door to the lemon tree, suc-
cinct in its alignment to the ground, an arterial spray of leaves and
fruit crowning a tight stem. The tree looks nearly artificial, sover-
eign and remote beyond the glass door, a transplanted god.

I close my eyes and concentrate. Perhaps if I really, really try.
The feelings are dark, a stressed-out sad mélange. But no tears. Not
even one. Oh, I manage a small moistness, hanging in wet anchors
tucked into the corners of my eyelids. Hurt wells up—that wet, salty
feeling tiny and spreading in my throat—but I can't push these sen-
sations forward and out into expression. Suddenly I feel an urge to
fly to the borders of the room, to smash with my fists all along where
the ceiling adjoins the wall. Smash in a riot of fists! Smash! Fucking
kill! Smash! Fucking break the goddamn wall!

The only release for these turgid feelings, pent up. Smash! Break!
Flail with a tight and evil fury!

I pause. This is a fantasy . . . a compelling one. Organic, spring-
ing out of my bones and muscles, into my jaw, clinched and tight. I
clench my fists and crank my head around with sheer stubborn frus-
tration. These feelings defy my endurance.

This fury is pain, not just anger; it is real, raw pain.

I can't release. So I wait. I think and wait. The dark, sad feel-
ings pass. I feel better in a few hours.

This entry captures my discovery early in transition of another aspect
of my changed emotional landscape. The experience brings an insight
I never thought I'd have. I begin to talk to nontranssexual men about
their emotional volatility—the number of times they cry every month
or year, the way sadness and tears feel, what makes them cry, what
they do whenever they want to cry and can't. I also discuss this experience with other transsexual men on testosterone. Additionally, I begin
to collect anecdotes from transsexual women about their emotional
changes after being on estrogen. I compare all of these feelings and

experiences to how I felt before, as female; I attempt to be honest, to extract a distilled, active truth.

Most of my nontranssexual male friends report weeping only once or twice a year. Generally, these guys start out this conversation telling me how very emotional and sensitive they are. Then, pressed for details, they report that they cry for five or ten minutes once or twice a year, unless there is some major heartbreaking or stressful circumstance. Then, possibly, they'll cry four times a year.

Aleister reports how, instead of crying when he's in emotional pain, he feels like smashing things. I think back to my initial testosterone-driven response to frustration and pain. The pounding of a fist into a wall was a sharp and blunt purgative, a drumming howl to make the tears come—like dredging up blood.

The only times I've really wept as male have been those instances when I have been in deep, agonizing, emotional pain, or stressed beyond belief: the loss of a major relationship or a cumulative onslaught, a dense configuration of stress. Even in these extreme circumstances, I cry much less than I would have as female. I probably cried more as Anita in six months than I have as Max in four years.

David, although a very emotional, sensitive, and volatile man, didn't cry as often as I did when we were roommates. I was, then, an ostensibly tough punk rock precursor of a riot grrrl. David tends to depression and definitely used to get hangdog and melancholy, often locking himself into his room in fits of feeling. Yet I always sensed more rage and frustration in his sadness than there was in mine. I remember him getting really upset and talking about "buying a machine gun" during one down episode. I don't think David has ever owned a weapon, but again, now I recognize his frustrated pain. A pain that, when pushed to extremes, is more apt to fantasize about striking out than about simply breaking down in tears.

Ron and I were roommates in the early eighties. A fantastic poet and saxophone player, he looks like Elvis Costello driven by a surrealistic id. When I tell him about this change in my emotions, he isn't surprised. Ron remarks how men, because of this hormonal difference, don't have the "luxury" of crying. "Actually," he says, "women are lucky that they can release their feelings so much easier." He also reports crying only twice a year.

Alexander reports the same pattern—about two cries a year. Certainly a sensitive person, not stereotypically macho, a guy who hates team sports and rarely raises his voice, Alexander is shocked when I tell him that I would often cry two or three times a month when I was a woman. Sometimes I even locked myself in my room and cried, literally, for hours! These crying spells were generally related to my hormonal cycle, at least to some extent. Though they could also spike up suddenly, a break in the levee. "Crying jags" is what these episodes are called, and I never thought I had them, until, as a guy, I no longer did. Considering this, Alexander recalls his female roommate's crying jags. Her bursting into tears, rushing to her room, and weeping. Or her moodiness, which always seemed to surface without warning. Alexander always thought this behavior was manipulative and phony, that she was playing a female game to attract attention. No, I tell him, that isn't necessarily true. That's just how she felt, really. He shakes his head in amazement. "Why would anyone cry so much? About what?"

Now I find myself wondering the same thing. *What in the world was I crying about?*

These crying jags were a part of the natural, discreet rhythm of my life. This rhythm and its attendant crying jag rituals have vanished, the tears have dried up. The weeping bouts were a spontaneous and powerful release, swelling to a crescendo. Will and I both remember with amazement pounding a pillow and crying till our eyes were red and swollen and our cheeks soaked with tears. A solitary pursuit, it was nothing I talked about with other people, like an odd hobby.

Many women have crying jags around the time of their periods. Or they occur with a random frequency. It isn't totally unusual for a woman friend to call me up and say, "I cried all afternoon," or to phone in literal, gnashing tears.

Certainly, there are differences in emotional volatility that also have to do with personality and culture. When I was female, I didn't consider myself emotional. In fact, Selene used to chide me for being "too much in my head." Rarely caught crying in public, I was not big on emotional displays. Some of this is my personality, some of it might be cultural. Although we aren't stoic, but actually huge jokers once you get to know us, Plains Indians aren't big on emotional displays. When I was a child, my mother and American Indian relatives encouraged me not to cry when I got hurt. After all, out on the Great Plains in the old days, too much crying and carrying on just wasn't suited to survival or to getting along with others in a closely knit tribal setting. (Though my mother certainly used to complain about her headaches, particularly while she was vacuuming the drapes! Okay, she didn't vacuum the drapes, but she did vacuum with a hell-bent intensity . . .) Generally, American Indian women never had a cultural directive to act like wilting hothouse flowers with hysteria or fits of fainting. Tepees had no "fainting rooms."

Nonetheless, testosterone appeared to affect my emotions dramatically.

Transsexual women have perplexed tales of how their feelings change once they are on estrogen. Stories of sudden emotional volatility—of feelings being closer to the surface, more accessible to tears. Cruising the Internet, I've read accounts of transsexual women writing in wonder to transgender bulletin boards about the emotional acuity and intensity they feel on estrogen, and how their emotional selves have transformed. They ask for advice from other transwomen who might be further along in the process: *Is this normal? Does anyone else cry now when watching a TV movie of the week, or to sad songs, or even when watching some sappy AT&T commercial about long-distance calling to rarely seen loved ones? Is this okay, or am I losing my mind?!* One transwoman friend, Ingrid, relates how once she was on estrogen, at work she had to stifle an urge to run out of the room and cry at least once a week. Suddenly, it is hard not to be devastated by someone raising their voice, a misunderstanding, or just the day-to-day stress of office politics.

Of course, it takes time to get used to the intensity of these feelings, and eventually, like all women, Ingrid learned to control her impulses. Most women don't feel like running out of the room just because they're yelled at. While pubescent girls tend to let these feelings run wild, adult women learn to get a handle on it. In some respects, these transsexual women, new to transition, are more like teenagers. Just as transmen experience our own emotional surges akin to those of teenage boys. And, like teenagers, we all eventually grow into our new emotional selves. Transwomen report that, although they may adjust, their feelings never "feel" like they did before. The new vulnerability, moodiness, and sensitivity remain.

Some transsexual women report feeling more nurturing once they are on estrogen. One reported that she had never before felt such deep, tender love for her children; she was now much more protective of them, worrying about their safety to the point of distraction. As male, she had been far more caught up in concerns about work and money, more driven. All of this within a few months: Moods sift and change, the hormones work their elusive yet concrete magic. As their skin softens and becomes thinner, it seems almost as though these women's souls, their emotional lives, become softer and their skin metaphorically thinner, as they bask in a translucent light of tender feeling. Estrogen—a sweetened, if stormy, world.

Will and I discuss the differences in the way we relate to women now. He reminisces about how he and his girlfriend used to hold each other and cry watching movies on television. He declares, "You know, I could never be that close to a woman now. We felt such similar things, we were on the same wavelength. Now, there is much more emotional distance. I mean, we did that for fun, Max, we pressed our wet cheeks together and told each other how beautiful we looked all red-eyed and teary!"

Will finds this lesbian bonding ritual hard to imagine now—it is the memory of another person in another time. I laugh, as I can remember doing similar things with my girlfriend Sarah. Holding each other and crying every morning for weeks on end because we were so much in love, or holding each other close and crying as we listened to the fog-horns off the bay. Now, a few tears of joy with a girlfriend, even a passionately loved girlfriend, is a huge event and not a daily mating ritual.

The emotional elements of so-called dyke drama have quieted and faded to a low background hum.

I'd believed that men could cry as much as women if they'd just let themselves go. Men were victims of a masculine ethos that forbade tears, that made them into unfeeling, seething septic tanks of repressed pain ready to lash out.

I was wrong.

Emotionally, I do have a thicker skin now. Certainly, I'm happier as a man since I feel more congruent, yet this change is not simply about general happiness: It concerns aspects of the primal state of masculinity. I can shrug off hurt feelings a lot easier than I ever could before. The hurt is quick and sharp, I'll feel it stab, then a clarity rings in with an emotional distance that contains and quells the pain—dissolving its sting. Women have told me that they notice that I will get hurt emotionally, then just as suddenly shrug it off and act as though nothing happened. Slights and painful emotions are easier to recover from. What might have upset me as female for a few days, might now upset me for a few hours.

Of course, these differences can and do cause a great deal of misunderstanding between men and women. I'd noticed, as female, that when I got into fights with my male friends, serious fights where we'd both be yelling, that I was invariably the one who burst into tears. I'd seen guys cry here and there, but it'd been frustrating to fight with a man and be the one more likely, almost guaranteed, to break down and cry. I resented this. I thought of men as somewhat cold. Even if they were emotionally gregarious, men appeared to possess a frosty tinge; you could see this propensity as strength or as a remote hardness. This masculine emotional atmosphere was mysterious to me, and I often attributed this quality to males simply being "assholes." Now, I understand it differently.

David confided to me that men often sit around and ask each other, behind women's backs, "Why are women so neurotic?" I remember thinking how this was terrifically sexist and inexplicable. How could men ever think such a thing? Now, without estrogen-driven mood swings and crying jags of my own, and after witnessing many a girlfriend's sudden, wild tears, I can see why men may have a perception of women as irrational or overly emotional. Many guys get irritated by these moods, seeing them as a female game or as simply inexplicable. These emotional episodes are not willful manipulation, but just the way women genuinely *feel.*

Women's arguments now often appear to me to be informed more by emotion than by logic (or at least by as much emotion as logic). This is an alarming observation. One transman, Rocky, summed it up like this: Men think about their feelings and women feel their thoughts. I do feel a driven clarity.

On the other hand, I know that often my girlfriends experience depths and ranges of feeling that I can barely touch anymore or, as time goes on, even remember without a sustained effort.

A woman I know going through menopause reports that she too feels this clarity, and sometimes feels like a wise old owl who can see for a very long distance.

On estrogen, every object had an emotional weight. A specific emotional substance, a gravity that pulled feeling into it. The world had an infusion of feeling—tender, sentimental, subtle, and deep. Everything around me was soaked in these feelings. Women's feelings are in Technicolor and men's are in black and white. It's true, except for the red feelings, like anger and lust, or sheer frustration. Being male,

I get stressed out faster now, but I don't feel blue as often, as sweetly sad, nostalgic, or weepy.

And although my sexual passions have been turned up many notches, and mad, obsessive lust makes more sense than ever, the poignant longing of solitary love songs on the radio has become fainter in my ear. Those aching violins play at a distance now.

I feel more emotionally self-sufficient, more independent. I've become more of a loner.

The emotions that each object of my life had accrued have become faint. Everything is flatter. Flatter yet brighter, as though a fog has lifted. I'm not as depressed. There's a freedom. A bright clarity. Will says the same thing. It's more than the relief of being male now; this is a sudden shift to a charged, slightly more euphoric state. A light euphoria. Testosterone is an androgen, there's more get-up-and-go.

Statistically, women experience twice as much depression as men. Men are more prone to "acting out" types of behavior, those smashing and plundering urges I feel when I'm in emotional pain. I spend more time wandering and walking outside, in the streets, exploring at random or covering terrain on long winding walks, and less time in bed, being quiet with a book or with my thoughts. I feel more restless—all that energy, a background buzz charging my life.

Will compares the difference in feeling between female and male hormones to a deep well (estrogen) as contrasted to a very bright light-bulb (testosterone).

Ingrid said that she was "frostier" on testosterone.

Neither is better.

Both have value.

For me, being hormonally male feels right. I slide into it with a rush. The hell with all that crying! Yet, I have to admit, men do miss out.

Women live inside an emotional realm that men cannot even completely imagine. It is lost to us. It doesn't exist, except as a faint color on our emotional palette.

CHAPTER 50:
SWITCHING PLACES

I haven't seen Gene in many years. Gene is now Jan.

When she announced that she could no longer live a lie, and would pursue sex reassignment, Jan's ex-wife had tried to take away her visitation rights. After a trying and painful battle, the courts awarded Jan the right to visit her son. Later, that decision would be reversed. Although she is currently unable to see him, Jan wishes very much to someday reestablish a strong, loving relationship with her child. Unfortunately, for many transsexuals who are parents, custody or visitation rights are denied or curtailed once they decide that they must undertake the life-saving process of medical sex change. This is just one of many areas where transsexuals need to fight for our civil rights. In spite of the burgeoning "transgender" studies in universities and a heightened public sympathy and interest, we have a long way to go.

Although her decision has made her pay a terrible price, I feel relieved for Jan. Automatically, I know she's making the right decision. I've watched Jan struggle, been privy to her guilt about her unexpressed female gender identity, her stifling unhappiness as a man. Clearly, this is the courageous and right path to pursue. Other avenues have been exhausted.

We've talked over the phone many times over the past few years, yet I'm not sure what to expect when I see her in person. She's moved away from San Francisco, lived in Seattle and then Chicago. And time has worked its magic. I have forgiven her for not supporting me in the beginning, understanding that Jan's unresolved gender conflicts had made it hard for her to extend support. It's also hard for people to let go of a cherished image of a friend.

Jan has declared several times that she has gotten big breasts, informing me that she's grown them all on her own—just estrogen, no implants. We decide to meet at the bus terminal before going to eat. Maybe at the Vietnamese place on Sixth Street—a cramped restaurant on skid row with food that's heavenly and reasonably priced. I comb my hair and peer into the mirror. What will Jan think when she sees me? *I* know that I've changed, but a part of me is always leery when I have to meet someone I knew in my previous life. Will they try and find the old me, erase the changes in order to feel comfortable? A small part of me worries that she won't even see the remarkable transformation, although I know that is impossible at this stage. However, people easily lapse into denial, sometimes they even militantly resist change. My ex-girlfriend Roxanne always says to me when we talk on the phone, "Well, you always had a deep voice, anyway."

"Not this deep," I reply.

"No, I guess. . . ."

Then, when we see each other after years, after I'm pretty far along, she says, "You don't look much different, you've only aged."

Roxanne actually stubbornly wanted to believe that the effects of the testosterone, the sharp virilization of my body and face, were only the coarsening effects of age. I was shocked.

I'm running late so I squeeze into a cab heading down to the Transbay bus terminal at the end of Mission Street. It's night and I see the crisscross of cables in the air, the buses waiting in windy concrete parking lots, people milling around. My eyes search the disorderly surface of faces, bodies, machines. Where is Jan? I look for a long time. I'm out of the cab now and walking around, turning my head around on my neck like a searchlight—right and left.

Jan is standing on a small concrete island waiting for me. She's wearing a light summer dress, too thin for most San Francisco summer evenings, a shawl draped around her shoulders. Nonchalant and perfect, she's different than before, almost someone else. I notice the changes with more startling feeling as I move in closer to her. Walking up to me, she smiles. *Jan is a woman.* She certainly looks like a woman to me, without a doubt. More than she had the first time she'd attempted to transition. This time around, there's an aura of composed completion, an ensemble of detailed feminine feeling effusing from her—curves, a thin waist, and a soft glow to her skin. I go up and hug her. Feel a nearly electric current. *Jan feels like a woman!* An unmistakable softness and vulnerability.

I am speechless. It's amazing to see this happen for someone, to become a witness to the effortless intelligence of the hormones guided by the will of someone determined to live their life out in a sex apparently opposite to that of their birth.

She's smiling, seeing the transformation in me, too, looking just as incredulous as I feel. "You look great!" I exclaim.

We walk down Market Street together on our way to the restaurant. I feel protective of her. I had never felt that way before. All the coarseness in Jan has leaked out. Instead of an impish yet sensitive long-haired dude,

I am now walking alongside a pretty woman in a summer dress who is painfully out of place on this long, dark, grimy stretch of Market Street. A woman who looks as though she might need a little protection.

It occurs to me just how vulnerable women in thin flower-print dresses really are at night on wide, abstractly spacious city blocks. I feel afraid for Jan in starts and stops of heart-shrinking anxiety. I don't even remember feeling this protective feeling before, as Anita, when I accompanied a woman in a dress down a street like this. Not with such startling acuity. She seems nearly fragile to me now. The contrasts between Jan and me, between my new perceptions and feelings and my previous ones, make me quiet with reflection.

We get to the restaurant and sit at a small table. Order. A formal feeling. Then lightening up as I talk about my life and she lets me in on hers. It's been a few years on testosterone, and although I am still binding, yes, the feeling I have is that I am now a man.

"Well, you don't look like you have tits. I mean, you look totally flat." Jan points her fork at my chest area in a delicate gesture, smiling demurely. Her energy feels quieter overall. Not as tense or keyed up.

"The binder is great. It works. I mean, I hardly think about it. I've gotten used to it. But still, I can't wait to get rid of these things. That's what they are now, things, you know? They've flattened out."

Jan looks disturbed for a fraction of a second. An eclipsing arc of facial muscles transmits small anxieties across her face. It must still be weird for her to think of someone who's been a woman and had breasts wanting to have them removed. After all, she's worked so hard to get hers.

"You have breasts now, I mean, they are pretty, uh, bi—" I begin.

"Decent size, huh?" She bursts out laughing. The old Jan, irreverent. "And they are going to get bigger. I know that the hormones can give me a C cup. I am seeing a doctor now who really thinks it's possible for me," she says with pride and a devilish smile. It feels great to fool Mother Nature.

"Really? You will actually grow to C-cup size?" I ask, incredulous, as a smile spreads slowly over my face.

"Yes," she winks. "I'll be bigger than any of the women in my family!" Another laugh.

We both laugh now. The food is great. Thai food, spicy and sweet in just the right proportion.

Jan keeps looking at my face and body, slightly stunned, taking me in. She's registering all the little and large changes. The shape of my eyes, the cut of my jaw, how it's gotten squarer, the muscles in my arms, the width of my neck, my nose that's grown stronger, particularly at the bridge. All the subtle and definitive characteristics that make a person look like either a man or a woman.

"You really look like a man," she says, wide-eyed, shaking her head in wonder.

"You really look like a woman," I reply, smiling a broad smile now.

She's doing well, working on graphic arts projects, moving into working on computers. She's dating men, although she is still attracted to women.

Jan tells me, as many people do, that I seem calmer now. Although I feel like I'm experiencing an overall increase in energy, the effect is converse. An object vibrating faster—so fast it appears stationary.

"It's as though a film has been peeled off your face. Now you're here, the real you that was underneath is revealed. I mean, you are really *present* now." Jan peers into my eyes for a moment with a concentrated look, an aura of awe. "It also reminds me of the story of the boy who comes back from the long journey. After the initiation in ash from ceremonial fires, he comes back to his old village, and they welcome him back. He has ashes all over his body from the rites of passage and they know he's not a boy anymore, he is a man."

I realize as we eat that we've switched places.

I catch her looking at me with surprise. She catches me looking at her with surprise.

"Jan, we've switched!"

We peer across the food at each other, eyes wide. "Yes, I keep thinking, you were the man and I was the woman. Now, I am the man and you are the woman!" I laugh again.

"Yeah . . ." she seems to drift off in thought.

"You know, you look great!" I straighten up and look at her with an unflinching eye.

"Thank you." Jan pauses, thoughtfully taking a bite. Looking across the table at me, she reflects, "It's true. I keep looking at you, I mean, I'll glance up and it's you . . . and I'll forget that you were ever female. I just think, I am sitting here with a guy, and a very good-looking guy, too."

CHAPTER 51: PHANTOM DICK

I feel the presence—spiritually and somatically—of a penis. A phantom dick. I have sex with women as though I genuinely have a penis. It seems natural.

Having sex and thinking of myself as having female organs feels unnatural. It always has.

Since my clitoris has grown, I have genitals that are noticeably different from my female partners'. Some have remarked that as far as they are concerned, my homegrown, small "neocock" is indeed a penis and they relate to it as such. I've also discovered, over time, that I'm able to penetrate. Although this is an amazing experience, I am not able to go deep enough to satisfy myself or my partner.

Like any person with a physical anomaly, I have to be inventive. I use my hands, or dildos that act as prosthetic extensions of my desire. Every guy should have a spare. It's great to be able to keep it up all night and to have at least a few different sizes available for her to choose from. Or, a different size and shape for a special occasion. Some lovers prefer that I always use the same cock, since we both can relate to it then as mine. For others, variety offers an advantage, since they might feel like being with a different-size guy on different nights. Also, I can always surprise them.

On the other hand, I can't say that being a man without a normal penis doesn't make me feel a bit insecure at times.

Considering the surgery to construct a penis, or "bottom" surgery as it's called, I'm alternately hopeful and depressed. A perfect solution does not exist.

There are basically two methods. The most common one is called metoidioplasty, a nearly unpronounceable word conjuring up a weird, terrifying operation. This clumsy term actually designates the preferred method for transmen to get a dick. Metoidioplasty is relatively safe and simple, and looks very natural. The surgeon frees the hormonally enlarged clitoris by cutting the ligament that holds it close to the body. This enables the new penis to hang freely, giving it the appearance of more size and allowing more movement. Because of hormones, the clitoris grows and does actually appear to be a small penis, complete with a head. Actually, since the clitoris is the analogue of the penis in the female, this isn't too surprising. All erotic sensation is maintained, and most of the transsexual men I've met who've had this surgery are very pleased with the results. The one glaring problem is that the penis it creates is extremely small, not a size most men would ever brag about or even show in the locker room.

But it's much less expensive than the alternative—phalloplasty.

Phalloplasty is also a lot more daunting. Lou called it "The Cadillac." You can get a large, sometimes *very large,* penis. Besides being expensive, the operation is also painful, arduous, and dangerous.

Phalloplasty is actually relatively uncommon. Most transsexual men do not opt for this risky, budget-busting surgery. However, the ones who do are often pleased with the results. They can, sometimes with prosthetic rods, or now, with surgical implants embedded in the penis, achieve penetration and have intercourse. To my mind, this alone makes a phalloplasty seem like a worthwhile endeavor.

However, there are serious drawbacks. For one, these full-size cocks do not have sensation unless another fairly radical and invasive procedure is performed using microsurgery to attach nerves and veins. Since the phallus is created from tissue harvested from the abdomen or thigh, the only way to obtain erotic sensation is to harvest tissue from another, more sensitive and nerve-saturated area of the body, usually the underside of the forearm, although now the thigh is beginning to come into use. If all goes well, over time, the two nerves become one and grow up the length of the shaft, awakening erotic sensation along the way.

Urethral extensions can be created in either type of surgery if desired, so transmen can pee standing up without using a device. Or, if a guy doesn't use an aid to stand and pee, he can avoid waiting interminable hours for a stall to open up. For some, the urethral surgery works like a dream. For others, this aspect of the surgery is the most problematic. Many men have problems with fistula or infection after the surgery is completed.

Balls are created by placing testicular implants in the labia majora, or outer lips, in both metoidioplasty and phalloplasty. These implants can be made of either silicone or saline, depending on the preference of both surgeon and patient. Depending on the skill of the surgeon, and the method preferred by the patient, the scrotum created can look very realistic, sometimes indistinguishable from a naturally occurring set. You can ask for small, medium, or large. I knew right away I wanted mine large, though tight and youthful. In this world, you need big balls.

In certain respects, I am attracted to the phalloplasty—big-cock surgery. It would be great to have a normal- to large-size cock, to be able to bone down my girlfriend without having to go fishing in the sex-toy drawer. However, the risks are enormous and the scarring is horrible. Although results vary, and methods are being evolved to create less vivid scars, generally the scars are pretty intense. Your forearm will look like it's been bitten by a shark, or mangled in some terrifying accident. Over time, of course, these scars will heal to some degree, but your arm will never be the same. Things can also go terribly wrong with this surgery. A man could lose movement of his fingers, or his entire hand, or, if the nerve graft doesn't take in the new penis, all erotic sensation could be lost forever. It happens. The surgery takes around twelve hours, which is risky in and of itself. And the appearance of these "neococks" leaves a lot to be desired. Results range somewhere between an oddly shaped block of flesh and a decently carved penis that still looks out of place alongside the flesh around it. Also, most importantly, these penises are not made of erectile tissue. At least with metoidioplasty, I would have a penis that was homegrown and composed of genuine erectile tissue that could react to touch and expand with desire.

I will always have the greatest respect for transsexual men who opt for phalloplasty. These guys are the risk takers, the big dreamers, the steely-nerved gamblers. By giving themselves up to a process that is so radical, still being perfected, often raw with experimental angst and danger, they pave the way for other transsexual men to find more ideal solutions. However, contemplating the risks and potential benefits of this operation gives me pause.

This chapter is not meant to be an exhaustive investigation of FTM bottom surgeries, but, there are new surgical methods, including Centurion, a type of metoidioplasty that can create a larger phallus from the released clitoral penis by using the round ligaments found in the labia majora. Also, some transmen go for partial surgeries, like a simple release of the enlarged clitoris. There is also an operation to remove the vagina, called a vaginectomy. Hysterectomy and oophorectomy, or removal of the ovaries, are also often performed. Many transmen opt not to have these operations, for many different reasons. I encourage the interested reader to browse the many Internet information sites on these subjects, as well as to investigate other sources of information, including Listservs or other books, to find out more.

Surgical techniques are changing and advancing quickly, and what is standard treatment today might change tomorrow. The decision as to which surgery to have, and why and when to have it, is very individual. I would encourage as much exploration as possible for anyone considering any of these options.

Considering my options, big or small, and with whatever combination of techniques, it's clear that I will never possess a normal, fully functioning penis in this lifetime. Looking ahead, DNA manipulation may open up new avenues; perhaps there will eventually be a method enabling the clitoris to grow even larger, into a normal-size penis. But right now, things don't look too promising. On the other hand, the small one isn't so bad. Even without the benefit of a metoidioplasty, the clitoral penis looks good: It functions, it's homegrown, and yes, I can achieve penetration, even if it's not enough to satisfy either me or my partner.

The fact that I would never possess a normal penis actually put me off the change for awhile in the beginning. If I can't whip out a nice, hard, normal-size cock, one attached to my body, and fuck my girlfriend silly, why bother? Also, as long as I don't possess a normal and functioning penis, I thought, many people would never consider me to be a man.

So, in the beginning, before even starting testosterone, I had to consider what makes a man. Does having a penis do the trick? Certainly, it's one of the components, but a cock isn't everything. Lou Sullivan points out in his book, *Information for the Female to Male Cross Dresser and Transsexual,* that there are men who have lost their genitals in war or by accident, or who've lost partial or full function of the genitals through disease or injury. Not to mention the John Wayne Bobbitts of the world.

Phalloplasty was first perfected for these men, some of them veterans. It's also performed regularly on nontranssexual men born with a condition known as "micropenis." These men are born with tiny, undeveloped penises, sometimes an inch and a half long. They are unable to pee standing up. The predicament of these men is actually not so different from that of transsexual men, and the integrity of their manhood is not impugned. They are considered to be "real men." A man is not a penis, although a penis is an important part of a man.

After a week of giving up the idea of sex change because of this problem, I decided that it didn't matter. I already thought of myself as possessing a cock when I had sex, and at least the rest of my body would be decisively male. And the clitoral growth would be an amazing improvement.

Lots of guys want bigger dicks, anyway. I would join the eternal sandlot of men who yearn to have big cocks. Monstrous, thick, superlative erections that awe women and fill other men with envy. On the other hand, I wouldn't be shy about grabbing a Jeff Stryker out of the top drawer and clamping it over my little dick, bending my girlfriend over, and letting her feel the pain and pleasure of a porn star–size cock.

CHAPTER 52:
ADAM'S APPLE

Man-size
Got my leather boots on
—P. J. Harvey, "Man-Size"

The veins came. Shooting up my arm and standing out in tension on my hands. At attention, just under my skin. Sculpting my arms and corded, shifting muscles.

Jack is impressed, and tells me that not all guys get them. "I don't have veins showing on my arms and hands, that's great you do."

It's odd to find myself thinking that veins popping through skin are a sign of physical attractiveness. Obviously my standards have changed. What once would have been a sign of aging or distended skin is now a distinguishing characteristic, emblematic of virility. Getting ripped.

I turn my arm in different directions under the light of a lamp and catch the shadows as they pop out in sculpted ridges. I'm still changing so much. Every few months I notice new masculine characteristics—more hair or veins, my muscles standing out in places where there were none before, hair creeping along my wrist and knuckles, eyebrows fuller, my hairline's changing, too.

I watch my hairline with bated breath. Some changes are hard. A male hairline is desirable. It's one of many cues that enable people to read you as a man. Women tend to have more rounded hairlines, which helps give an overall appearance of roundness to the face, softness, more curves. Even so, I don't want it to go back too far. I don't want to have to consider joining the Hair Club for Men. That curse of manhood, the scourge of male-pattern baldness, hormone induced, genetically programmed. Not everyone goes bald; the thing to watch is the guys in your family. If your brothers are bald you might one day be, also. It's known to pass down through the mother's side, with the X chromosome, but I watched a show about hair transplants that claimed that 20 percent of a person's hair comes down from the father. The fact that transmen, unlike genetic males, have two X chromosomes might throw this formula off. Whether or not you lose your hair really is dependent on what genes you've got, a roll of the dice.

So I'm already watching those hair-transplant shows. Like all my nontranssexual male friends, I watch my hairline with mild trepidation. In time, my hair begins to go back on the sides and recede a bit on top, and I have a "male hairline." I watch and pray it won't keep receding. "You can stop now," I tell my hairline in the mirror.

One thing women don't really have to worry about. Even so, one could take it as a mark of virility, that shiny bald head. Very manly, no doubt. Certainly, a male hairline, that V shape, is seen as attractive by many people.

Mr. Clean, Yul Brynner, Henry Miller, Montel Williams, skin-heads . . . baldness proliferates all around me. All guys are nervous, rubbing their heads, checking the mirrors. I watch the patterns, there are all types: V shapes, round shapes, chrome domes, square patterns at the temples, and receding. Almost every man has a little of it as he ages. Will speculates that yarmulkes were originally designed to hide the patch of hair that many men lose at the crown. Baldness, some pattern of hair loss, even if it's a tiny loss on the sides, helps to make the man, to age him, to cultivate his masculine visage. I watch my friends' hair thin, in front or in back. I look at the bright, shiny chrome domes of my Hispanic/Sephardic ancestors, with their big handlebar mustaches. I comfort myself that American Indians don't go bald—certainly not classic Hippocratic baldness, the fringe around the head. When there is more hair on the body, there appears to be less hair left on the head. White men go bald four times faster than any other racial group. But since I'm not a full-blood and have those Caucasian genes as well, who knows what roll of the genetic dice I will get. I gaze into the mirror, inspect my hairline, and tell myself not to worry.

I don't look like a teenager any longer, but clearly like an adult man. Fully grown, I've arrived.

When I go to the gym now, I find that I progress much faster. I've gone from lifting 50 to 120 pounds on a machine in two weeks. My muscles pump up faster and so the results are also easier to see. Testosterone is anabolic, and creates muscle from protein. So these results, while seemingly spectacular, are not unusual.

My jaw is more defined and square, the muscles in my face are set into a harder expression. Men's facial muscles show more because they just generally have less fat on their bodies, and the muscles tend to be larger.

It's gotten to the point that if I tell someone I once was a woman, they don't believe me. I told a gay man one night and he began yelling,

"You are lying! You are lying!" This guy was from Iceland, stocky, with a thick accent. He'd been fag-bashed in New York and had sustained a serious brain injury that had changed his brain chemistry so that he could drink tons of alcohol, straight from the bottle, and not feel it. I watched him drink an entire bottle of rum that night, straight, in a tall glass. Like it was Coke. He didn't appear at all drunk, which I found very odd.

My revelation was extremely upsetting to him. Possibly he had thought I was an attractive young man, and the idea of me being born female disrupted his worldview almost violently. The Icelander got crazed, screaming over and over that I was lying, that this couldn't be and wasn't true! Finally, to put him out of his misery, I said, "Yeah, I am joking." He chastised me that I shouldn't joke about such things, he knew real transsexuals, this was a very serious matter, and I should not make light of it.

Since many doctors are still unfamiliar with FTM transsexuals, they have often assumed that I'm transitioning from male to female when I state that I am a transsexual. Often, they are puzzled that I am not "trying very hard" to pass as a woman. Sometimes they sneer at what they see as a futile and pathetic attempt to attain femaleness. One woman doctor snidely informed me that the hormones wouldn't change my voice. I replied, "They have, though." She smirked and said, "No, estrogen does not affect someone's voice." I looked at her for a moment, perplexed. It is true that estrogen will not alter a person's voice, but testosterone will. I proclaimed, "I'm taking testosterone, not estrogen!" She blinked back disbelief. "You mean you used to be a woman? Oh my god! Why, why on earth would you want to be a man? Men have much more difficult lives!"

People's reactions rarely fail to entertain, surprise, and provoke me. I understand why transpeople were associated with tricksters in tribal cultures. We reflect back at people their hopes, fears, and beliefs without even trying.

When I tell a gay male roommate of Alexander's that I am a transsexual man, he is convinced it is a hoax. "Max could never have been a woman, he wouldn't even make a good drag queen!"

This isn't just my experience. Most of the transsexual men I know have similar tales to tell once they have been on testosterone for a couple of years. For transsexual men on testosterone, passing as a nontranssexual man, an "ordinary" guy, is generally not an issue. However, we have to worry about whether or not to disclose our past, and to whom and under what circumstances. This is the life sentence, and the cost of passing as genetic males. Certainly, I am not complaining. The alternative, not being convincing as a man, is far worse.

Friends are adjusting, even the few who resisted initially. Kate, who had predicted I would be like Alan Alda or Phil Donahue, had wanted to sever our friendship. As a dyke, she didn't feel she could be close friends with a straight man. Eventually she learned to accept me, although I don't think that the man I've become reminds her anything of Alan or Phil.

Over coffee, eyes scanning my face, she said to me, "I look at you now and I think about when you used to be Anita, and I find it hard to believe. It's like a dream." Kate continued wistfully and in wonder, "The other day I saw a woman walking down the street and I thought, that's Anita! You know—spiky hair, black leather jacket. Then I remembered, oh, yeah, that's not her. Anita's a man now. A man called Max."

When I was female, I felt more limited as to what I could wear, since I had to try harder to maintain a boyish or androgynous look. Now I can wear what I want. I experiment with different fashions that might have been unthinkable before—baggy or tight, suits or leather jackets—now that the clothes fit the way they should. When I look in the mirror I see a guy. When I dance, my body looks entirely different than it used to, each movement translates into sharper lines and angles. My silhouette is longer. It's a joy to look at my reflection and see a man looking back at me. And to know that man is me.

It's been years since I began taking testosterone. My face is leaner, my body harder, my shoulders broader; my beard continues to come in. I had to throw out most of my old shirts and I can't fit into my old punk dyke leather jacket anymore, since my shoulders are broader; it barely covers my chest now and rides up high on my arms. I can't zip it up. When I buy boots, I find that my feet have continued to grow. I can't wear a size 7 in a male shoe anymore, and had to try an 8½ or 9. I started out as a man's 6 ½!

The energy I felt initially, so overwhelming, has quieted. I've grown into it. With time, as you become larger, more muscular, the energy begins to fill in a space appropriate to its circumference. In other words, you grow up.

I take the same amount of testosterone that I did initially, one cubic centimeter every two weeks. This will go on for the rest of my life; after all, genetic males have testicles that produce testosterone. I don't. Although this may appear to put me in a position of extreme dependence on the medical industry, it is no different from the fact that I also have to wear very strong prescription glasses or contacts in order to see the expression of whoever is speaking to me or even to cross the street safely. Some transmen experiment with lowering their dosage as they age, but most of us continue to use the standard dosage to feel healthy, vigorous, and vital. The testosterone maintains the secondary sexual characteristics that we've acquired, although many of these—the voice, hairline, body hair, clitoral growth, and some changes in bone structure—are permanent. Other changes could be reversed without testosterone, such as body-fat distribution, and certainly, our increased muscularity. In my opinion, the dosage that I take keeps me youthful and promotes a sense of well-being. At this time, it works, and I see no reason to tamper with a positive experience.

The change has affected more than just my body. Many people who knew me before report that I seem happier, more alive somehow. I know I'm not as angry, I've opened to the world in degrees over time. I am more outgoing, even gregarious, some people tell me. More than a few friends have told me that I was comparatively quiet before. Others say

I seem calmer. And at least one acquaintance said that Max seems like a much nicer person than Anita. I know that I'm not as depressed; I'm less on the defensive, more relaxed, and genuinely at ease.

Without a doubt, the experience of no longer being "trapped" in a sex and a social gender that felt inauthentic has opened me up to life. I feel both happy and lucky that I actually have had the opportunity to take this leap, and that I went ahead and did it. If I can do this, I can do anything.

Although shocked, my mother and father have been working toward accepting me. My mother asked at one point, "Why couldn't you just stay a lesbian?" My father chided me almost immediately to make more money, something I have never been really spectacular at. "You'll have to earn money like a man now." Certainly, I have found that an important part of the male role is that of provider, and that a man who is poor appears to be judged more harshly than a woman in the same position. There are different expectations. I did not grow up with this expectation, and have learned about it over time in my male life. Dad gave me some practical advice, too, telling me that I would have to change my ID. Something I had already done. I was surprised that he was so matter-of-fact and helpful, right away. My father has always been more accepting of me in general, and this change was easier for him than it was for my mother.

My mother has had a difficult time with the change. It has been an up-and-down battle. Contrary to what many believe about American Indians, my mother and her people didn't immediately declare that I was a shaman. Instead, my mother forbade me to set foot on her reserve ever again. She felt that no one there would understand, and that she would be a laughingstock.

After many years in virtual exile from my relatives on the reserve, I recently reconnected with them. I'm happy and impressed that they have accepted me with love and sensitivity. It's also true that my aunt Florence found out years ago, on an unexpected visit to San Francisco with my grandmother. She was the image of sagacity, letting me know that she respected my choice. My late grandmother Kate remarked matter-of-factly, "Oh, no wonder your voice is so deep." To her, it never seemed to make any difference.

In time, I will tell my father's side of the family, as well. I anticipate that their reaction will be just as accepting.

Counting my blessings, I am impressed that both my parents call me "Max" and refer to me, at least when I am within earshot, as "he." They have continued to be there for me, and we celebrate holidays together and have extended visits. The support they have given me is not taken for granted.

My siblings, two younger brothers and a younger sister, have been a dream—never wavering in their support. This has been a grace; not all transsexuals are so lucky.

It is light outside the window of my small room. The beginning of summer is coming—I feel it in the air, a lightness that is ephemeral, a buoyancy. The clarity and tone of the light outside is transforming. It is May. I stop for a moment in that light, sitting on a small metal chair enclosed by the blue walls of my room. There isn't far for my eyes to look. Ahead and outside into the street, where a group of teenage boys in hoods sell crack and children ride bicycles up and down the narrow alley, then farther out and beyond to the deep cobalt blue sky.

Finally, after six years on testosterone, I got my chest surgery. The money I received as the advance to write this book is actually what made that possible, a surprise solution that I had not anticipated. With the chest surgery, I now experience a feeling of completion, of newfound comfort in my body that has made my life more satisfying. The sensation of having a flat chest is liberating. And is it ever flat! When I first got the surgery, I was amazed at just how flat I felt. Walking down the street, I realized that this was a new and entirely different sensation from what I had been used to. Even when I was binding, and my breasts were flattened out and virtually undetectable (so convincing that many people thought I had gotten the surgery already), my chest felt weighty, with a fullness in front. Now it's like being a knife in the breeze. My body has a compact lightness, which undoubtedly makes me feel more complete as a man. It's a relief to be able to take off my shirt with lovers; I even walk around shirtless in the house or outdoors. Initially, if the doorbell rang or a housemate's friend or lover was over and I hadn't yet gotten dressed for the day or had just gotten out of the shower, I would instinctively cover my chest with a towel. Or wonder, *Where is my binder?* before I went out for the day. A wave of relief would come over me when I looked down and remembered that I didn't need one anymore. And a smile.

There are people who ask, "Do you regret getting the surgery?" The answer is a resounding no. I only regret that it took so long to get since I did not have the money, or an insurance plan that would help cover at least some of the costs. For a transsexual, surgery is corrective and not merely cosmetic; it enables us to feel free and at home in our bodies.

I look forward to eventually getting bottom surgery, which will most likely be some version of metoidioplasty, the easier and more natural solution. In fact, by the time this book is actually published, I may have accomplished it. The day may yet arrive when I actually can grow a normal- or nearly normal-size penis that is virtually undetectable in appearance from the penis of a nontranssexual man. Recent medical advances involving genetic manipulation, such as the grafting of skin tissue grown from fetal cells for burn victims, offer hope. Also, experimentation with growth hormone holds possibilities. I scan the future from the threshold of this hope, expectant yet resigned, nearly content with the results that many of the current surgeries offer. After all, my sex life works. I have found that the penis is not the only measure of the man. So far, my variance hasn't impeded my having relationships with a range of women, most of whom identify as heterosexual, or occasionally bisexual.

I have been with some gorgeous, talented, and exceptionally interesting women who have taught me a great deal, as well as providing enjoyment, passion, and inspiration. I've also had odd endings and strange, unbidden experiences with textures and qualities very different from what I experienced as female. Some of this has to do with the inevitable tensions associated with being a transsexual. However, many of the conflicts I experience with my partners are part of the "war between the sexes" that I couldn't have known in a lesbian relationship but which I am experiencing firsthand and up close for the first time in the arena of heterosexual relationships.

I've learned that the trust level between men and women in romantic relationships is in the basement compared to the level of trust that I experienced in lesbian relationships. Women often think I am angry when I'm not. I'll feel as though I am engaging in a spirited conversation, emphatic, possibly heated, but not angry. Girlfriends have told me in moments like this that I appear to be very angry, which catches me by surprise.

Mina considers herself to be a feminist, but is also antidogma and a freethinker. She cherishes art and the imagination, and possesses a resolute critical faculty. Mina opened to me with an immediacy and freshness that felt fated. I have never known anyone quite like her. I can never predict what she will feel about any particular topic, she is fearless and penetrating in her investigation of ideas. So it feels odd when we begin to clash about ideas and attitudes.

She shows me her collages, landscapes of images that resonate with my own poems, dissonant and blazing with visual music. Mina points to a collage on her wall containing an image of a Heruka, a wrathful Tibetan deity, gazing down in flaming anger, cleansing anger with eyes slanting and brows flaring. "You are like that," she tells me. She points at another image, a golden statue of a muscular man with a penis for his head, a literal dickhead. The statue has a furious energy, emanating a maleness that is extreme, angry, threatening. The penis head is a force blasting out of a glistening, metallic, muscular torso. "And you are like that," Mina says as I scrutinize it more closely.

In my estimation, I am barely angry, but engaged in sensible, logical, although passionate discussion. I can't understand how Mina can see me as so menacing, so forceful, angry, male, and threatening when I am only emphatically disagreeing with her. Or, possibly, attempting to present another perspective without feeling as though I need to quash her. To my mind, her perception of me is inexplicable. I contemplate it for a long time, attempting to understand.

Mina and I have been walking around town all day, kissing in the park; she gets ice cream for me and watches me eat it. We walk among the lovers embracing on park benches and stroll around a lake. I am planning to move in with her in the fall. Everything has been going well, but sometimes now, cracks appear. There's trouble in paradise.

It is more difficult for me to communicate with women. Is it because I have changed so much more than I realize and in ways I don't completely comprehend? Or am I missing some essential ingredient now in terms of communication?

Mina and I argue about Andrea Dworkin, about free speech and sexual harassment, about pornography. She thinks I don't listen to her, she tells me that I am trying to shut her up. It occurs to me: *I am arguing with my feminist girlfriend about feminism. I never thought this would happen to me.*

I flash back to when I marched in the first "Take Back the Night" march in San Francisco in 1978. I was only twenty-one and fresh as a spring leaf, naive, winsome. I joined in the surge of women as they flooded Broadway Street, shouting out to the strip joints, "Shut it down!" We stormed the Condor, where Carol Doda's nipples blinked neon on and off above the entrance. A papier-mâché effigy of a woman with meat hanging from her was held aloft in the all-female crowd. I remember being overwhelmed by the energy surging through the crowd, the piercing intensity of feeling. It was all so new to me. I think about how much I have learned and lived since that time.

Mina calls me "sexist" one day in an argument. My mind is pulled into a vise. Clamped down, I struggle in the heat of contradictions. *How can she say this to me?* I can't believe it. How come I am finding it so hard to communicate with the women I care the most about?

Mina and I have similar perspectives, or so I thought, on censorship, pornography, and free speech. Suddenly, the ground shifts and I am no longer entirely sure where she is coming from.

Exasperated, I blurt out, "You can't say that. I was a lesbian! I was a lesbian feminist! You can't say that!" This declaration sounds puny, and like a refuge of last resort, which it is. Even if I wasn't such a "good" lesbian feminist, I nonetheless knew that language, lived it as best I could, understood the finer points of the discourse, the irrefutable holy gospel. Now I find myself on the other side.

"You cannot use that anymore in an argument," she announces, protective and mischievous at the same time. "What if I were arguing with Norman Mailer and he suddenly shouted, 'You can't say that! I was a lesbian feminist once!'?" Mina is laughing, but she is dead serious. In that moment I grasp how she sees me, as a man like any other, claiming to have once been a lesbian. Now I am laughing, too.

The other night I had a dream. There is going to be a play and I am to take part in it. I go up onstage. Looking around at the set I realize that everyone in the play is male. John, the roommate who gave me the advice about guys and fighting, is in it. There are a number of men there, most of whom I don't recognize. All types: construction workers, men in tuxedos, nondescript men in khaki slacks, African American men and white men, Latinos in T-shirts, motorcycle guys with long hair and black leather jackets, men in glasses and men in dark suits with sunglasses and cell phones, American

Indian men with long black hair or in cowboy hats and cropped hair an-
gling around the stage practicing their lines. There are men whose race or
ethnicity is indistinct, or that changes as I watch them. Their names are
all simple. There is no mystery as to what they call themselves. Each one
is sure of his part and his place in the production. My name in the play is
uncertain, however. In fact, everything about my part is uncertain. I don't
know what my lines are or what I'm supposed to do. All this uncertainty,
this unknowing, is upsetting. I panic. When my turn comes to speak I'm
silent. I have no idea what to say. I'm expected to know my lines, but no
one has told me what they are. The audience waits, sitting quietly, expec-
tantly. I face away from the audience, hoping no one will notice. The au-
dience starts stirring and laughing. I start to feel resentful, thinking that
someone should have told me what I'm supposed to do, what part to play,
what my lines are. Then, someone—one of the guys onstage—tells me that
my part is to be the joker. "Of course, I can do that!" I say and get up and
slide around the stage, skinny and slinky like the Riddler or Jim Carrey in
The Mask. *I catch myself in a mirror and see that I am wearing a shiny*
red shirt and that my hair is jet black and slicked back, rockabilly look-
ing, yet elegant. I'm wearing a zoot suit and a lime green fedora. I can see
myself from a distance parading at the edges of the stage, unafraid of the
audience, laughing, feeling seductive and powerful. Being the joker is easy,
natural. I slink around the stage with ease, liquid, inspired, lithe. A sin-
ewy provocation of energy and intelligence.

One night, Will and I sit in his car talking a moment before I go up to
my apartment. We've been out for the evening, caught a movie, had a
burrito. The evening is dark and a streetlight is shining on my profile in
the car. I pause before I get out. Will is looking at my profile in the deep
light, focusing shrill on my face and neck. He discovers: "Max, you have
an Adam's apple!"

I feel my neck. He's right. There it is, a hard knob under my fingertips!

I swallow. The knob bobs up and down, stiff and sharp, a rigid pointed growth on my throat. I'm amazed. Happy and amazed. I keep feeling this new Adam's apple over and over again. It's there, it's *really* there, and it will never go away!

I discovered a new, large vein throbbing on my forehead the other day. It's taken a few years to make its appearance. Now it throbs, swollen and manly, a pulsing signature.

ACKNOWLEDGMENTS

It was Marie-France Boisselle who first taught me about risk, ambiguity, and peril. Then Marie-France Alderman, she wrote, "The thread that runs through Monika Treut's *Female Misbehavior* . . . is about imagining and imagination's conditions; mainly, willingness to befriend ambiguity and peril. . . . Ideologies cannot accommodate such adventurous goals. Art can. People can. We go on imagining; that is how the civil rights movement started, that is how feminism started."

By connecting the pure power of the imagination with the two great political liberation movements of our time, Marie-France helped to provide me with the foundational concepts that would animate *The Testosterone Files*. Her announcement that a preoccupation with safety and ideology was not conducive to igniting imagination's liberating potential became a touchstone for my subsequent writing and life. Marie-France also wrote specifically about the film *Max*, a documentary about my early transition that is a part of the larger feature *Female Misbehavior*—directed by Monika Treut, with the late Steve Brown as cinematographer—in the summer 1993 issue of *Visions*, the cinema and television arts magazine she published and edited. *Max* was shown worldwide throughout 1993 and Marie-France and I would meet because of that film review. Our meeting would become the catalyst for creating this memoir.

Marie-France concluded that Monika, like Virginia Woolf in *Orlando*, had captured the "essence of immortality—(which has) more to do with the intricate workings of human connection and with the time-bent ability to love amidst the betrayals, the bewilderment, the passion and the ambiguity than transcendence." Transcendence she wrote, is the stuff of "angelic bliss," and removed from the transforming power of life's hope and fear in an ornamental stasis. Lately, when gender has been discussed, and transsexuals are involved, the idea of transcending, or even destroying, the binary gender system is considered the goal of our struggle. I've never thought so. For me, the binary of male and female is a primary and enduring source of human potency—the same "human potency" that Marie-France declared to be "a very real source of hope." The binary of male and female is hopeful because it is filled with the force of life, even in its dark sexual essence and irresolvable conflict. These ideas were entities I grappled with as I wrote this book and bridged my own understanding of man and woman, of biology and social construction, the places in-between: human potency, imagination, peril, passion, ambiguity, risk, and the limitations of "transcendence" or "safety" over gambling—and gambling big. I remain indebted to Marie-France's visions and their revolutionizing effect on my life and work.

By the time *The Testosterone Files* is published, in 2006, I will have been a man, by some definition, for seventeen years. This memoir is mainly about that first fresh and joyful surge of discovery—those first five years of transition. I have been writing this memoir for more than a decade, and as I think back upon my experiences, I realize that I couldn't have begun it now. It remains edgy, irreverent, and unapologetic. It is my hope to immerse the reader in my transformation and the demands that process made on me. It was Marie-France's appreciation and acknowledgment of the raw intelligence of the transformational process from female to male, and of the individual integrity needed to live it out, that created a context and impetus for this work to move from experience to language. Without her guidance, persistence, and love, *The Testosterone Files* would not have been written. *I thank her.*

During the twelve years that this book has been in the making, there have been many highs and lows; at one point, it looked as though the project was permanently stalled. I had a publisher, and then that publisher was lost. For a time, the manuscript was in boxes, and the boxes were in storage. I never gave up the certainty, however, that someday this book would be published. Many people helped me along the way, with their support and encouragement, both personally and professionally:

I want to thank my first agents: Lane Zachary and John "Ike" Taylor Williams, as well as Elaine Rogers, for their support and enthusiasm about this project in its earliest phases. I want to thank Liza Dawson, my first editor, for her ear, her care, and her ability to see the potential in this work.

I also want to thank Klara Lux for introducing me to Monika Treut; Jill Enquist, for giving me the use of her computer to bang out my first proposal and for publishing my essays in her magazine *TNT* (*Transsexual News Telegraph*); Shane H., for being my buddy in early transition and discussing these topics endlessly into the night and through the days—we were mad explorers of sexual politics and the effects of testosterone; Kevin Horwitz, for his friendship and more laughter than I've ever had with anyone. I also wish to acknowledge the talents of Kyle Zimmerman for the cover shot and the photo that appears in Part Three—your work is like a painting; of Maria Elena Boyd for the captivating author photograph; and of Tracy Mostovoy, who is responsible for the photo of me as Anita—no one has ever captured that time in my life better.

Many transsexual men have provided special and enduring friendships through the length of this endeavor. Others have been casual friends and colleagues—arguing, laughing, hanging out, and sharing their lives with me. I don't always see eye to eye with each and every one of these men, but they are all important. Thank you to all of you. Special thanks to the trans-advocacy and inspiration of Jamison Green and the photographic art of Loren Cameron. Thanks also to Dean Kotula for his artful photographs, for including me in *The Phallus Palace,* and for his early support for my work. Jayson Barsic, for your inspiration. (Lazlo) Ilya Pearlman—thanks for making me a movie actor in *Unhung Heroes.*

Other transmen are deeply cherished friends. I want to thank Chuck Kussoy for believing in me and for listening to my girl problems and talking transpolitics—you are a true and rare friend. His girl, Marty, too. John Otto, for your energy and intelligence—you have helped me to get here, really. Carlos Gonzales, you saved my ass a few times with loans and your patient and caring ears. Martin Inane Macor, you are my punk rock buddy. Jordy Jones, I have loved watching you become you— you are a scholar, an artist, and an intellect. Stafford, no one is more resourceful—thanks for all the help all these years.

I have known many transsexual women who were instrumental in my political formation as a transsexual, and my growth as an artist and in my personal life. Special thanks to Teggan McKay, my dear, close friend who helped show me the way. Anne Ogborne, who influenced my transpolitics early on more than anyone else—you taught me I was "real," and that I had a right to claim my gender, like any nontranssexual would. Gianna Israel, because you helped me get my testosterone, you opened my path—you have the spirit of the joker. Margaret O'Hartigan, you tell it like it is for transsexuals everywhere—you are a working-class activist and a formidable political thinker. Shawna Virago, you are my rock-and-roll partner in crime—thanks for defending my voice to those who didn't understand. And Julia Serano, thanks for the readings, the shared political engagement, and the energy.

Canadian transwomen are the bomb! These women deserve spectacular mention: Thank you Viviane Ki Namaste, Mirha-Soleil Ross, Trish Salah, and also Xanthra Mackay. Without your humor, your no-nonsense advocacy for transsexual rights, your amazing films, scholarship, and writing, I would have felt quite alone in the late 1990s. You made sure that my voice was heard. Also, I thank Mark Karbusicky, Mirha-Soleil's wonderful boyfriend, who has been a quiet and vigilant supporter and buddy.

I would like to thank some nontranssexual women as well, notably the late Gloria Anzaldúa and AnaLouise Keating. Gloria was a mentor and early friend. Her visionary politics endure, and her compassionate soul will always be missed. I wish to thank her and AnaLouise for publishing my essay in *This Bridge We Call Home: Radical Visions for Transformation.* They braved controversy and political fallout to do so.

Thanks to Kerwin Kay for including the chapter, "Cock in My Pocket," in his groundbreaking anthology on male sexuality, *Male Lust: Pleasure, Power and Transformation.* Thea Hillman, thanks for taking a chance on me at "Intercourse" in 2001, and for not backing down when people protested. Natalie Watters, thank you for bringing my writing to Australia.

If Lou Sullivan were still alive, I would thank him for being the first transsexual man I ever met, and for showing me that becoming a man was possible with his life and tireless work for transsexual men. Lou, who is featured in this memoir, died of AIDS in 1991. He is not forgotten.

Thanks to the late Byron Perrin, a close friend and a writing companion whom I will never forget. Byron will always be a true poet.

Thanks also to my dear friend for almost twenty years now and my best support during early transition, Anthony Raynsford. You never stopped believing in my writing and my projects, even through the hard times. I can never thank you enough. And to Greg, who helped make those first years fun.

Other people have contributed over the years to events that made this story live. Most of them are still friends, a few of whom I no longer keep in touch with. Nonetheless, they contributed to this time of my life and this book: Karen Wheeler; Cathy Shore; Lula Perla—thanks for over twenty years of great hair styles and punk rock energy; Kat Page, Ellen, and Laura; Luna Olcott—my friend and spiritual guide; Cheryl Wallace; Ray Rea; Bonnie L.; Jeff (Rev. Adtrian Cain); Al Roth; Timothy O'Neill for the art and the work—we will complete our poetry/music projects yet; Kristine Ambrosia—ahead of her time performance artist; Frank Discussion—friend, punk artist, Babalawo, mentor and inspiration; Tracey Livezey; Missy Zwigoff; Ken Morris; Zoon—for the computer, the emergency money when I was running low and lean, and the always-perceptive ear for my life and work—you are irreplaceable. Valerie—thanks for reading the manuscript.

In 1997, *Gendernauts* was released (now available on DVD), another documentary film by Monika Treut and Elfie Mikesch, which is about gender expression and gender fluidity in the Bay Area. I am featured again, as a blonde! Besides boxing the camera again, I read from this memoir, then called *A Man*. I thank Monika and Elfie again. I also wish to thank Bestor Cram and Candace Schermerhorn for including me (and mentioning *A Man*) in their informative and wonderful documentary, *You Don't Know Dick: Courageous Hearts of Transsexual Men*. *Octopus-alarm (Tintenfischalarm)*, an Austrian film about intersex FTM Alex Pum, is soon-to-be-released, and I wish to thank filmmaker Elisabeth Scharang for including me, along with an excerpt from *The Testosterone Files*, in her brave and wise documentary.

Many thanks to Diviana Ingravallo, a true artist who always reminds me that art heals. Your amazing talent and persistence inspire me to keep creating, and living on that edge where creation becomes conscious.

Thanks to my parents, who call me "Max," and who have tried to accept me as a man. In particular, thanks to my father, who is one of the most wonderful dads any child could hope for—gentle, funny, and supportive. My mother's early and strong belief in my talent and potential remains my earliest source of optimism and drive. Also, to my siblings, Frank, Steve, and Bonnie, who understand and have always been there for me. My relations on the Blood Reserve have amazed me with their warm acceptance. This is what real family is about. If only all transsexuals were so lucky!

Amy Lightholder for being my true angel, my tender lover—passionate, patient, insightful, and kind. Thanks also for loaning me your computer when mine crashed on a deadline! You have been my muse, and my sweetheart. Because of Amy's encouragement, I took this manuscript out from the box it was in for so many years and tried again to get it published. If Amy hadn't believed in me and motivated me, this book might still be in that box. Your love lifted me up.

My godmother Christina, in Lucumi, for her spiritual guidance, patience, and love—and for making the Orisha, Eggun, and Oludumare manifest to me.

Thanks to Charlie Anders for the readings, in particular the one where I met Michelle Tea. To Lynne Breedlove, for trying to help me get an agent and a publisher. Thanks especially to Michelle Tea, a fellow writer with talent to burn and energy to spare, who brought me to Seal Press. You opened the doors. When I was down about the prospects for this memoir, you enabled me to get back on track. Thank you, Michelle!

Finally, I wish to thank everyone at Seal Press for making me the first male author Seal has ever published! It is brave of you to take on this work, and I can never thank you enough. Thanks to my editor, Brooke Warner—you saw the potential in the proposal and swiftly brought this book to completion with me. Your guidance and editorial eye have been indispensable. Also, an enormous thank you to my publisher, Krista Lyons-Gould, and managing editor, Marisa Solís. And to Seal's publicist, Krista Rafanello, whose enthusiasm I know will take this book far.

Lastly, I want to acknowledge the ancestors—all the transsexual men and women who have come before me. My life is a cakewalk compared to what they lived and experienced, and because of their determination and belief in who they were, I have been able to become who I am. It is my hope that this book will help, in some small way, to make that becoming possible for other transsexuals living now, and for all those who will follow us.

CREDITS

ABOUT THE AUTHOR

Max Wolf Valerio is a transman and an American Indian (Blackfoot)/ Latino Sephardic poet, performer, and writer. He has appeared in a number of documentaries, including the *Max* short in Monika Treut's *Female Misbehavior* and *Gendernauts*. He has also acted in several films, including *Unhung Heroes* and *Healing Sex*. Valerio's writing has been published in *This Bridge Called My Back* (pretransition under his female former name, Anita Valerio); *This Bridge We Call Home; Male Lust; Transgender Care; The Blythe House Quarterly* (online); *Transgender Warriors;* and *The Phallus Palace.* He was also photographed for *Body Alchemy* and *The Phallus Palace.* Valerio lives in San Francisco; his day job is enterprise software sales.

SELECTED TITLES FROM SEAL PRESS

For more than twenty-five years, Seal Press has published groundbreaking books. By women. For women. Visit our website at www.sealpress.com.

Cunt: A Declaration of Independence by Inga Muscio. $14.95 1-58005-075-1. "An insightful, sisterly, and entertaining exploration of the word and the part of the body it so bluntly defines. Ms. Muscio muses, reminisces, pokes into history and emerges with suggestions for the understanding of—and reconciliation with—what it means to have a cunt." –Roberta Gregory, author of *Naughty Bitch*

The F-Word: Feminism in Jeopardy by Kristin Rowe-Finkbeiner. $14.95. 1-58005-114-6. An astonishing look at the tenuous state of women's rights and issues in America, and a call to action for the young women who have the power to change their situation.

Lesbian Couples: A Guide to Creating Healthy Relationships by D. Merilee Clunis, PhD, and G. Dorsey Green, PhD. $16.95. 1-58005-131-6. This popular guide for lesbian partners has been extensively updated to reflect the current cultural and political landscape, including the debate over same-sex marriage.

Reckless: The Outrageous Lives of Nine Kick-Ass Women by Gloria Mattioni. $14.95. 1-58005-148-0. From Lisa Distefano, former playboy model who captains a pirate vessel on her quest to protect sea life, to Libby Riddles, the first woman to win the legendary Iditarod, this collection of profiles explores the lives of nine women who took unconventional life paths to achieve extraordinary results.

Waking Up American: Coming of Age Biculturally edited by Angela Jane Fountas. $15.95. 1-58005-136-7. Twenty-two original essays by first-generation women caught between two worlds. Countries of origin include the Philippines, Germany, India, Mexico, China, Iran, Nicaragua, Japan, Russia, and Panama.

Without a Net: The Female Experience of Growing Up Working Class by Michelle Tea. $14.95. 1-58005-103-0. A collection of essays "so raw, so fresh, and so riveting that I read them compulsively, with one hand alternately covering my mouth, my heart, and my stomach, while the other hand turned the page. *Without a Net* is an important book for any woman who's grown up—or is growing up—in America." —Vendela Vida, *And Now You Can Go*